BOOKS IN THE SERIES

DEVIL'S GATE. THE TOLL GATE, ON ROAD TO THE COMSTOCK LODE, VIA SILVER CITY

An Editor on the Comstock Lode

by WELLS DRURY

FOREWORD BY ELLA BISHOP DRURY

Illustrated with Photographs

UNIVERSITY OF NEVADA PRESS

Reno   *1984*

An Editor on the Comstock Lode, by Wells Drury, was originally published in 1936 by Farrar & Rinehart of New York. A second, somewhat abbreviated edition was published in 1948 by Pacific Books of Palo Alto, California. The present volume reproduces the entire first edition except for the following changes: a Vintage Nevada series logo and book list have been added just ahead of the frontispiece; the title and copyright pages have been modified to reflect the new publisher; a foreword to the new edition has been added between pages viii and ix.

Library of Congress Cataloging in Publication Data

Drury, Wells, 1851–1932.
  An editor on the Comstock lode.

  (Vintage Nevada series)
  Reprint. Originally published: New York: Farrar &
Rinehart, c1936.
  Includes index.
  1. Virginia City (Nev.) — History. 2. Virginia City
Region (Nev.) — History. 3. Silver mines and mining —
Nevada — Virginia City Region — History. 4. Drury, Wells,
1851–1932. 5. Journalists — Nevada — Virginia City —
Biography. 6. Virginia City (Nev.) — Biography.
  I. Title. II. Series.
  F849.V8D73   1984   979.3'56   84-20870
  ISBN 0-87417-093-1

University of Nevada Press, Reno, Nevada 89557 USA
© University of Nevada Press 1984. All rights reserved
Cover design by Dave Comstock
Printed in the United States of America

CONTENTS

Contents

LIST OF ILLUSTRATIONS

FOREWORD TO THE NEW EDITION

Over the years no period or aspect of Nevada history has proved to be as fascinating as the Comstock mining rush. For more than a century writers have perpetuated images of huge fortunes, wild mining towns, gunfighters, stage robbers, and the dangers of underground mining at the desolate, windswept site on Mt. Davidson. Those who "lived" the Comstock, particularly in its bonanza years (1860–1880), and later wrote about it seem to have shared Miriam Michelson's view that, for all the hardships of the cruel land, theirs was a priceless experience. They sensed that they had lived in a very special place at a special time. As she put it, "we lived at a Happening Time, one of the epochs of the world's life."[1]

That epoch has produced a wealth of literature. Although the rich mines of the nation's first silver strike played out by 1900, the lore remained. Between 1905 and 1940 at least five Comstockers attempted to convey and preserve the spirit of that intriguing place in published memoirs and histories. One of the best of the studies is Wells Drury's *An Editor on the Comstock Lode*.[2] When it first appeared in 1936 reviewers welcomed Drury's book as a well-written, engaging, pungent reminiscence by a keen observer who knew Nevada as a newspaperman, elected official, and political leader. Harry Gorham, in his memoir published in 1939, wrote that in many ways Drury's book "grasps the 'atmosphere' of the life there more closely and accurately than any of the other modern works." Gorham, a Comstock mining superintendent for twenty-six years, felt that Dan De Quille and Drury had come closest to providing a true sense of the "soul" or "aura" of that place and time.[3]

Drury's reminiscence is a lively, entertaining, anecdotal account of Nevada's journalism and its social and political life as he knew it from the time he arrived in the Silver State in 1874 until he left in 1888. Mark Twain, Dan De Quille, Alf Doten, Arthur

McEwen, John Mackay, James Fair, Leland Stanford, Eilley
Orrum Bowers, Hank Monk, and Ambrose Bierce — he knew
them all, and many more. However, he was as interested in the
life of those at the bottom of society as he was in the aristocracy.
Unlike others, particularly Michelson, he wrote as a friend to
all, discussing individuals and their conduct without criticism or
comment. Consequently, the reader may be left wishing for
more but is grateful for the insights Drury provides.

Wells Drury was twenty-five and well prepared when Alf
Doten hired him as a reporter on his Gold Hill *News*. Already a
college graduate, Drury had held a federal post as an Indian interpreter at the age of eleven and had published a newspaper in
Oregon at nineteen. In Nevada he made the most of his opportunities, and they were many. He rose to prominence in that
talented Comstock journalistic fraternity which Charles Shinn
described as "the most virile, rollicking, merciless, tender-
hearted quill drivers in America"[4] and at various times was city
editor of the Virginia City *Chronicle*, *Daily Stage*, and *Territorial Enterprise*. Later Drury served as deputy secretary of
state for Nevada (1882–1886) and was speaker pro tem of the
Nevada Assembly (1887–1888). In 1884 he was a delegate to the
Republican National Convention, where he became well acquainted with Theodore Roosevelt. Later that year he stumped
the state for Blaine.

With the Comstock in decline, Drury left Nevada in 1888. A
seasoned newspaperman, he found work over the next two
decades as reporter or editor on nine papers in Denver, Kansas
City, Chicago, Sacramento, Los Angeles, and San Francisco. In
1908 he joined the Berkeley (Calif.) Chamber of Commerce and
for thirteen years served as its managing director and secretary.

However, he continued to contribute articles to magazines and newspapers and wrote several books: *Berkeley, a City of Progress* (1909); *To Old Hangtown or Bust* (1912); *California: Tourist Guide and Handbook* (1913). He made his home in Berkeley, and at the time of his death in 1932 was chairman of the board of Drury Advertising Company of San Francisco.

Drury's sons, Aubrey and Newton, with whom he was associated in the family firm, also left a legacy. Both were active in the conservation movement and particularly prominent in the campaign to save the California redwoods. Later Newton Drury was director of the National Park Service (1940–1951) and of the California State Parks (1951–1959).

An Editor on the Comstock Lode was published after Wells Drury's death through the efforts of his widow, Ella Bishop Drury, and son Aubrey. They organized Drury's material, written over the years, and prepared it for publication. Part of the chapter on journalism had appeared earlier as an article Drury wrote for Sam Davis's *History of Nevada*. An excellent foreword by Mrs. Drury, his wife of forty-four years, provided a biographical sketch and insights into Drury the man. The first edition, published by Farrar & Rinehart, also included a thirty-four-page appendix of articles and poems, some written by Drury, which had appeared in Comstock newspapers.

In 1948, as part of the Gold Rush centennial celebration, the book appeared in a second edition with the appendix and five photographs omitted. This "Centennial Edition," published by Pacific Books of Palo Alto, California, reflected a renewed interest in the mining West as a tourist attraction and subject for writers and film-makers. Drury's memoir remains a Comstock "favorite," and the University of Nevada Press now makes it more accessible for the enjoyment of old and new readers by reprinting the first edition in its Vintage Nevada Series.

Robert W. Davenport
Associate Professor of History
University of Nevada, Las Vegas

August 1984

Notes

1. Miriam Michelson, *The Wonderlode of Silver and Gold* (Boston: The Stratford Co., 1934), p. 9.

2. John Taylor Waldorf's memoir of his Comstock childhood appeared as a series of articles in the San Francisco *Bulletin* in 1905. It was first published in book form as *A Kid on the Comstock* (Berkeley: University of California Press, 1968); Michelson, *The Wonderlode;* Wells Drury, *An Editor on the Comstock Lode* (New York: Farrar & Rinehart, 1936); Flannery Lewis, *Suns Go Down* (New York: Macmillan Company, 1937); and Harry M. Gorham, *My Memories of the Comstock* (Los Angeles: Suttonhouse Publishers, 1939).

3. Gorham, *My Memories*, pp. 10, 158–159.

4. Charles Howard Shinn, *The Story of the Mine* (Reno: University of Nevada Press, 1980), p. 247.

ACKNOWLEDGMENT

Thanks are given to *Sunset Magazine* for authority to include in this book a copyrighted passage by Wells Drury on John Mackay, originally published in *Sunset* in 1903; and to Mrs. Fremont Older for permission to quote from the book of reminiscences, *Growing Up,* by Fremont Older. Considerable material by Wells Drury, incorporated in the present volume appeared in a different form, in the San Francisco *Examiner* more than forty years ago. Part of the chapter on Journalism originally appeared as a signed article by Wells Drury, in the Sam Davis *History of Nevada,* to which appreciative acknowledgment is made.

Thanks are given to the Wells Fargo Bank and Union Trust Company, San Francisco, for historic photographs and records from its collections; and to Mr. Will J. French, of San Francisco; to Mr. Henry Slosson, of San Francisco; and to Mr. Herbert Thomas, of Cornwall, England, for illustrative or other material. In the Scrap-Book section at the end of this book, part of the text on Placerville appeared in a little volume, "To Old Hangtown or Bust," written by Wells Drury in 1912 to commemorate the visit of Mr. John M. Studebaker to that picturesque Mother Lode camp.

To Mr. Herbert S. Howard, of Berkeley, California; Mrs. Mary Alt Dickey, of Reno, Nevada; Mrs. Mary Rolfe Lemery, of Oakland, California; and the late Mrs. Lola Watts Lee, of Carson City, Nevada, thanks are given for allowing the author to consult valuable old Nevada scrap-book material in their possession. Mr. Joe Farnsworth, State Printer of Nevada, kindly supplied a number of old photographs. Thanks are given to the staff of the Bancroft Library, University of California, Berkeley, and especially to Miss Edna Rodden Martin, who is a member of a pioneer Nevada family. Counsel and assistance from the Nevada State Library, the California State Library, the Nevada Historical Society and the California Historical Society are gratefully acknowledged.

FOREWORD

Wells Drury and I were married in Reno, and at the Insane Asylum—and that's a combination hard to beat! Nowadays, *Amo,* I love, is often succeeded by *Reno,* I do not love, but in the '80s this negative significance did not yet exist. My father, Dr. Simeon Bishop, was the superintendent of the State Hospital, and it was at our house on the ample grounds of the asylum that I married Wells Drury. He visited it in an official capacity, as a committee member of the Nevada State Assembly, of which he was Speaker *pro tem;* and I had come over on vacation from school-teaching.

Our paths had first crossed a few years before at the railroad depot at Reno, as I was arriving from California after my graduation from Mills, and as he was departing for Carson City, the State capital. Our family's light rig was parked, as we might say now, in a crowd of carriages, and to prevent the necessity of making King, our big gray horse, turn the buggy at such close quarters, he lifted up the back of the carriage (with me in it) and pivoted it bodily around, pointed for home. It took my breath away, and probably took his for a moment, but he didn't let on. Thus he got us started, with King a poor second in the effort, but the old horse had got his racing legs limbered up and I had only time to wave my hand, and call back, "Well, I'll surely vote for you, when you run for Governor!" Women did not have the ballot in those times, but it is worth noting that in the Legislature, with a natural gallantry supported by a sense of justice, Wells Drury was an early advocate of woman suffrage.

Whether or not it was love at first sight, before I had even been introduced to him on that occasion, I had a premonition, "That's the man I am to marry."

Some months later, as many tourists do today, I went to see the over-size footprints (made by giant sloth of prehistoric age) in the stone formation on the grounds of the State Prison at Carson. A manly voice was heard singing, off-scene, in that unpromising environment. But this was not a "Prisoner's Song;" instead, the refrain was, "When the Bloom is on the Rye." Upon discreet inquiry, for I was charmed, I learned that this was the baritone of Wells Drury, who had driven out to see his friend the warden, and was enjoying the advantage of the fine swimming-pool within the walls. I was later to discover that he always sang in the bath!

Happily, our meetings embraced other locales than the Insane Asylum and the Penitentiary. With Wells and my sister Persia I went on a tour of the Comstock, his old stamping-ground. On that storied mountainside (no pun intended) he recounted to us innumerable happenings during his adventurous life as a reporter and editor in Gold Hill and Virginia City. We delighted in his talent as a born story-teller, with good-humor overflowing.

Of course, Virginia City, where we prospected around together, was familiar to me from early childhood. Born in Illinois on April 5, 1863, I had come in an overland stage-coach with my parents at the tender age of three months, crying (as they later told me) all the way. The parties immediately preceding ours and following ours were attacked by Indians. We paused first at the hospitable ranch of George Alt in the Truckee Meadows, and then fared on to Washoe, receiving hearty welcome to that desert metropolis from Sandy Bowers and his wholesouled wife, Eilly Orrum Bowers, who was ever a lover of children. When she heard me fretting, she gathered me up in her large, capable arms and directed, "Sandy, you go right out and get milk of that Jersey cow of ours. This child *must* have the rich milk. " Perhaps she saved my life, for I gained strength from that Jersey's milk. My parents and the Bowers couple were warm friends, and the little Persia Bowers in after-years had as playmates the little Bishop children.

Our family lived in Virginia City in the early '70s, and my husband-to-be was a citizen of the same community, but we were blissfully unconscious of each other's presence. If I saw him at that time, I didn't know it. I may have passed him often in the crowds, for a young reporter must be everywhere; but as I never broke a bone on the very dangerous streets, I was possessed of no news value. Anyway, he was a dozen years older than myself, and a young man of twenty-two seems ancient to a girl of ten.

On Saturdays and Sundays we children used to take long walks, frequently up the slopes of Mount Davidson, carrying our lunches with us and making picnics of the outings. My school-lunches I used to eat in the shadow of the steeple of the church which towered near the big school-house. Even in those early times, and in that remote mining-town, the church and school structures were such as would do credit to cities of this day and age. We were conscious, though, that civilization on our mountainside was not perfect, for there was a deal of strife. My father had been an army surgeon, and his practice in Virginia City in treating wounds was large.

Wells Drury thrived on danger. It seemed, indeed, to heighten the gaiety of his spirits. From his very first year, his had been an adventurous life. He had been born on September 16, 1851, in New Boston, Illinois, near the Mississippi River. His parents, Squire Thompson Drury and Rebecca Newton Drury, inspired in 1852 by the spirit of adventure, with their five children left their comfortable home with a covered-wagon train on the old Oregon Trail. They never reached the Pacific Coast, but died within four days of each other, from the Asiatic cholera then sweeping America, and were buried on the North Platte. The children continued on to the Far West— Melissa, the eldest, was nine years old; then there were Celinda, Emily and Newton, and the baby, Wells, only ten months old. On arrival in Oregon, each of the orphaned Drury children was taken into a different household, but all retained their own family-name. There was a strong bond of love between them, and in after-years they were happily reunited.

Alfred Ridgley Elder and his good wife, attracted first perhaps by the baby's bright eyes and merry manner, took Wells into their home. Elder was a farmer and clergyman of Yamhill County, in the Willamette Valley. In his family were twelve children; yet Wells was received as the thirteenth and treated as one of their own. Alfred Elder and Abraham Lincoln had grown up as boys together, on adjoining farms in Kentucky. The Elders freed their slaves, and removed to Illinois; and in that newer land the youthful chums again were neighbors. When Lincoln was elected President, he offered Elder a high post, but his friend preferred to remain in the Northwest, and told the President he could do most good as Superintendent of Indian affairs on Puget Sound, with headquarters at Olympia. Forthwith he received the appointment, and Wells, who had played with the Indian children and knew several of their languages, was made Interpreter, after a competitive examination in which he finished far ahead of older men. Yes, he was an office-holder under Abraham Lincoln, though his age was only eleven! Self-reliant, from that day he made his own way in the world.

When Andrew Johnson became President, the young interpreter moved to pastures new. He had received only a small salary in his Federal position, but he saved a modest nest-egg to help put himself through college. To earn more, at the age of fourteen, he began his apprenticeship in the trade of printer in Seattle and Portland. Like so many who became Western editors, he started his literary career at the compositor's case; and soon he had experience as a reporter on the *Colonist* up in Victoria, British Columbia, and on the *Oregonian,* in Portland. When nineteen he owned and edited his own little newspaper, the Monmouth *Messenger,* as he worked his way through Christian College, Monmouth, Oregon, where he was graduated with honors. Avid for learning, his special aptitude was in the classics—English, Latin and Greek—and he studied these in company with his bosom friend, George McBride, afterwards United States Senator from Oregon.

During college years, he was sprinter as well as printer, and a baseball player, too; and though athletics were not highly organized, Wells had lots of fun. In later times he took up boxing and fencing.

Often he had exciting adventures in those Oregon days—on one occasion he nearly perished, rafting on the Willamette, when the river was booming in flood. The youth enjoyed hunting expeditions in the primeval Northwest, and became a sureshot with the rifle, though he was best with his own Colt revolver, which he treasured all his life. He came naturally by the instincts of a frontiersman, for his father, Squire Thompson Drury, was a relative of Daniel Boone and Squire Boone.

His family had been in America for about a century, yet Wells Drury was the picture of an English squire—ruddy in complexion, though with dark brown eyes and dark hair. In later years his hair, so fine in texture, was silver-white. Albeit he worked hard, his hand-touch was soft as a woman's. Though short in stature, he was a man of remarkably strong physique, and his perfect health and vitality were reflected in his buoyant spirits.

The immigrant ancestor, William Drury, born in England in 1750, came to Pennsylvania before the Revolution; and at the dawn of the next eventful century the family were established in Kentucky, whence members went to Ohio, Indiana, Illinois, Iowa and the Far West. (His mid-Western cousins are truly "noted for their piety and learning," and many have gone as missionaries all over the world.) The center of the English family is in East Anglia—Norfolk and Suffolk—and Drury Lane, in London, derives its name from that branch. The Newton family, to which the mother of Wells Drury belonged, also of English descent, were from the Shenandoah Valley, Virginia.

After his graduation from the little Oregon college, Wells decided to attend the University of California. He went to San Francisco in 1873, gained employment on the *Alta* and made a call upon the campus at Berkeley, across the bay. In those pioneer days, entering students sometimes enrolled with the President. When President Gilman noted by his application that he was a practical printer with much experience, he asked him to help in the inspection of some printing equipment which the University was just purchasing—the start of the great University of California Press. Wells was glad to aid in this manner, but when the next term opened he was not in attendance at Berkeley—instead he was 250 miles away, on the Comstock. He had made money in mining-shares, and had followed it to its source, Nevada. The abiding thrill of the big Bonanza camp was too much for him; he had to stay.

Of his eventful life in the Silver State you may read in these pages. It is because his earlier career throws light on his Comstock days that this much has been told about it. As a journalist, he had a high sense of his duty to the public. He never hesitated to denounce any wrong-doing among officials or influential politicians. Sometimes he was referred to as "the Fighting Editor of the Comstock," and doubtless he often had to hold his ground in that tumultuous frontier community. But he was not belligerent. Except when aroused, his was the most genial, generous, easy-going nature imaginable. If a man would attend to his own affairs and let him attend to his, without any unnecessary comment, he was indeed "a peaceable party."

When he struck the Comstock, it was a lively camp, and the excitement was exhilarating, especially to a very young man. And here appears the best evidence of his good birth and upbringing, for with no restraining influences whatever, being utterly a stranger in the place, and having no kith nor kin within hundreds of miles, he passed through the life of those wild bonanza days unscathed, maintaining his own standards, emerging after the stampede for wealth and fame into the quiet of domestic life, as an honored citizen, husband and father.

Wells was always remarkably independent. He would do what he thought right, in spite of the view others might take of his seeming eccentricity. If he felt like leaving a gay party and going home to read Tennyson or Meredith, or *Hamlet* maybe, or even Demosthenes on the Crown (these were among his favorites), it was not long before people found out that it was not well to interfere with his predilections.

His way was to keep quiet, until it was necessary to speak, or to act, and then he was the first to speak or to act, without waiting to see what others would do. He was a law unto himself.

At the time of our marriage in Reno, on May 23, 1888, he

told me that he was tired of the turmoil of politics. The Comstock had sadly declined, and San Francisco was inviting. Thither we went, and he entered newspaper work again with zest, enrolling as one of that alert, adventurous crew of reporters (he became city editor) on the San Francisco *Examiner,* the first Hearst newspaper. A few years later he was managing editor of the *Call,* and news editor of the Sacramento *Union.* During his long career, he was on the staff of several other leading California newspapers.

A certain restlessness was to be expected. He longed to join the Klondike gold-rush. He volunteered for service in the Spanish War, but he was nearing fifty and was denied, although he had served as Captain in the Nevada National Guard.

His literary labors continued. My husband was a voluminous writer for magazines, as well as newspapers. He trained many young newspaper writers, and was on friendly terms with such men as Ambrose Bierce, Franklin K. Lane, Joaquin Miller, Jack London and Robert Hobart Davis. He was one of the first presidents of the Press Club of San Francisco. Bret Harte and Mark Twain were among his acquaintances, and he met Robert Louis Stevenson when the gifted Scot was in San Francisco in 1888 on his way to the South Seas. Stevenson left a large collection of books in San Francisco, and Wells Drury had the pleasure of helping to catalog and appraise these volumes for the bookseller who disposed of them.

To the great Panama-Pacific Exposition of 1915 he lent effective aid in several ways. He it was who suggested that the Liberty Bell be brought from Philadelphia to California, which resulted in an outpouring of patriotic sentiment all across the continent. Love of country was inborn in him.

Whenever stirring patriotic speeches were given, or poems of true patriotic ring recited, his eyes were wet with tears of emotion. If he tried to read them aloud, invariably he would "choke up" and find it difficult to go on. Ordinary sentimental poetry or prose did not affect him, but noble actions and deeds of valor did—especially "bidding defiance," like Horatius at the bridge.

It was in his latter years that this book was written, our son Aubrey aiding in the editing and arrangement of the material. In the course of this congenial activity, Wells returned in fancy to the Comstock of his youth; and the awakened public interest in the old camp, accompanied by a measure of heartening revival of mining there, gave timeliness to the work. It is even more timely now, for Virginia City is staging a valiant comeback.

This book may be considered in a way unique. The *Nevada State Journal* had commented that he "could have written with more first-hand knowledge today of the pristine glories of Virginia City and Gold Hill than any other person." Happily, he did write, and we have a contemporary account of the rich and racy era of the Big Bonanza, by one who was an active participant.

I wish that everyone who reads these pages could have heard Wells Drury in conversation. He was a "single-handed talker" (as Westerners used to phrase it) who could, and often did, keep a whole roomful of people interested all evening.

Yet fond as he was of company, and social in his instincts, he had resources within himself which were unusual. At the time of his passing, John D. Barry wrote, in his column of comment in the San Francisco *News:*

"When once I met Wells Drury, he said, 'Last night I read

an article of yours on Loneliness. It may amuse you to hear that, in my whole life, I've never been lonely for an instant.' I can see his face now lighting up with amusement and friendliness. He may have realized the implications in that remark of his. What a vista he opened up!"

ELLA BISHOP DRURY

An Editor on the Comstock Lode

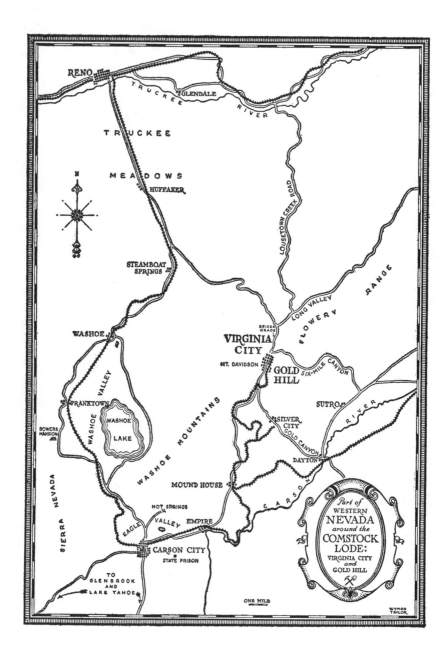

Part of
WESTERN
NEVADA
around the
COMSTOCK
LODE:
VIRGINIA CITY
and
GOLD HILL

ONE MILE

BY WMAN
TAYLOR

CHAPTER ONE

First Day

"Can you shoot?" questioned Alf Doten as I stood before him, asking for a job as reporter, in the little grimy office of the Gold Hill *News*. "Will you stand without hitching?"

With as much modesty as I could muster, I softly admitted the twin virtues which this frontier editor set store by. Alf grudgingly allowed, when I told of ten years' dabbling in printers' ink, that he guessed I'd do. No wonder he looked doubtful, for I was in my early twenties, and the line on my upper lip might have been the single light stroke of a camel's-hair brush.

"You write what you please. Nobody censors it. But you must defend *yourself,* if anybody has a kick." Alf Doten frowned as with his free arm (his other arm was in a sling that day) he indicated to me a big dragoon six-shooter, carrying an ounce ball, which was placed convenient to hand in the half-open upper drawer of his desk. A villainous-looking weapon, this mainstay of the Gold Hill *News* armory, and I regarded it uneasily. These gamecock editors, be it known, all went heeled; this formidable shooting-iron constituted the heavy artillery, in reserve.

"We call this peace-preserver 'the family Bible'," said Alf, showing his teeth in a smile. "You may not need it, and then again you may. Be careful—it has a feather-light trigger."

I was taking the place of a six-foot Scot, Donald McTavish

Scrymgeour, who had wandered off the reservation. My pay, I learned, was to be $7.50 a day, plus an allowance of $2.50 a day as "whisky money." This last, which never proved enough, was not so much for the scribe as for the entertainment of the citizenry interviewed (saloons were the invariable meeting-places) on his rounds as news-gatherer.

Early next morning I made my appearance at the *News* office, eager for my first day's reporting. With trepidation I heard Alf Doten confiding to his friend, Steve Gillis, "I have just hired a pink-cheeked Sunday school chap. He's too light in the saddle, but the best I could get. I don't think he can possibly stick, but we had to have somebody." Steve Gillis, boon companion of Mark Twain, and high among the illustrious on the Comstock, regarded the tenderfoot stripling with amused tolerance.

Mark Twain recounting his arrival in Comstock journalism, more than a decade earlier, complained that nothing happened on his first day, and he had to reel his fine-spun yarns out of whole cloth. But the Big Bonanza had "livened up" the camp and no such paucity of incident beset my own modest advent. Almost before the office shutters were down, we were told breathlessly that a man was lying dead over on B Street in Virginia City, and we hurried to see him. He was sprawled on his back in the street, his chest bare—and on it a small bullet-hole showing. There had been no bloodshed in this killing; all the blood from the wound apparently was flowing internally. With its delicate pink edges, it was the cleanest, prettiest wound that ever I saw.

The slain man, we learned, was John Dalley, killed by Richard Carter, a case-keeper for Tom Buckner's faro game in the old Sawdust Corner. The fight had been over a woman, Katy Twist. Carter was universally known as "Brigham" (he was a man of many women) but he proudly told the coroner's jury which exonerated him that this was not an alias, only a nickname.

After viewing the body, my companions (to my surprise) expressed themselves about ready for breakfast, and soon we were regaled with broiled chicken and crispy bacon. In the craw of the chicken I found a little nugget of gold, and by camp custom this treasure trove was handed over to the *restaurateur*, Charlie Legate. The precious metal when later assayed totaled $4.85, just about a British pound sterling; and I bought it, carrying the gold around with me in the form of cuff-links, to recall my first "strike" on the Comstock.

We were not to linger long that morn at Charlie Legate's. Again we rushed over the Divide, to Gold Hill. A Concord coach—an old-fashioned "thoroughbrace wagon," a huge lumbering affair which had been used as a stage—had been wrecked. On a steep grade the brake-beam had given way and the four horses streaked down hill at runaway speed. At the Empire mine the road turned almost at right angles. Bill McFarland, the driver, was wearing out his semi-annual drunk, but he drove by instinct, anyway. If the stage continued straight ahead, it would plunge into a deep ravine. Bill, with fine abandon, drove that careening coach into the bank at Sandy Bowers' old diggings, overturning it but preventing a worse disaster. As I viewed the wreckage, I noted that the coach when it gouged into the hillside had uncovered a piece of rich-looking quartz. I picked it up: it later proved to carry $12 in silver.

Almost daily mishaps marked the development of the Comstock mines, and that afternoon it fell to me to record two accidents, in one of which a carpenter had been crushed by falling timbers, while in the other several miners had been maimed by a premature blast of giant powder.

To add to the excitement, mining-stocks had suffered a big break; several men were lodged in jail for disorderly conduct, including Mike McGowan the Man-Eater; and a dog-fight, in which the favorite lost, had attracted a big crowd.

When the *News* went to press late that afternoon, I was cheerfully informed that the custom of the shop commanded that the new man on the staff must stay and look over the sheet as it came wet off the press, making any amendments necessary in proofreading. All the rest of the thirsting staff filed across the street to Tim Dumars' saloon—The Fashion— for refreshment.

Standing back scanning a rough proof, I was almost hidden behind the big desk when a great, hulking fellow stormed in and banged his hand down on the desk, demanding to see the editor. On a platform slightly raised above the main floor of the office, I found myself next to the drawer which held the six-shooter. I recalled Alf's parting words, "Be careful—that gun has a hair-trigger." As soon as I saw the big stranger come stalking in I naturally thought of the revolver, and wondered if it was really loaded.

"I'm John Somers," he announced in stentor tones. "I want to see Alf Doten or whoever is in charge. You people have slandered me and I came to get an apology or get satisfaction. I cowhided an editor of this paper once, Conrad Wiegand— you may have heard of that little picnic."

"Did you?" I mildly confessed my ignorance of this episode.

"Well, I had to horsewhip *him,* and I guess I'll have to repeat the dose. Are you an editor?"

"N-no," I faltered. "I'm just one of the reporters—a *new* one. The managing editor is across the street, sir, getting a drink. If you'll wait just a few moments I'll run right across and tell him you want to see him."

"Oh no, you don't," roared Somers. "Not much! If I can't find the editor, by thunder, I've a mind to take the first man here I *can* find."

His hand manifestly was against all scribes, and as he raised it in menacing manner and made a move in my direction, almost involuntarily I picked up that pistol. It had a hair-trigger, all right; and, sure enough, 'twas *loaded,* for it went off—with a terrific bang, almost at my merest touch.

With his face white as chalk, Somers cried, "Hold on! Don't kill me!" turned and ran, breaking the glass doors of the office as he slammed his way out. He was never seen again in Gold Hill.

At the sound of the shot and the shattering glass, all the staff of the *News* came running back across Main Street. I told the truth, that the gun went off accidentally.

"Oh yes, it did!" chorused the gang. "But you can't make us believe that you didn't try to wing Somers. Serve him right, too!"

This time *all,* man and boy, went over to the bar. Overnight I found myself pitchforked into a small reputation as a gunfighter, strenuously as I disclaimed that doubtful honor.

CHAPTER TWO

A Roaring Camp

*B*orn in a log cabin; carried across the Plains in a prairie schooner at the age of one, losing my mother and father on the way, from that dread scourge, Asiatic cholera; an Indian interpreter at eleven; earning my way through college by "sticking type" on a frontier newspaper—is it any wonder that my heart beat faster when I heard of the Big Bonanza on the Comstock?

Before reaching my majority, I was admitted a member of the art preservative of all arts, and allowed the title of master printer. It was while a compositor on the *Alta California,* in old San Francisco, in 1873, that I listened to the glowing tales of the treasure-hills of Nevada. More, I set in minion and nonpareil type the astounding news of the bonanza, such as now would be blazoned in banner heads and boldface text in every newspaper in the country. The very types seemed transmuted to silver as my eager fingers set the names: Ophir, Mexican, Kentuck, Chollar, Potosi, Savage, Exchequer, Yellow Jacket, Crown Point, California, Consolidated Virginia. Those blessed doublets—Gould & Curry, Best & Belcher, Hale & Norcross—rattled off the cases with a merry click.

Ophir and Crown Point were my fancy; a fellow-craftsman introduced me to the stock market. My stocks skyrocketed,

© *Behrman Collection*

VIRGINIA CITY, NEVADA, WHEN WELLS DRURY FIRST WENT THERE, 1874

MOUNT DAVIDSON AND VIRGINIA CITY

VIRGINIA CITY FROM CEDAR HILL

SILVER CITY, NEVADA

and before I knew what had happened I was notified by my broker that several thousand dollars stood to my credit. From that I incubated the idea that it was my pleasant duty to go to the Silver State for an inspection tour of "my mines." I left intending to be away a few days—stayed fourteen years.

Virginia City in 1874 was on the swift-rising tide of its prosperity. I came upon it, as most do now, by way of the town of Gold Hill, neighboring it upon the south. The central points of the two mining-towns are about a mile apart, but the interval between was becoming so thickly settled that a stranger could scarcely guess where either left off. Between the Comstock communities is the wind-swept rise known as the Divide, and above towers Mount Davidson, the "Sun Peak" of early explorers.

My heart gave a skip of exaltation as first I saw it, lying sprawled there in its canyons and along the scarred mountain-side—the greatest mining-camp ever in America!

From this lofty vantage-point my eyes swept the vast panorama of mountain and desert, in matchless combination, gleaming with mineral colors. So clear was the mountain air upon that May day I could see canyons criss-crossing the ranges more than a hundred miles away.

And here before me, the hustling settlement overlying the Comstock Lode, that treasure-vein whose wealth was yet only partly guessed—but known to be rich beyond the fabulous mines of Ophir and Golconda. No wonder that a hint of mystery was in the sage-scented air, along with the eager excitement of exploration.

It was not long before I imbibed the legendry and history of the camp, from hospitable old-timers. Already the Comstock, they told me, had produced a quarter-billion in bullion—

about 60 per cent in silver, 40 per cent in gold, by value. It was destined to triple that astounding output.

The development of the Comstock mines was a natural sequel to the discovery of gold in California. Early in the '50s the metal had been found in the Washoe district of Nevada (it was western Utah then), including the canyons which lead down from the Comstock Lode; and following up their course, red-shirted miners toiled and moiled. All the first mining around Mount Davidson was for gold. The black sulphurets, so rich in silver, were cursed as worthless and cast away.

No one can say with certainty who discovered the Comstock Lode, but the same uncertainty as to priority of discovery (as my old mineralogical friend, Gilbert McMillan Ross, stated it) prevails as to germs and continents. The credit is usually given to a couple of prospectors from Pennsylvania, the Grosh brothers. These youths, Hosea Ballou Grosh and Ethan Allen Grosh,[1] were well educated and possessed some skill in mineralogy. It was in 1853 that they crossed the Sierra from California to engage in placer mining in Gold Canyon, one of the ravines heading on Mount Davidson; but the yellow dust was not all they sought, for within the next few years they did much prospecting, evidently convinced of the presence of important deposits of silver in the uplands, and the presumption is strong that they made a big find somewhere about Mount Davidson, quite possibly along what was soon to be known as the Comstock Lode.

The premier chronicler of the Lode, Dan De Quille, who prospected in Gold Canyon in 1860 and saw the little smelting furnaces used by them there, often talked to me about the brothers and their tragic fate. "In the fall of 1857," he

---

[1] This family name was often spelt Grosch.

recounted, "Hosea Grosh, while engaged in mining, stuck a pick in his foot, inflicting a wound from the effects of which he died in a few days. In November of that year, while on his way to Volcano, California, Allen, the surviving brother, was caught in a heavy storm in the Sierra, and had his feet frozen so badly that amputation was necessary, from the shock of which he died. With the brothers was lost the secret of the whereabouts of their silver mine. There was much search, but no mine was ever found."

Before their death, the Grosh brothers are supposed to have made an assay which showed the abundant presence of silver in the ores. "Out of that little assay glass," wrote Sam Davis with native eloquence, "came a giant more powerful and relentless than the awful shape that sprang from the pan in the Arabian story."

In January, 1859, a rich deposit of free gold was struck in placer diggings on a small eminence above Gold Canyon, promptly named Gold Hill. A rough mining-camp sprang up overnight.

Henry T. P. Comstock, who had come West as a trapper, followed the Grosh brothers, whom he knew, and tried to relocate their ledge. Some say that he was entrusted with the Grosh cabin near the later settlement of Silver City, when Allen set off on his ill-starred journey to California, but this is disputed. At any rate, when the miners began swarming to the Lode in 1859, Comstock ("Old Pancake" to his familiars) was already there, "claiming everything in sight." Assuredly Comstock was not the discoverer of the rich ledge which bears his name any more than Americus Vespucius was the first to behold America, but he swaggered to the fore and won the credit. At least, he was one of the first locators on the great vein, having somehow horned in on the rich claim discovered by Peter O'Riley and Patrick McLaughlin.

It was in June, 1859, that they made this marvelous strike, in a prospect hole near a spring on the rugged slope of Sun Peak. With the gold in their rockers was "heavy black stuff" which puzzled and baffled them. Some of the ore was carried for assay to Placerville and Grass Valley in California, and thereupon it was revealed that the cluttering stuff was black sulphurets of silver, and the ore astoundingly rich both in silver and gold. Other assays verified these. Intense excitement reigned, for this was the first great silver strike north of Mexico. Then began the famous "Washoe Rush" to the new diggings, which were in a barren region often called the Washoe country after an Indian tribe which wandered over it. Claims were staked out in mad haste. The Ophir was the first location on the Comstock, the discovery claim; others followed in rapid succession as an unlovely town of tents and brushshanties and dug-outs made its appearance on Sun Peak, soon to be renamed Mount Davidson, in honor of an ore-buyer.

Among the earliest locators on the Lode was a wanderer named both Finney and Fennimore—he found it convenient to pack an alias. This roistering blade was better known among his fellows as "Old Virginny," in delicate tribute to the State of his birth. On one of his sprees, while carrying a precious bottle from saloon to cabin, he fell down and broke the bottle on a rock. Always a man of ready resource, he arose with the dripping bottle and proclaimed, so loud that the whole camp might hear, "I christen this ground Virginia!" And thus came the name Virginia City.

That time he was thrown by John Barleycorn. Three years later, Old Virginny came to his end, thrown by an outlaw mustang.

Ill luck dogged all the pioneers of the Lode. Comstock, millions within his grasp if hℯ had but realized it, sold his interest for $10,000; then tried store-keeping, but lost his stake, and drifted to the Northwest. He came back to Virginia City in 1870 to testify in a trial and on his homeward journey, in Montana, he either committed suicide or was murdered. Peter O'Riley, when he parted with his mineral holdings for a sum around $50,000, built a stone hotel for the new city, speculated in the somersaulting mine-stocks and soon found himself penniless. After losing his fortune and his mind, O'Riley tunneled for gold, guided by spirits, and died in an asylum for the insane. McLaughlin became a camp-cook and later a hobo, dying a pauper. "Manny" Penrod, partner of Comstock, perished long afterward still looking for the precious stuff which he had found and lost again. Of the other early locators, John Bishop and J. A. Orsburn or Osborn (Kentuck) did not long hold on. More fortunate was Lemuel Sanford Bowers, first millionaire created by the Comstock; and of him and his consort I shall write more expansively later.

With the spring of 1860 came the peak of the mad rush to the mines. Men thronged over the route from Placerville, the historic old emigrant road, placed again in repair and improved as a toll-road. By the northerly route from Downieville and Nevada City they swarmed, too. The traffic by team and stage over these highways soon became staggering.

In May, 1860, a war with the Piute Indians flared up for a few weeks, but it put only a temporary blight on the mushroom growth of the camp. Before long, Virginia City boasted many substantial structures. Mines were actively developed, money flowed freely, prices (and wages) were the highest in America, and the community gloried in a crude opulence. Adventurers and adventuresses poured in. Those were lively days in Comstock history, as Mark Twain recorded in ROUGHING IT.

Nevada was organized as a Territory in 1861, and was admitted to the Union as a State on October 31st, 1864, at the height of the Civil War. Throughout the great conflict the Comstock was producing treasure which helped the Union mightily to win the ultimate victory.

Virginia City, during and after the war, had a troubled career. Holdups, slayings and incendiary fires were so frequent that a Vigilance Committee, known as the "601," took charge and cleaned up the camp, around the spring of 1871. The rough element was never entirely dispersed, but marks of civilization—schools and churches, societies and clubs, theaters, newspapers—multiplied. With brilliant lawyers and engineers, journalists and other professional men, whose eminence in achievement was recognized throughout the nation, it can be well imagined that when on its good behavior at least part of Comstock society was distinguished by intelligence and culture. This was in contrast to the riotous activities characteristic of mining-camps, into which it must be admitted all elements, high and low, good and bad, entered upon occasion.

Leaders arose in the community such as William M. Stewart, keen young lawyer, who gained Ophir and other important mining-companies as clients and who, rich from retainers, went to the United States Senate in 1864; William Sharon, sent up from San Francisco in that same year to represent the Bank of California interests, and who succeeded in establishing a milling monopoly and control of most of the producing mines; tenacious Adolph Sutro, mill-owner, who during a period of depression in the early '60s devised a plan to drive a tunnel through a mountain above Carson Valley to tap the Comstock mines on the 1600-foot level—an audacious project, on which actual work was begun in 1869 and carried to completion in the face of stern opposition and discouragement.

New impetus was given to the development of Nevada as the Central Pacific was built across the Sierra and across the sagebrush desert, the transcontinental railroad being completed at Promontory, Utah, in 1869. Charles Crocker had charge of the transportation of those who went to Promontory to witness the driving of the last spikes—there were two spikes. California gave one of gold and Nevada gave a silver spike, both regulation railroad size. In the notice in the *Territorial Enterprise,* Crocker announced that he had provided free transportation on flat cars and in freight cars for all firemen in uniform, and several hundred firemen from Virginia City, Carson and Reno accepted the invitation.

The mineral production of the Comstock dwindled, then increased again as John P. Jones developed the rich Crown Point mine. Mackay, Fair, Flood, and O'Brien joined forces to explore new ground. The Big Bonanza was discovered in the Con. Virginia mine in 1873, and following that was when the greatest influx to the Comstock came—my young self along with the rest.

Life was at full tide on the Comstock—for every grizzled old-timer and every Johnny-Come-Lately. When once fairly launched in Comstock journalism, accredited with the privileges and perquisites of a reporter, I had the run of the camp, and reveled in its animation. I was a part of it all, eager, alert to every new flurry of excitement. Contests and intrigues between the financial titans for control; the fevers of the stock-board crowds; wildly-flying rumors of new bonanza strikes; sudden death in the mine-depths; giant-powder explosions; fires and floods and blizzards; stage-robberies and hold-ups; street-duels and bar-room fights, cutting-and-stabbing affrays; rows in the brothels along D street in Virginia City; raids on Chinese opium-joints; gambling-games for high stakes; boxing, wrestling, cock-fighting and all the sports patronized by the bloods; political campaigns, parades, picnics, arrivals of world-celebrities; play-acting, circuses, grand balls, target-shooting bouts, walking-matches, spelling-bees, jamborees—it was my job to cover them all, to record everything from deep tragedy to broad comedy in the close-set columns of the newspapers on which I wrote—on the Gold Hill *News* for several years, and later on the Virginia City *Chronicle* and *Territorial Enterprise*—the three leading journals of the Comstock Lode. They were flourishing sheets then, with generous public patronage.

During the era of the Big Bonanza, for a distance of five miles reached a continuous line of roofs through Gold Hill and Virginia City, sheltering more than 30,000 people.

This roaring camp in reality presented the last phase, the climax, of the mining excitement begun in California with the discovery of gold. Nevada's early history, in a sense, was merely a continuation of the history of California. After the discovery of rich mines in the sagebrush territory, and particularly following the development of the Washoe diggings, including the Comstock Lode, Californians fairly swarmed over Nevada and took possession. Of course, there were Mormons from Utah, and always Missourians—but the Californians dominated the scene.

The Comstock then had all the carefree zest and abandon of a '49 mining-camp beyond the Sierra. It was, so to speak, a suburb of California. One could cite a long list of Californians, some known to fame, who at different times inhabited the lower slopes of Mount Davidson. The list would range from miners like John Mackay, and writers such as Sam Davis, down to the "bad-men" of the camp. All and sundry went in for living again the excitements of the days of '49 and they succeeded to their hearts' content. To illustrate how thoroughly Virginia City was Californian, it had a Society of Pacific Coast Pioneers as large as the parent body in San Francisco, and every man had come in '49 or '50.

Not only the officials were from California, but also most of the miners, merchants, editors, hightoned gamblers, hightoned gun-fighters, stage-drivers and stage-robbers, lawyers, mining magnates, prize-fighters, artisans and courtesans, hotel keepers, cooks, waiters and bottle-washers.

In keeping with '49 tradition, on the Comstock almost all the men carried guns, so that all were on an equal footing, regardless of education, breeding, wealth or poverty, race, color or previous condition of servitude. Zinc Barnes, the law-sharp, said that Colt's revolver did more than the Declaration of Independence to make men equal. And ordinarily these were probably the most polite lot of men ever herded together in such a region of sagebrush and cactus. When every man is the judge of his own conduct and is swiftly resentful of even the slightest insult, the standard of behavior is necessarily marked by a high degree of punctilious courtesy that would under less strenuous conditions make the polished Chesterfield look like a rube at an afternoon tea. But even so, there were frequent disagreements among those polite gentlemen, and in almost any history of Nevada you may pick up you are likely to find from 20 to 30 pages of fine print giving just a partial list of the shooting affairs, mostly fatal, which punctured and punctuated the current of social events. These records, to be sure, did not include the ordinary robberies, highway holdups, and such vulgar crimes as are indulged in by inferior elements of society.

The arena for these exploits was an oversize mining camp—it was all one big camp—which from a straggling village came to be a city in fact as well as in name. City-of-Six is the truth-telling name of one Sierran camp; Mammoth City, which now cannot muster a solitary inhabitant to wake the echoes amidst its tumbling walls, never lived up to its brag. But Virginia City hummed with industry and traffic. Its mills and hoisting-works were on a gigantic scale; great piles of waste rock arose around the works—giving the lower section of the city a strange and unique appearance. Eager thousands surged through C street, which in the city's heart was lined with buildings of imposing front.

Hanging precariously on the sides of a bleak mountain, Virginia has streets which in winter are like toboggan slides. Perhaps the steepest is Union street between B and C. Unwary folk venturing down, particularly after a sleet-storm, were likely to perform "the Comstock glide" to the foot, unless they caught anchorage at a saving lamp-post. Runaways, of constant occurrence on these steep streets, added to the excitement, especially as they often ended in tragedy.

On the heights, the back-roofs of the houses were often set into the mountain-side. The goats living in old tunnels and foraging for scant herbage on the slopes of Mount Davidson ran out on the flat tin roofs of the houses and their clattering hoofs kept the inmates awake. Several goats, mascots of saloons mostly, were public characters—notably Black Billy, who lived and chewed tobacco on C Street. Goats had the run of the city. Maybe that is how I came to some understanding of the proud spirit of the mountaineer breed. I admire a goat. See how independently he stands! Nobody can insult *him!*

Doors in Virginia City often would not close, and many were the broken windows, because of the sliding and slumping of the surface soil. The town of Gold Hill (it lies mostly in a canyon) was actually settling into the old workings of the Yellow Jacket, Crown Point and Belcher mines.

The infamous "Washoe zephyrs" sometimes swirl around the flanks of Mount Davidson, blowing with titanic force. Dan De Quille used to relate that during an historic windstorm on the Comstock, "when boulders as big as pumpkins were hurled through the air, and water pipes were being ripped out of the ground," an old be-spectacled Chinaman was observed seated on a knoll calmly flying a kite—an iron shutter with a log-chain for a tail!

The windiest place is the Divide, between Virginia and Gold Hill. There the blasts blow almost without cease. A dreary spot at night, it was notorious for its holdups.

Whether the Washoe zephyrs were blustering or still, the Comstock was always a roaring camp, especially after lamps were alight. With the miners divided into three shifts, and with hundreds of men coming on and going off duty all through the night, the community was irregular in its sleep. It was said of some of the handsome lads who made their appearance after dark that they had worked so long underground they were afraid the rays of the sun would darken their fair complexions. Many places of resort never closed. Virginia City was far from being a nine-o'clock town.

CHAPTER THREE

Dramatis Personae

*B*efore me as I write lies a well-worn volume, a dusty old directory of Virginia City, Gold Hill, Silver City and other hustling western Nevada towns in the '70s. Worthless to others, perhaps, this weighty tome to me is precious, a golden book, for in its pages I read the names of my familiars, those who crowded the stage on the Comstock in its heyday. Here again, as in review, pass the *dramatis personae* who enacted events tragic, serio-comic and downright funny. Even to be a spear-carrier in that drama, even to be a scene-shifter, even to stand around in the wings—that was to look upon spectacles stirring and amusing. Of course, the innocent bystander did sometimes have to hunt cover when ornery scene-shifters tried to shift scenes too swiftly upon others who perchance had looked cross-eyed at them.

As I shuffle the pages, the personages of the old camp arise from the musty past. Rich man, poor man, beggar-man, thief, doctor, lawyer, Indian chief—all made up the roster of the citizenry of the Comstock. Few beggar-men, though: in bonanza times the nearest to utterly indigent campfollowers were Needles, "the Comstock Tragedian," and Sleepy, the opium-smoker, but they were rather of the *lazzeroni*. True, the Comstock was a paradise for tramps as well as dogs: fleas did not care to live at that altitude.

In the old directory, John W. Mackay and James G. Fair, mightiest magnates of the Comstock, are presented with the single word "mining" after their names. Their humbler helpers are cataloged in due order—superintendents, shift bosses, outside foremen, carmen, miners, pickmen, surfacemen, pumpmen, engineers, watchmen, firemen, melters, retorters, tankmen, battery-men, amalgamators, bulkheaders, fuse-makers, wood passers, wire rope workers, giraffe-men, oilers, sluicers. Even the names of their callings are obscure. L. Larson is set down as "agitator, California Mill," but his work was in refining noble metal, rather than the stirring of base human passions to strife.

After many a name is frankly put "speculator"; after many, "bartender" or "saloon-keeper."

Mine superintendents were universally entitled Colonel. The Comstock went in for honorary titles. All lawyers and leading saloon-keepers were also Colonels, excepting those called Judge. That rule was laid down by John Kittrell, when he was Attorney-General of Nevada, and nobody ever dared to dispute Kit and his bowie on such a proposition as that.

It was bewildering to read the report of a trial in a Comstock court: "Judge Whitman contended that certain evidence was inadmissible. Judge Mesick read from decisions of the Supreme Court precedents clearly establishing its admissibility. Judge Leonard and Judge Belknap held that the evidence was pertinent, but Judge Seely took diametrically opposite grounds. Judge Rising thought that the precedents cited in support of the admissibility of the evidence were not in strictly analogous cases, and that the evidence should not be admitted in this case. Judge Aude then addressed the jury, urging the acquittal of the prisoner." No wonder the casual reader was puzzled to find which among all these judicial alumni was really *the* Judge!

California's bench and bar were recruited later with distinguished legal lights from the Sageland. Take Chief Justice W. H. Beatty, to begin with, and John Garber, too. Both of them served on the Supreme bench of Nevada. Garber resigned to take a fee of $100,000 to argue the Raymond & Ely mining case. That talk was worth the money, for he won the mining claim that yielded $5,000,000. Judge Coffey of the Probate Court of California took his first practical lessons in Virginia City. Colonel Billy Wood, Colonel Hank Mitchell, Colonel Bob Taylor, Judge John Boalt and Senator Pat Reddy also did their share of lawing in Storey county's brick court house. It was the most prolific place for litigation and lawyers on earth, for every inch was covered with claims three or four deep. Mackay, Fair, Flood and O'Brien had to fight a dozen contesting titles to the Big Bonanza before they were allowed to dig out their millions in peace.

Most eminent and affluent of the Comstock lawyers, from early days, was William Morris Stewart. As a youth, after some study at Yale, he went to California, gaining experience as a miner and then entering the practice of the law. He settled in Nevada in 1860 and won repute not only as a lawyer but as a fearless fighter, on one occasion standing off Sam Brown, the desperado, who came into the courtroom to try to intimidate him. Stewart was a giant, and not to be cowed. "Bullyragging Bill" Stewart, he was called by Mark Twain, who was for a brief time his secretary.

Going to the United States Senate from Nevada in 1865, and serving four additional terms (as later herein recounted), Stewart did more than any other man to formulate mining law, not only for Nevada but for the nation; and he was a stalwart champion of silver as a monetary metal. He promoted the one-ledge theory, "a mixture of law and geology," contending that the claims extended the width of the Lode rather than a limited number of feet, and after long litigation he and his clients won out.

Senator Stewart was a man of tremendous energy. As a lawyer, in the matter of fees he was long the foremost in the United States, his earnings far exceeding those of the leaders of the New York bar. He owned interests in a number of newspapers in Nevada, which ownership generally lasted merely through the political campaigns in which he was a candidate.

In the course of my work on the Comstock, it was part of my reportorial duty to visit the courts frequently, including the police courts, where the seamy side of life was outermost, and there and elsewhere I became acquainted with virtually all of the bench and bar of western Nevada.

Among the well-known lawyers on the Comstock may be recalled Richard Mesick, Thomas H. Williams, who made a couple of million dollars through Con. Virginia stock taken as a fee, Tom Fitch of whom more later, as orator and editor, "Sandy" Baldwin, Charles H. Bryan, Charles De Long, who had been ambassador to Japan, Jonas Seely, William W. Bishop, B. C. Whitman, William H. Claggett, and a host of other brilliant ones.

Of the Bonanza team of mining magnates, Mackay and Fair dwelt much of the time in Virginia City during the '70s, Flood was there seldom, O'Brien almost never. With the members of the famous firm, except O'Brien, I was well acquainted. I often interviewed Mackay and Fair as to mining developments. Both were democratic, approachable men, and journalists who entered their presence, although frequently bent on asking prying questions, stood with them upon a footing of absolute equality. Oh, yes, there was the discrepancy of a few millions in financial ability; but the scribes were mostly young, very young, with their fortunes (such was their bright hope) fair before them.

While we might not be stacking up the twenties rapidly in journalism, all of us dabbled in mining-stocks, and Lady Luck sometimes favored us. Everyone, even the lowliest, believed that somehow he would share in the Bonanza—if not now, then presently.

Thus it was that a pencil-pusher on a pittance felt in the presence of the grand nabobs of the Lode who were in the midst of piling million upon million. We were bewildered, maybe, but not awestruck; and surprisingly free from the gnawings of envy. Instead of feeling that he was "on the outside looking in," the Bonanza journalist was more likely to consider *himself* an insider.

That other Big Four, the magnates of the Central Pacific Railroad, who often found it hard to raise money, sometimes visited the Comstock. Leland Stanford, Mark Hopkins, Collis P. Huntington and Charles Crocker were familiar figures in Nevada. I knew them all. Senator Stanford later remarked, "Virginia City, that little mining town, bought more of our stock than did the whole city of San Francisco." Virginia was ever a camp of speculators, willing to take a chance.

But enough of the "big guns." It was a motley crew of humbler personalities that gave the old Comstock Lode the variety which is the spice of life. They were characters all, originals.

To me, the worthy who personified the carefree spirit of the camp was Colonel K. B. Brown, one-time Chief Engineer of the Virginia City volunteer fire department. I can see him now as he swaggered along C street. His glossy silk hat had a rakish tilt, his immaculate shirt-front was resplendent with a sparkler as big as a pigeon's egg, and he wore a red flannel shirt inside his vest to show his allegiance to the profession by which he earned so much fame and his title of Colonel.

A portly figure was James Brown—"K. B." Brown, he was universally called, in the press as well as on the streets. He was sometimes referred to by his full nickname of Kettle Belly Brown.

When his health failed, "K. B." became watchman at the old Yellow Jacket works in Gold Hill, and later wandered away to California, where he settled in one of the Mother Lode mining towns. But he promised to come back, for he had abiding faith in the revival of the Comstock workings. "When they are going again," he would say, "from the Geiger Grade to Devil's Gate, as I hope and believe they will, I'll stand on C street in front of the Sawdust Corner and welcome back the prodigals. They'll come in droves." "K. B." has answered his last alarm. No call came from the Comstock.

Some years after he (and I) had left the Comstock, I wrote a series of Colonel K. B. Brown sketches for the newspapers, "dramatic monologues" in his character, and these enjoyed a degree of popularity.

One of the personages of old Nevada who has gained more than local fame, was Mrs. Sandy Bowers, "the Washoe Seeress." The book EILLY ORRUM is on the fiction shelf of most libraries, but it tells her story with spirit and is in the main a true account. She was a familiar and pathetic figure on the Comstock, and made a precarious living as a fortune-teller and prophetess after her great wealth had gone. Her brother,

James Oram (he also spelled the name Orrem), lived at Gold Hill, a wood-chopper.

Mrs. Bowers came to Washoe Valley as the young wife of a Mormon emigrant, but she separated from him and was located near the spot where she and her next husband later built the magnificent Bowers Mansion, when Sandy found her. She was glad to have a husband in whom no other woman had a partnership, and Sandy certainly was worthy of her devotion. While they were considered poor when they married, both owned some interest in the mine which afterward made them wealthy. They each owned ten feet on the ledge. They had an idea the mine was likely to turn out well, but had no conception of its immense value. Sandy got his interest in the mine in payment for work, and she got hers the same way, for she was not too proud to wash clothing for a living when she first arrived in Nevada.

There is a story, too—Sam Davis used to tell it—that they worked for a time in a Gold Hill restaurant, and that some of the miners who wolfed their food there urged Sandy and Eilly to get spliced, and amid uproarious laughter gave them as wedding gift "a million dollars." This million dollars was the face value of mining stock, which the jokesters believed virtually worthless. Not long after, fabulously rich ore was struck, and Sandy Bowers unloaded his stock, selling it for about what the hilarious miners had promised him. With reckless extravagance he celebrated, and that quite explainable occasion when he went out on the porch of the old International Hotel and proclaimed that he "had money to throw at the birds" has given many folks the idea that he was a drunk. When I asked his family physician, Dr. Simeon Bishop, about this, he replied: "I don't recall that I ever saw him take a drink of spirituous liquor, though he kept a liberal sideboard, and everything in his cellar was as free as water. The hospitality of Sandy Bowers was ideal. It was cordial without being insistent; free-handed, open, frank.

"Two better people than Sandy Bowers and his wife never lived," exclaimed Dr. Bishop, with depth of feeling manifested in his voice. "They were plain folks, both of them, though she was somewhat more pretentious than he. She was Scotch, a Highlander, and the broad accent with which she pronounced the name 'Sawndy' was a delight to her husband.

"He was a frontiersman; his ancestors had been pioneers of Kentucky, and his was the blood of a chivalric race. He was a gentleman without trying, and without knowing why. Besides, he was one of the handsomest men as well as most modest that I ever knew.

"My brother, Frederick Bishop,[1] was at one time superintendent of the Bowers mine and milling plant, and he told me that the average net earnings of the outfit amounted to about $18,000 a week. As the mine was a booming success for about five years, Sandy and his wife must have handled fully $4,-000,000. They were the first real millionaires of the Comstock.

"Nobody could make them believe that the mine could ever be worked out, so they spent their money as they went. When they visited England and Scotland and France in 1862 they took probably $100,000, but Sandy telegraphed back home for $45,000, and when he landed in Gold Hill all of that was gone."

In the flush of their good fortune they built the Bowers Mansion, of which so much has been told, twenty miles south of Reno. This supreme achievement cost $300,000, but in its

[1] Frederick Aubrey Bishop came to western Nevada with Fremont in the '40s, and settled at Genoa before 1853. His brother William was a leading attorney; his brothers Simeon and Alva Curtis Bishop were prominent physicians—all pioneers of Nevada.

construction the middlemen got most of the money. The stories about doorknobs and hinges made of silver bullion are true, as also are the tales of marvelous prices paid for pictures and statuary, and a bronze piano with mother-of-pearl keys. The library was a chamber of wonders, containing rare books and curios that cost many times what they were worth. The windows were of French plate glass and the entire mansion was most opulent in its furnishings.

Sandy Bowers was a rich man when Sharon was a bank manager at a modest salary; when James G. Fair was mining at Angels Camp; when John Mackay was just about getting away from the diggings in the neighborhood of Downieville; when Flood and O'Brien were unknown to financial fame; when John P. Jones was a sheriff of a California mountain county; when William M. Stewart was just commencing his great career.

But Sandy's glory was short-lived. He died at the age of 35 or so, and left a widow who he thought would be provided for to the end of her life, but she quickly lost what was left of the Bowers fortune and suffered dire privations. Her daughter, Persia, died in 1874, and after that it seemed that she never again cared much what happened.

Matters went from bad to worse, and soon the little money that was left at Sandy's death melted away and Mrs. Bowers lost possession of the mansion, which was quickly dismantled. For thirty-five years she fought against poverty but seldom protested. She eked out an existence, pretending to foretell what was going to happen in stock speculations and the like. Her calling appears as "clairvoyant" in the old Virginia City directory. She may have been sincere in her predictions, for all I know. At any rate, nobody complained, and those who patronized her were of the wealthy class who could afford it.

AN EARLY-DAY PARADE, ON C STREET, VIRGINIA CITY

GOLD HILL, COMSTOCK LODE, NEVADA, 1875

COLONEL K. B. BROWN, CHIEF ENGINEER OF THE
VIRGINIA CITY FIRE DEPARTMENT

Sandy Bowers died a few years before I arrived on the Comstock, but Mrs. Bowers I knew well, and later when she went to San Francisco to set up as a seeress, I did what I could to help her. After struggling for a long time there she returned to Nevada, where she fell sick and was sent to a county poorhouse. From that she was rescued and again went to the San Francisco Bay region, where she lived until her death in 1903. She who had been presented to Queen Victoria of England in costly gown passed in poverty.

For a long time the Bowers Mansion was owned by Theodore Winters, the racehorse king of Nevada; later the historic place passed into the possession of Henry Riter, who endeavored to restore it to its former splendor. On learning of Mrs. Bowers' death, and knowing that she had always expressed a longing to be laid at rest by the side of her husband and daughter on the hill back of the mansion, Riter made arrangements for this at his own expense. There she reposes. Other owners now have the mansion, once more bright with lights as a gambling casino and resort, and now, as before, a favorite picnic-place in summertime.

There was plenty of work cut out for the sky-pilots in those early days. The primitive church in Nevada was beset with hardships of a barbaric wilderness. Often the earliest services were held in saloons; over at Eureka the Episcopalian church gathered its first congregation in a tent bearing the sign, *Antelope Restaurant*. Now and again the cry of "keno!" from down the main street punctuated the discourse, by way of emphasis.

Bishop Ozi William Whitaker was the founder of the Protestant Episcopal Church in Nevada. He gave service which called for the physical energy and mental force of a noble manhood. This "missionary bishop," as his official title was, endured the hardships of the frontier, sharing the dangers and tribulations of the unsettled regions to the amelioration of which he gave the best of his life. As a tribute to his memory, a bell has been dedicated for the new Episcopalian church in Reno, by the alumnae of Bishop Whitaker's School for Girls, pioneer educational institution in Nevada.

A bell of Comstock silver hangs in the belfry of the imposing Catholic church in Virginia City, "Father Manogue's church," to all the old-timers. Just the man for the salvation of the Comstock was good Patrick Manogue. He had a rollicking wit and he understood the spirit of the camp, having been a miner himself.

Doing good in another way, Dr. Simeon Bishop, whom I have mentioned as a friend of Sandy Bowers, was one of the quaint and lovable characters on the Comstock in early days. His work carried him often for hundreds of miles through the snow and sleet of winter, and through terrific dust storms of the desert, in summer. Dr. Bishop kept no books, indeed sent few bills; nevertheless, he received a princely reward, that I know of. When he was superintendent of the Insane Asylum at Reno, one of the inmates presented him monthly with a check reading five figures!

The old "Doc" was of the early American type, in appearance remarkably like Uncle Sam. His native humor was unfailing and he had a great flair for forceful characterization. Of someone he disliked he said, "His eyes look like two rotten apples in a swill barrel."

Upon a lovely spring day the "Doc" was driving along a desert road, in the glory of a new long black coat. Suddenly came a drop of rain splashing the new apparel. With a troubled glance he handed the reins to his youngest son, who sat beside him. "Here, Frankie," he said, "you drive while I look for a rain-cloud."

Dr. Bishop gravitated to the mining-towns. After he left Reno he was a beloved figure in Columbia, Sutter Creek, Angels Camp and Iowa Hill, along the Mother Lode in California. He hated a city. When he was resident in a dark house in San Francisco, walled in between others, he said, "I wish I could gather all the sunshine in this house—I'd bottle it for ink." Scornful of the home life of the city-dwellers, he gave his definition of a modern family: "A man, somebody else's wife and a dog—in an apartment!"

Another quaint character on the Comstock was Metaliferous Murphy, ore-expert. When a sample of rock was referred to him as an exhibit, he would cock his head knowingly on the side and would invariably say, "This *spicimen* is highly *mitaliferous.*" To me one day he said, "This spicimen is highly mitaliferous . . . the component parts of which is antimony and lid"—dashing my thought that I had discovered a new gold-and-silver bonanza.

Metaliferous Murphy was not noted for restraint of utterance or fancy. When he praised a certain site for a mine he enthused, "With all Niagara for water power and all hell for a dump, that mine would niver be worked out in tin thousand years!"

The rise and fall of a mining magnate was relentlessly reflected in the salutations of the community, according to Patrick Quinn. From poor prospector he gradually became rich mine-owner, and when his gold ledge near Devil's Gate petered out he fell accordingly in public estimation. The summary of his life and fortune was contained in the way general reference was made to him. This is as he gave it me:

Quinn
Pat Quinn
C. Patrick Quinn
Col. Cornelius Patrick Quinn
Col. C. P. Quinn
Patrick Quinn
Pat Quinn
Old Quinn

"Lightnin' Bill" Jones, in the play made famous by Frank Bacon and Will Rogers, told about driving a swarm of bees across the Plains and never losing a bee. But Lying Jim Townsend would have been an overmatch for Bill. He swore that he had invented a grindstone that turned both ways at the same time. After taking a breath to rest himself he said "that he had just made a list of the three biggest liars in Virginia City and that he was one and Hank Blanchard was the other two."

Hank was a big teamster—owner of great ore-wagons, a leading citizen in the community. He drawled in rough Missourian phrase until he was excited, then spoke in the most classic of English.

More about Jim Townsend later, when we review Journalism—for this cheerful liar habitually prevaricated in print. So did editor Fred Hart, author of THE SAZERAC LYING CLUB, whose adherents carried little hatchets as tokens of their craft, and usually resorted to Billy Eckhoff's Sazerac Saloon when around Virginia City. They vied for the title of Monumental Liar of America.

The most desperate lie of all was told by "Noisy" Kelly, a lookout for a faro game. "Noisy" derived his name from the fact that he scarcely spoke a word except once a year, and then he would talk "like a house afire," as the boys said. Every Christmas Eve he would get drunk and would tell big stories about his adventurings and exploits. Those who knew him would gather around to lend encouragement. One Christmas Eve when the thermometer marked 10 degrees below zero, "Noisy" warmed up on hot Tom-and-Jerry. Just before midnight he became greatly agitated—a sign that the brainstorm was about to start. Leaning his back against the bar he began: "With five companions I was in the fiercest Indian battle that ever was fought. We had killed about a score of Apaches the day before, but just at dark we discovered that we were surrounded in a cabin in a box-canyon by swarms of howling savages. We stood them off all night and kept them from getting in or burning our cabin. Just at daylight our ammunition gave out. All of my companions lay dead in the cabin leaving only me as the sole survivor. When the redskins saw that I was defenseless they rushed in, broke down the door and twenty of them, yelling like devils, attacked me with knives and tomahawks."

"Noisy" was so excited that he forgot his drink and had to stop for breath.

"I should think they would have killed you," mildly suggested a listener on the edge of the crowd.

"By God, they *did*!" shouted "Noisy," and we knew that his annual celebration had been a success. Then he lapsed into silence for another year.

Johnnie Skae, later the head of the Sierra Nevada mine, was in charge of the wonderful water system at Virginia City. There arose quite a dispute between him and the aldermen, who wanted a one-third reduction of the water rate. Skae stuttered, and on this occasion he spluttered, "Pre-pre-preposterous! Why, that s-s-system cost us a million a year ago, and we haven't got our m-m-money back yet." Such was the story "told for true" on the Comstock.

Skae had another lively dispute, with Colonel Gillette, the new superintendent of the Savage mine. Gillette objected to being scandalously overcharged for water. He approached Skae and challenged, "We w-w-want a reduction." Skae flashed back, "You d-d-don't get it."

"But that ch-ch-charge is a d-d-damned outrage."

"D-d-don't you mock me," cried Skae. "I'll c-c-cut your heart out!"

Little did Johnnie suspect that Gillette also was a stutterer, especially when excited. My recollection is that he raised the charge. There were no regulatory commissions in those days. Johnnie Skae, by the way, was a great practical joker. You may read about him in Mark Twain's early writings.

A wanderer who drifted into the camp at odd times was Kelly the Fiddler. How Henry Ford, patron of the artless art of fiddling, would have enjoyed him. Old John Kelly would have scorned the title "violinist." He was just a fiddler. That was all. And it was enough for him and his admirers. He improvised and composed, yet Kelly knew not a single written note. Though a giant in frame, he had infinite delicacy of touch; "his music charmed the birds." Yet this was the man who, popular legend insisted, scraped the catgut for the first stag dance in San Francisco in '49.

On the Comstock, in the Mother Lode district of California, in the Salmon River and Owyhee mining regions, among the placers of the Rogue River valley, in the lumber camps of Puget Sound, and even as far north as the Fraser River mines, Kelly the Fiddler played himself into the hearts of his companions. No mere violinist ever gained such applause. At his will he swayed the men who heard him—melted them to tears or aroused them to enthusiasm.

All frontiers are alive with fiddlers, because the fiddle is the only complete orchestra that can be carried in a green flannel bag under your arm.

There is all the difference in the world between a fiddler and a violinist. Anybody who is industrious can learn to be a violinist, but only the gifted few can be fiddlers. Judge Charlie Goodwin, who went from a Downieville editorial chair to Virginia City, and then to Salt Lake City, was a marvellous fiddler. Bill Sharon, magnate, and Steve Gillis, journalist, could "fiddle a man's shirt off." Dave Scannell, longtime fire chief of San Francisco, who often came up to Virginia City for a good time, was another natural fiddler.

The Comstock saloons were visited by a poorly-dressed couple, the Maziotts, a woman fiddler and her husband, who accompanied her on an Italian harp. She played like a backwoodsman, with an astonishing swing to *The Arkansas Traveler* and *Lanagan's Ball*.

True, catgut-scrapers were not universally popular. In one of the early playhouses on the Comstock, when a fight flared up in the gallery, a gigantic fellow was seen lifting an adversary above his head, ready to hurl him over the balustrade. Someone below was heard to yell, "Don't waste him! Kill a fiddler with him!"

No review of the Comstock characters would be complete without mention of Conrad Wiegand, the most peculiar man who ever tramped the trails through the sagebrush. An assayer by profession, he was a deep student of the question of metals as a medium of exchange and wrote voluminously on the subject—it is claimed that the idea of the Government issuing silver certificates originated with him. But it was as editor of a newspaper that his eccentricities became apparent. When he was whipped by a politician whom he had criticised, so completely was his gentle spirit under control that he found it possible to obey the injunction to forgive his enemies. Most any other editor would have had recourse to a six-shooter.

Lovers of good living, the Comstockers accorded generous patronage to *restaurateurs*. Charlie Legate has been mentioned—he prepared my wedding dinner, to perfection. In one restaurant establishment I myself was passed as a graduate *chef* after a complete course in French cookery.

Some of the French cooks were from Canton. A couple of patrons were in an eating-place, and didn't seem to relish the steaming *potage*. "Sim, don't you think there's too much *caloric* in this soup?" asked one. The proprietor overheard, and left hurriedly for the kitchen, vowing that he'd have to take an ax to that Chinaman, so heavy-handed with the caloric.

One of the favorite restaurants was run by "Porky" and "Big Nell," who, as everybody knew, lived together—simple, jovial souls, both. Not having been there for some time, I said to one of the boys, "Let's go over to Porky's and get some luncheon."

"Why, didn't you know?" he answered. "The place is closed."

"Closed!"

"Yes. Porky and Big Nell were persuaded to get married— and they were so ashamed they had to leave town!"

Almost in defiant mood, another Comstock couple had their marriage license framed and hung up over the head of their bed.

Would that I could ramble on about so many other Comstock characters: hefty Uncle George Tufly, for instance, who was long State Treasurer and always one of the best-loved men in Nevada; "Joggles" Wright, Robert E. Lowery, Jason Baldwin; Pat McCourt, sometime chief of police, who told hair-raising tales of the Piute War, in which he served as a young soldier. Zinc Barnes, whose exploits have made him a kind of legendary figure, was a lawyer known for his cuteness. Judge Charlie Goodwin wrote, "Zinc's character was in the main fine, but there were holes in it." Then there were originals like Little Griffin and old Sam Wagner, the negro bootblack, who was almost a "centurion," so he said. Sam was the bell-ringer and town-crier of Virginia City, and a political wiseacre as well. Old Henry, likewise a sagacious negro bootblack, was considered one of the landmarks of the country; but drifters such as Medicine Bill, Buckskin Bob and Grizzly Dan came and went. William Sadler, universally known as Prospecting Bill, Nevada's long-distance walker, flung a defiant challenge at champion O'Leary.

Little Butch, otherwise George Elston, the bill-sticker, shone as an entertainer, and when he sang "My heart is bruk, God knows it is, since Terry joined the gang," he left the sides of his listeners aching. Mike Kennedy, boss fireman of Gold Hill, was another public figure—his cry, "Git off de hose!" Then there was old John Gilrooney, picker up of ashes and other inconsidered trifles, the scavenger whose dearest aversion was John Chinaman. His goat was Gil's valiant auxiliary in cleaning up on the camp and Chinese.

"Needles" is to have a chapter by himself, and others of the *dramatis personae* will parade in later pages—gamblers and gun-fighters, firemen and sheriffs, editors and printers, and the battalions of politicians who kept things humming. This story will range, as they did, pretty freely about Nevada—but stay on the Comstock most of the time.

"Indians and Chinamen not counted," many a bad-man of

the wild days would say when he modestly indicated the notches on his gun. The Chinese were particularly numerous in the early years of Comstock history, and a few of them lingered on in the camp after almost all but they had fled. The Hop Sings and Sam Sings carried their tong wars up from San Francisco's Chinatown, with the usual accompaniment of killings; and other tongs had their bloody feuds, too. As usual, the Chinese in Virginia City were inveterate gamblers.

With the Indians, *our* first families of Virginia, I never fraternized much, for I had known nobler redmen "in a cleaner, greener land"—and anyway I carry the deep mark where an Indian spear drilled into my lower left leg. No pension is paid in this case, as my wound was not in a regular Indian War—just a little private war.

Passing reference has been made to Indian chiefs. We had Old Winnemucca, head of the Piutes, with swarthy courtiers like Captain Bob, Captain Sam and Big-Mouth Jim from Pyramid Lake, and Princess Sarah Winnemucca, who turned out to be an authoress as well as a leader of her people. She married an army officer and wrote, LIFE AMONG THE PIUTES. Then, too, there was Johnson Sides, the Piute cop, about whom Bob Davis wrote a lively yarn telling how that dusky brave had been absolved from the sin of taking a drink of fire-water by act of the State Legislature.

Johnson Sides bore a name identical with that of an early settler. Leading citizens of the Comstock region had a hard time preventing the Piutes and Washoes from naming their children after these great ones—personal and family names both were appropriated.

Indians rode free on railroad trains—still do. No doubt there is a liberal ruling as to those who are "half-Injun, half-injineer," as the familiar saying goes.

The Indians all turned out in war-paint and feathers when General Grant came to Virginia City. Captain Lord's artillery thundered a salute. I was lieutenant of the Sarsfield Guard and was arrayed in my sprucest regimentals. A Cornish widow on the sidelines was heard to say, "Isn't he the *fitty* little chap!" But the General, when he had responded to my salute by taking his cigar-butt out of his mouth and putting it back again, came up to me with a tolerant smile, "Young fellow, I never had as fine a uniform as that all the time I was General of the Armies!"

Grant and his party went through the mines, as did General Logan, when he called on us some years later. The "Black Eagle," after visiting the depths and seeing the men at work under terrific hardships, came to the surface vowing that "a silver dollar is worth all of a hundred cents."

General Sheridan, General Sherman, President Harrison, James G. Blaine, Henry Ward Beecher, Thomas A. Edison, Henry George—a succession of notables came to visit the Comstock, and it was my privilege to interview most of them.

Colonel Bob Ingersoll was guided to the hottest part of the mines and he candidly confessed that if he had been led much farther he would have been swayed to belief in the actuality of hell.

CHAPTER FOUR

Aunty's Big Pension

*D*o you want to know the spirit of the camp?

Well, some wiseacre has said that a people is to be judged by its amusements—and I guess that goes for old Virginia City, too. So I can give no better first presentment of the carefree life of the mining metropolis than by telling of some of the high revelry and deviltry on the Comstock.

Mark Twain querulously complained in his autobiography that the people of Nevada in that day were addicts of practical jokes, which he branded as signs of a barbaric culture. Lack-wits parrot the libel that the pun is the lowest form of wit; those who have been their victims aver that the practical jokes are the lowest form of jokes—in fact, mudsill jokes. It would be lese majesty and worse to charge the king of all humorists with lack of a sense of humor; but perhaps Mark may have been in this case unappreciative of the broad and boisterous practicality of some of the Comstock fun because he was himself the butt of so much of it.

Of course, all right-thinking folk will agree with Mark that jokes of the practical kind are vulgarian. It is the more painful to record, therefore, that the camp's Best Minds—lawyers, doctors, bankers, editors, gentlemen gamblers—entered with zest into such gigantic sells, along with the rest of us. Much of this activity centered about the theaters and music halls.

Max Walter's Music Hall used to be a favorite place in early times on the Comstock, and his patronage was something immense. His place was not as "high-toned" as some, but he paid big prices, though many of the shows were so poor that if there was to be any fun in them the fellows had to make it themselves.

Manager Walter used to visit Gold Hill once or twice a week to tell the boys what he was preparing for their amusement on the other side of the Divide. Of course, he advertised in the newspapers, but that didn't count. A man had to be sociable in those days if he expected to get business.

Max was a character in his way. He had a great habit of putting his finger alongside his nose when about to make any kind of important announcement. Taking this favorite position, he would say: "I dell you vat, poys: you shoost gums oop next Monnaday oond see der g-r-r-and opening nacht. It'll make you laugh more as you effer vas."

Whenever Max's shows didn't please the gang they let him know it and he'd change things mighty quick.

Sometimes the boys were a little original in their manner. Once Max imported an old-maid vocalist from San Francisco to do the Jenny Lind part of the program. She called herself Antoinette Adams, and said Boston was her home. She was nearly six feet tall, with a decided stoop to her shoulders, long neck, light blue eyes, a Roman nose, a crooked mouth and faded blonde hair that was frizzed with little curls around her forehead.

Antoinette, or "Aunty," as she was dubbed for short, had a voice that was a cross between that of a Washoe canary and a squeaky wheelbarrow. She couldn't sing "a lick on the round green earth," as the boys roundly stated it, so they concluded to "put the kibosh" on the show until she quit.

That evening word was sent around Gold Hill and the gang began to congregate.

"Look here, fellows," said Hank Blanchard, one of the leading teamsters of the place, "I for one think it's time to retire Aunty from the stage. Let's pension her and let her go!"

"Agreed!" said Mike McClosky, husky miner.

"Agreed!" cried all the rest, eager for the lark.

"Fall in by fours!" was the order, and up the hill they started.

"The boys are out for a jinks!" everybody said, and all who were not compelled to stay at home joined the procession. Business men closed their stores and hastened after, hoping to get into the tail-end of the crowd before it was all over.

Not one in ten knew what was going to happen, but they all knew it was going to be fun. The crowd marched through Virginia City just as if going to a funeral. Nobody said a word. The Virginia City fellows, of course, knew nothing about the scheme, but several hundred of them joined in just as silently and solemnly as the rest, as they marched right into Max Walter's hall and took the front rows. No reserved seats in those days. First come, first served, was the rule, and it's a good enough rule for me yet.

The Gold Hill crowd nearly filled the place and it wasn't ten minutes till every hole and corner was jammed. Everybody wanted to see which way the cat was going to hop.

The pride of the Comstock's manhood was assembled. A justice of the peace, constables, leading lawyers including the city attorney, mining magnates, all mingled with the throng.

When all got in, Max was around rubbing his hands and sending out for more chairs and campstools to set in the aisles. Never had he such a big house before. Of course, everybody paid—there was little deadheading in those times.

The gang sat still as the grave until four numbers of the program had been reeled off. Then it was Aunty's time to appear. She came out and made her usual prim bow, first to the front, then to the left and then to the right. As she concluded her bowing and scraping, a leader in the crowd stood up and called out:

"Now, boys, three cheers for Aunty!"

Those cheers fairly raised the roof. The boys sat down again as still as death. Not one of them cracked a smile. Aunty was so flustered with surprise and joy that she could scarcely catch her breath, but she finally came round, and started on her favorite ditty:

> " 'Under the willow she's laid with care,'
> Sang the lone mother while weeping,
> 'Under the willow with golden hair,
> My little one's quietly sleeping.' "

Well, to make a long story short, Aunty got through the song in her usual squeaky way, and just as she left the stage the gang began to applaud, wild with pretended enthusiasm. They whooped and stamped, and hammered the floor with canes and sticks and barrel-staves with which they had provided themselves for the occasion. There weren't any bouquets, for there was scarcely a flower within twenty miles of the camp, but half-dollars were shied onto the stage by the handful. That was the Comstock custom for giving a benefit. The money went straight to the person intended.

Aunty came back all smiles and blushes, and in an instant there was perfect order. She sang "Under the Willow" again, though her upper register began to show weakness, and once more the boys whooped it up on the applause. She attempted to bow herself into the seclusion of her dressing-room, but it was no use.

The third time Aunty looked over the coal-oil lamps which served as footlights and tried to sing, the exertion was just about all she could stand. It was apparent that the light mountain air was telling on her lung-power.

Again the thunders of applause greeted her rendition of the song. Aunty did not respond quickly enough, and the stamping was redoubled. The appearance of any other performer was prevented by the boisterous marks of appreciation for the songstress. Another hatful of silver coin was hurled on the stage. Manager Walter came out and tried to speak. He wanted to explain that the lady thanked her admirers for their appreciation of her talent as a vocalist, but that she begged to say she was unable to sing any more. He failed to stem the tide of her popularity.

"Take him off! Gag him!" yelled the savage crowd.

"Aunty! Aunty! Give us Aunty! We want to hear Aunty!" was shouted in chorus from a thousand throats.

Aunty panted as she came to the front once more. She looked slightly disfigured, but still in the ring. She tried to sing again, but her bellows wouldn't work, so she had to back out, bowing and smiling and waving her hand.

Then there was another storm. Max came before the curtain, held out his hands imploringly and finally made himself heard.

"Miss Antoinette begs me to say dot she cannot sing any more to-nacht," said he, "but she danks you for your courtesy, oond hopes to see you—"

"Oh, cut it! We want to hear Aunty sing. If we can't have what we want, we'll go home," protested the spokesman, and with one accord the Gold Hill contingent got up and filed out.

THE BOWERS MANSION, ABOUT 1880

VIRGINIA CITY IN WINTER. MOUNT DAVIDSON ABOVE

PARTY OF PRESIDENT HARRISON WHEN VISITING THE COMSTOCK MINES

PARTY OF GENERAL GRANT AT THE BONANZA MINES, 1879

Everybody else did the same, leaving the house as empty as a pauper's purse.

Next night the same crowd marched up from Gold Hill. The stragglers following were even more numerous than before. After re-forming in line on B street in front of Colonel Bob Taylor's law office, they advanced again. All drew up in front of the concert hall and called for the manager.

Max came out, hat in hand, as smiling as a basket of chips.

"Vat can I do for you, shentlemen?" he asked anxiously.

"We came to find out if you are willing to arrange your program to suit your patrons," said Alf Doten, who had superseded Blanchard as leader of the claque. "That's all the boys ask. We want to know before we go into your show tonight whether you will let Aunty sing all the time or not. We pay our money to hear her sing, and if that is denied us we'll go home."

Max threw up his hands in despair. "Vell, shentlemen, certainly Miss Antoinette vill sing shoost so long as her preath holds out, but she can't sing all nacht, of course. If you vill—"

"About face!" shouted the leader, and the procession marched to the Sawdust Corner, everybody in town following.

When the time for raising the curtain came, there was only a handful of people in the concert hall, and two of these were policemen. Nobody wanted to go to the show that night—there was too much fun on the outside for nothing.

Max blew out the lights and swore at his luck. More mystified than ever, he was still more thoroughly convinced that the camp had gone crazy. He couldn't see how men who admired a singer so much could give up the chance of hearing her at all just because she couldn't sing all night. Max would never have tumbled in the world if somebody hadn't told him. He hadn't the slightest idea of the merits of his actors except by the scale of their salaries. Aunty had been shrewd enough to ask a big figure, so he ranked her as a blazing star.

When Max found out what it all meant, he lost no time in releasing her, and the next coach which went over the Geiger Grade carried Aunty and two sacks full of the half-dollars which had been showered on the stage at her, and which she providently had swept up after she had somewhat recovered from, "Fair, fair, with golden hair, under the willow she's sleeping." The prima donna had enough to last her the rest of her natural life.

That's the way the Gold Hill boys took for giving Aunty a pension.

CHAPTER FIVE

The Professor Morse Slippers

*O*f all the "hoorays" the Comstock ever saw, the wildest and jolliest was at Pat Holland's Music Hall in Virginia City. Pat succeeded Max Walter in the show business and made a big success. He was particularly strong on practical jokes, and when he gave the tip that something unusual was going to happen his place wasn't big enough to hold the crowd.

Pat always was known as one of the gentlest-hearted practical jokers out of jail, and would never think of doing anything more serious than breaking a man's leg. His handsome countenance was always beaming with the pure light of brotherly kindness and love. But Pat did like a joke, just like Lincoln and Socrates, and Bismarck and Billy Emerson and many other good men.

You see, we were away up there in the mountains, shut off from the rest of the world, and ordinary humdrum shows and such-like didn't satisfy the yearnings for excitement. To be sure, we had the *E Clampsus Vitus* to help out, but nothing was considered so good as catching a real live "jay" and putting him through the paces at Pat Holland's show.

One day a tall, angular, actor-looking fellow, who called himself Elliston Trevillian O'Neil, showed up and struck Pat for a job.

"What kin ye do?" asked Pat.

"Do! Why, I kin do 'most anything. I'm an actor, I am."

"Kin ye dance?"

"Yes."

"Kin ye sing?"

"You bet!"

"Lemme see ye cut the pijin-wing, and sing me a stave of Joe Bowers."

The actor-man pranced around for awhile and did well, for he was really a clever Eastern comedian, but Pat tumbled that he was a tenderfoot who was on his uppers, so he decided to work him for a game.

"You're not exactly up to our style for singin' and dancin'," said Pat sorrowfully, "but ye seem to have good action, and I think ye could do well in one of our specialty acts."

The poor fellow looked hopeful.

"Say, did ye ever try to wear the Professor Morse slippers?" blurted out Pat.

"No. Never heard of 'em."

"Well, so much the better. Ye look like ye could do it, and if ye're willin' to try I'll give ye an engagement. Ye see this is the way it is. We have a pair of galvanic slippers, and we offer a prize to anybody who can wear 'em and not dance. Ye understand, of course, that these slippers are connected by wires with a strong electric battery, and there are mighty few men who can stand the shock without cavortin' and faunchin' all around the stage.

"Why, only last night we had the Governor and our Congressman goin' through their paces on this here platform, and everybody in the audience a-hollerin' and goin' on like mad. Hundreds of fellows have tried it and got left. If we could find a man who could stand it we could win a barrel of money, for they'd all play agin the game. Ye look like a man of nerve, and if ye've a mind to try it, we'll go ye one."

O'Neil was hungry and needy, so he was willing to risk anything short of death, and told Pat to bring on his slippers. Calling to him his stage manager, Jim Eddington, Pat winked and asked for the galvanic slippers.

O'Neil put them on in trepidation, expecting every minute to get a shock that would paralyze his backbone. Finally he ventured to take a step or two. He couldn't feel anything unusual, only the soles of the slippers were of copper and somewhat cold.

"Is that battery on full tilt?" yelled Pat to Jim.

"Not quite, sir!"

"Well, jam it all on."

Jim made a great ado about adjusting the screws and so on, striking the table three times with a hatchet, and soon O'Neil felt the pleasant warmth of a gentle stream of electricity tickling the soles of his feet. He walked about with perfect freedom, and would have danced had he not been cautioned that this was the thing of all others which he must guard against.

"What do ye think?" asked Pat, in his kind, smooth innocent way. "Think ye can do it?"

"Do it! Well, I guess. Just see me. Don't ye call this doin' it?"

"Ye're right, by jingo," said Pat. "And now for ropin' in the huskies. Ye must keep quiet and not give the snap away. Tomorrow night we'll win the majority of the money on the eastern slope of Mount Davidson, and ye shall have half of all we win. Here's $100 for ye to git any little things ye may need," shoving five gold cartwheels into the fellow's hand.

The next day Pat got out flaming posters proclaiming that

he had found a man who could wear the Professor Morse slippers without dancing.

You ought to have seen the throng that jammed into Pat's place that night. Pat was as proud as a monkey with a tin tail, and Jim Eddington was flying around like a pea in a skillet, seeing that everything was in readiness for the occasion.

There was the usual program of variety acts, with songs and dances, but nobody cared an ounce of porphyry for that. They wanted to see the circus. Finally the card of the evening was announced. The curtain went up and Pat Holland stepped forward and introduced Elliston Trevillian O'Neil. The audience fairly rose up at him and his self-complacency was elevated several notches. It was a reception of which any man might be proud.

Pat cleared his throat violently, and said: "Gents, ye see before ye the stranger who proposes to show ye that he can wear the Professor Morse slippers five minutes without dancin' or jumpin' around, or conductin' himself in any wild or unseemly way, such as I've seen the most of you do. Now, I believe he kin do it, and if anybody wants to gamble on the proposition, he's my Injun."

In a second the place was in pandemonium, everybody holding hands up filled with $20 gold pieces and offering to bet it couldn't be done. The Eastern fellow turned pale, for he had never seen so much heavy money before.

"One at a time, gents," yelled Pat, as they were nearly killing each other trying to get near enough to catch part of the money that Pat stood to lose.

Waving his hand majestically, Pat said: "Gents, we've got big money to gamble on this here proposition, and after consultin' with my pardners, we've concluded not to take any bet less than $1000 a rattle. So pool yer bullion, gents, and as fast as ye kin scrape yer thousands together ye kin be accommodated right up here."

The tenderfoot was fairly burning up with excitement, and Pat was telling him all the time to keep cool. A stakeholder and clerks were selected from the audience, and they took their places at the table on the stage. Stack after stack of twenty-dollar pieces were piled upon the table, and after each bet had been recorded the money was sacked up and carried to the back of the stage for safe keeping. Finally, when the books showed that $10,000 had been put up on each side, the gamblers in the audience began to weaken.

Then Pat started in to taunt them for not having any nerve. "What's the matter with you fellers?" he sneered. "Have ye run out o' cash? Ye're a pretty lot of fellers to call yerselves gamblers, now, ain't ye? After me a-goin' to the expense of sendin' clear to Philadelphy to get an electrician to wear these here Morse slippers, now ye squawk at $10,000. Why, blast yer stingy skins, that'll hardly pay his expenses by the stage line, to say nothin' of insurin' his scalp agin Injuns."

The boys admitted that Pat's complaint was just, but averred they were broke, so a committee was appointed to put the slippers on O'Neil and see that everything was done fairly. The committee, with Tom Gracey as the chairman, took off his boots and socks and fastened on the slippers with copper wire. Pat objected to this, protesting that it had never been done before.

"Oh, let 'em nail 'em on, ef they want to," said the Philadelphia man. "It's all the same to me. I could walk across the great American desert with them slippers and never make a skip."

A minute after, he stepped off the little carpet where he

had been standing and struck out like O'Leary in a six-day go-as-you-please.

"Turn on yer steam," he shouted to Jim Eddington, who was acting as chief engineer. Jim did so, and O'Neil kept on placidly tramping around.

"Do I dance?" he said, turning to Pat. "Well, I guess not. All that wealth is ours, or I'm a goat."

Pat smiled approvingly and the exultant comedian looked first at the audience and then at the timekeeper, who was calling the minutes.

"Three!" shouted the timekeeper.

The time was more than half over and the actor-man started out to make a speech, though Pat tried to keep him from it.

"You fellers must've been a weak-kneed lot o' cattle if you couldn't stand more than—"

"Four!"

"More than this. I've only a minute longer to stand here, and I'd like to bet a thousand dollars that I can last all night till broad daylight and go home with the gals in the morning. Just to make it an object, I'll call it two thou—"

"Whoop! whoopee! Wow! wow! Help! help! Take 'em off! Murder! Wow! wow!" and, with a shriek like a Comanche, the tenderfoot began turning flipflops and doing double song and dance business with himself. Over and over he went, and for your life you couldn't tell which was on top, he or the slippers. The stage-manager at last had "turned on the heat."

Did the boys laugh? Well, now, that doesn't express it. They howled and carried on and threw their hats away and smashed the benches and raised merry perdition generally. But, of course, it only lasted a minute or so, for Eddington turned off the electricity and let the actor-man loose. It didn't hurt him a particle, but it wilted the starch out of his self-conceit.

He was pulling on his boots when Pat Holland came out from behind one of the stage scenes with a big navy six-shooter in his hand. The poor fellow was so broken-spirited that he didn't look up at first, but Pat woke him from his reverie by cocking his gun.

"Villain! Ye've ruined me!" hissed Pat, "and I've a notion to murder-rr ye!"

"Don't shoot, Mr. Holland, don't shoot! For sweet heaven's sake, good Mr. Holland, don't shoot! I couldn't help it. Didn't I lose $5,000 myself? Ain't I a humil—"

"Out of my sight, thou base ingrate, lest I may forget myself and do thee har-r-m," shrieked Pat, flourishing his pistol. "Git!"

The electricity seemed to have done O'Neil good, for he sprang off the stage and ran right over the tops of the benches, knocking down everybody in his way, Pat shooting his pistol at the ceiling as he went, and jumped out of the back window, which was fifteen feet from the ground—but as it was winter, he landed in a ten-foot bank of snow and wasn't hurt.

He struggled out of the snow somehow, and next day left town $100 better off for his night's work. Pat made $500, the boys celebrated, and everybody was well satisfied.

You want to know where they got all that money, do you? Borrowed it from broker Joe Douglass on "jaw-bone security."

CHAPTER SIX

At Piper's Opera House

*7*he Comstock had a fine sense of the dramatic. Of its several theaters, foremost by far was Piper's Opera House, in Virginia City. Really, there were three theaters upon its site, for Piper lost his opera house twice by fire. This temple of the arts welcomed the most brilliant stars of the era. For some years, the companies which played in Maguire's Theater in San Francisco also appeared at John Piper's opera house.

Shakespeare had no lack of avid admirers on the Lode, and his plays were staged by a succession of repertory companies, all of them good and several outstanding. *Hamlet* was most often presented. Edwin Booth, Lawrence Barrett, John McCullough and Tom Keene were Hamlets who trod Piper's ample boards, besides several others of magnificent talent, though not so well-remembered. When he explained to the stage-manager his requirements for the fifth act, Edwin Booth was assured that he should have a practicable grave. He was astounded at the thoroughness in executing this promise. A section was sawed out of the stage-floor, a couple of Cornish miners did valiant pick-work, and that night the yokel grave-diggers shoveled some interesting specimens of ore onto the stage and were able to hand up Yorick's skull from the profound depths of a real grave. When Booth cried out, "This is I, Hamlet the Dane!" and leaped into Ophelia's grave to tussle with Laertes, he had the experience, unique in his long stage career, of landing on bed-rock.

Even the Shakesperian actors had their fun on the Comstock. McCullough and Barrett, great cup-companions, romped through a burlesque production of Richard III in Gold Hill in 1872 which must have made the immortal Bard turn over in *his* grave.

Edwin Booth played there a few years before William Withers Jr. arrived as premier violinist of the orchestra in Piper's Opera House. Withers had been director of the orchestra at Ford's Theater, in Washington, on April 14th, 1865, when President Lincoln was shot by John Wilkes Booth and he was standing in the wings when Booth rushed toward him. Not realizing what had happened, Withers placed himself in front of the assassin to demand what he was doing on the stage and was stabbed in one shoulder as Booth fled.

A Comstock musician possessed a rare Stradivarius, much praised by Wilhelmj, the Hungarian virtuoso, when he came to Piper's Opera House. Ole Bull had performed there, at an earlier time, and Edouard Remenyi came, also, to delight the multitude of Comstock fiddlers, to whom I have referred.

Always an ardent admirer of the theater, I was one of the faithful in attendance at the Opera House, reveling in its varied attractions, though truth to tell, in merit these must be described as "uneven." Many were the dramatic criticisms from my hurrying pen. For a time, in addition to other newspaper work, I was proprietor and editor of *The Daily Stage,* a little journal devoted to comment on the current dramatic season and printing the programs of plays at Piper's Opera House, whose officially approved news-medium it was. Naturally, many of the actor-folk became well known to me, and I was a frequent visitor in the Piper green-room.

The dramatic offerings were most varied. In the '70s and '80s, when I was on the Comstock, we were entertained by presentations such as *Camille, Lucretia Borgia, Ten Nights in a Bar-Room, London Assurance, Ticket-of-Leave Man* (again and again), *Rosedale, The Forger's Daughter, Monte Cristo, The Two Orphans, Galatea, The Octoroon, Under the Gas-Light, Led Astray, Mexican Tigress, Leah the Forsaken,* and a series of Drury Lane melodramas. *East Lynne* and other tear-jerkers had a poignant appeal. *The Lady of Lyons, or Love and Pride* was a prime favorite; I essayed the part of Claude Melnotte myself in an amateur production—"Dost thou like the picture?"

The Comstock had a big quota of enthusiastic Irish, and they (and the rest of us) were gratified by a goodly assortment of plays such as *The Shaughraun, Arrah-Na-Pogue,* and *Rory O'More* with Dion Boucicault, Shiel Barry and others as the leads.

One of the most popular actors, who came time after time, was Frank Mayo, in *Davy Crockett.* As he placed his brawny right arm athwart the door in place of a bar, his "Consarn them tarnal critters", hissed at the off-stage wolf-pack, won wild applause. Joe Jefferson never failed to delight with *Rip Van Winkle* and *The Rivals.* James A. Herne was *his* rival in the Sheridan play; that was before *Shore Acres.* Fay Templeton, as a girl, was with the Herne company—her father was the owner-manager. Also in the same cast with Herne appeared James O'Neill, father of Eugene O'Neill, the playwright. Nat Goodwin, Denman Thompson, the Lingards, Tony Pastor and his troupe, were among the stars of that era who got lots of fun out of their Comstock appearances.

Emilie Melville and her company rendered *Chimes of Normandy, Pirates of Penzance* and other tuneful offerings.

There was quite a run of Gilbert and Sullivan. "Lotta" and Maggie Moore, and Nellie Gilson, "The California Diamond" (she was a Nevada girl, though), were darlings of the day. Annie Pixley, another Nevada lass, was lovely in "M'liss". Hers was an appealing beauty.

In the earlier days, as "Aunty" could so well testify, silver coin was often showered on the stage as tribute to talent, but later the tokens of esteem took the substantial form of silver bricks, presented with appropriate addresses. One such was described in the local press as "of solid silver bullion, 50 ounces in weight; handsomely proportioned, polished and suitably engraved." And, then, of course, there were the inevitable "benefits."

It was the custom for some of the newspaper boys to participate in benefit performances for popular (and sometimes, alas, necessitous) actors of stock companies on the eve of their departure for other triumphs. Sam Davis, then a young reporter on the Virginia City *Chronicle,* and myself were among those pressed into service behind the footlights. Sutherland of the *Chronicle* was a skilful swordsman, and he was called on to fence with Borthwick Reid, a visiting Scotchman, who could do wonders with the claymore and the razor-edged sword.

Tremendous excitement was created, of course, when *The Black Crook* came, with its sumptuous ballet. Then, the troupe of Red Stocking Blondes, who filled the house as well as their hose. That other rollicking contingent, the Victoria Loftus' British Blondes, could not complain of their welcome to Virginia City, either, unless indeed they objected to being gazed at by the curious. When their train puffed in, at least five hundred males, mostly white-haired, bald-pated or red-headed, assembled around the depot, and a cheer broke from the throng as the blonde beauties passed up Union Street to Piper's Opera House, where a much better view was gained that night.

Helena Modjeska and Patti had graced this stage, but the miners applauded most vociferously for *Mazeppa* and other equestrian pieces, played by Adah Menken, Fannie Louise Buckingham and a succession of buxom performers.

A rather good story is told about Modjeska, Jim Fair and Sam Davis which may not be authentic—it is recounted sometimes with another set of characters—but which is characteristic of the camp. The great Polish actress, the tale goes, expressed a wish to see the Con. Virginia mine and Sam Davis volunteered to pilot her. After being rigged out in the necessary costumes, the party descended to the 600-foot level, where Senator Fair met them. The multi-millionaire superintendent, wearing jumper overalls and slouch hat, in his dress was not distinguishable from the miners around him. Sam Davis introduced the fair visitor with the remark, "This is the celebrated actress Modjeska, Jim," but vouchsafed her no information as to the identity of her new acquaintance. The Senator personally conducted the party through the underground passages, and after they had seen the mine Modjeska asked Davis if she had not better tip her guide in appreciation for his services. Sam unblushingly replied that it was a good idea, whereupon the actress drew a silver half-dollar from her purse and dropped it in the Senator's hand. Noting his look of astonishment, she asked Sam the reason, and he hinted that possibly it was not as large as the man had expected. So another half-dollar was added to the Fair fortune, and the lovely Helena had left before the Senator regained his usual composure.

All kinds of political and social meetings were held in

Piper's Opera House. With its dress-circle, parquet and gallery, it seated more than a thousand people. Lectures were far more popular in those days than they are now, and Henry Ward Beecher, Colonel Robert Ingersoll, Henry George and other nationally known personages were heard, sharing attention with Hermann, the Wizard, and Professor O. S. Fowler, the famous phrenologist who so captivated me that I paid good money for a course in the then-budding science which somehow has failed to come to fruition in half a century.

Maybe I secretly envied Addie, the page, who assisted the great Hermann. As a boy I *almost* was engaged in that capacity to travel with the Faker de Bordeaux, itinerant magician of marvelous powers.

Among the notables, Buffalo Bill appeared on the Comstock with a show, *The Red Right Hand; or, The First Scalp for Custer,* and with him was Captain Jack Crawford, "the poet-scout," with whom I became friendly when he sojourned in our midst for some time, after he had been accidentally shot in the groin during that blood-and-thunder production. Genial Captain Jack, who had been one of the bravest and most enterprising of the scouts and dispatch-bearers attached to General Crook's forces in the war with the Sioux, possessed all the engaging characteristics of the Western frontiersman. While he was in the hospital, his company having moved on, some of us gave a benefit for him. Among the amateurs who participated, I recall, were Judge Robert H. Taylor, Sam Davis, myself and George Gedge, who made an instantaneous success. Gedge served as an engineer at the Con. Virginia shaft, and at one time was associated also with the Ophir. Becoming a professional actor, assuming the name George Osbourne, he moved into higher histrionic circles.

Captain Jack Crawford came a few years afterwards with

his own show, and later sent to the Comstock for some Piute Indians to stage a war-dance in a new spectacle, *Through Death Valley,* but the wily sons of nature demanded a year's pay in advance.

Of course, we had the usual visits by "Tom shows," and these productions, especially when the players doubled in ebony and we beheld two Topsies and two Uncles Tom, seldom failed to draw. "A double quartette of educated bloodhounds was supported by an excellent dramatic company," one critic opined.

Minstrel shows were a perennial delight, notably Haverly's Mastodon Minstrels. The forty troupers fared well at the box-office, but after they undertook to buck the tiger in the faro-banks they carried away with them little more than bones and tambo and a few miscellaneous props. Billy Rice, the so-funny endman mournfully contemplated bankruptcy when he rendered, *Over the Hill to the Poor House.*

Emma Nevada, when she came to the Comstock, sang to a rapt audience—a Nevada girl she was, daughter of William Wixom of Austin. Later, we loved to hear the sweet voice of Dick Jose, big-hearted Cornish lad who left a Reno black-smith's forge to go on the stage as a ballad-singer, beloved by all the world. Informality of the old days was Dick's. One night in Los Angeles I sat with a thousand others to hear him sing. Dick spied me in the audience—we hadn't seen each other for years—came to the footlights, and heedless of the rest waved his hand, calling in greeting, "Why, *hello,* Wells!" Then he sang *Belle Brandon.*

Converse between audience and performers was as usual in Comstock playhouses as it was in "merrie England" of Shake-speare's time. I recall when John Mackay, patron of the theater, brought Dan O'Connell, poetical grand-nephew of the great Irish patriot, to Piper's Opera House to lecture and recite on *Gems from the Poets of Erin*. But there was a Cornish wrestling-match in Miners' Union Hall that night, and the theater presented an array of many empty benches, though all of us newspaper writers were there in force—Denis McCarthy, Arthur McEwen, Dan De Quille, Sam Davis, Ned Townsend, Alf Doten and myself.

Mackay, who had a genuine admiration for the genial O'Connell, was in a stage box. Dan's pride was somewhat piqued at the small turnout, yet he approached the footlights, manuscript in hand. His opening was very pretty, but Mackay evidently thought it a waste of poetical gems to cast them before only scribblers.

"Cut it short, Dan, and we'll go down to Fatty's and get some oysters!" called Mackay in a real stage whisper, as O'Connell paused at the close of his brilliant exordium. And Dan did cut it short with a vengeance. He stopped right there and bowed himself from the stage. The audience may have been slightly surprised at the abrupt ending of the lecture, but nobody objected, as that was a country where everything went. Over the oysters and ale that night, O'Connell regaled us with Celtic wit and poetic fancy.

CHAPTER SEVEN

Bonanza Kings and Minions

*P*eople who live in mining regions have a theory, amounting to a superstition, that money made in mining is cleaner than money made in almost any other way. There may be no valid foundation for such belief, but it is well nigh universal, down among the ravines where the stamp-mills roar, and along the sloping reaches of the placer diggings. The idea seems to prevail that the miner who digs metal out of the ground gets a clear and indefeasible title from the Creator, higher and brighter than any that can be obtained from the result of bargaining and chaffering in markets, big and little, or in matching wits even in the highest forums. The miner feels himself to be in partnership with the Dread Power that threw up the vast mountain ranges and tossed them about so carelessly that sometimes occur prodigious rifts—subterranean chambers, broad and deep—like the one which eons ago opened along the side of old Mount Davidson on the Comstock Lode and which in the course of the ages, by the process of volatilization, condensation and precipitation, became filled up, and grew into the marvelous body of ore known in history as the Big Bonanza. It is a cardinal belief of the miner that in rescuing the precious metal from rock or gravel he is harming no man, but is actually lending a helping hand to Providence in the work of benefiting all humankind. That is why the

miner habitually speaks of the proceeds of his industry as
"clean money."

Such was the view of John Mackay, as expressed to me
many times. Mackay, Fair, Flood and O'Brien were the
Bonanza quartet. Originally, James M. Walker was a partner—a Virginian he—his brother was Governor of that State.
He went back to the Old Dominion, declaring that he was
rich enough anyway, and he sold out his share to Mackay, so
that Mackay had two-fifths of all the Bonanza earnings, as
against the one-fifth share of each of the others. That's why
John Mackay was known as the boss of the Comstock.

Mackay and Fair were both practical miners, and men of
great discernment and strength of character. They had
worked in the mines of California before coming over the
Sierra to the Washoe diggings. Mackay began his career in
Virginia City as a skilled manual laborer in the mines, and
Fair as a machinist, but both soon rose to superior positions.
Joining forces, they secured control of the Hale & Norcross
mine in 1869, then of a number of others, including the Gould
& Curry. Steadily gaining capital they were in a position to
start exploration of the area where they thought the bonanza
lay, and they called to their assistance James Flood and William O'Brien, who were proprietors of a saloon near the water-
front in San Francisco. These affluent friends agreed to aid
them with funds, and the pooled resources of the four developed the Big Bonanza.

With a definite plan of campaign, the firm took over control
of a group of somewhat obscure and unproductive mines lying
between the Ophir on the north and the Best & Belcher on the
south, comprising the California mine and several properties
which they combined into the Consolidated Virginia. It was
by following a slender meandering clay seam, bearing par-

ticles of quartz, from the bottom of the Gould & Curry shaft through the Best & Belcher zone into Consolidated Virginia ground that the bonanza was found in March, 1873, the richness of the ore increasing as the development was pushed.

It may be true, as so many insist, that the Big Bonanza was struck through the persistence of James Fair, but his partner, John Mackay, was not the man to be turned back without getting what he was going after.

Public imagination was fired by the news of the find. The vaulting values of the Con. Virginia and California stocks in the market carried virtually all Comstock shares with them. Intrinsic worth was forgotten as stock quotations reached a dangerous point of inflation, out of all reason, even considering the richness of the Lode.

Each of the Bonanza Four had become as rich as Fortunatus. For quite a number of years, after 1874, their Con. Virginia and California mines had an average monthly output of a million and a half. Altogether the yield of the two mines was about $190,000,000.

How to be happy though a millionaire was a problem that John Mackay solved. He managed to get a whole lot of quiet satisfaction out of his money. Great wealth did not make Mackay miserable, as it does so many who have the unlucky fate of gathering together more of this world's goods than they can use. The reason for this was that riches did not cause him to forget that he was once as poor as the rest and he, like a true miner, considered it possible for nearly everyone to strike "the bonanza lead" in some kind of business if they only prospected long enough. So he was never distant or offish, but valued his friends for their personal qualities, not for their bank accounts.

It was only at the bank that Mackay's second initial "W"

was generally known. Everybody everywhere called him plain John Mackay. His name was used as a synonym for the superlative in everything. The idea of high quality and good luck were throughout the community typified by the term, "It's a John Mackay." He never had any title, not even so much as "Colonel," which (as I have noted) was bestowed by right of courtesy, *ex-officio,* so to speak, on other mining magnates of the Comstock Lode. And he refused three times to be named Senator to represent Nevada at Washington, though the post was assured him if he wanted it.

His benefactions were many. Of John Mackay it can be said that "good deeds stand beside him like Angels of Light."

Because he always remained plain John Mackay, and was their consistent friend, the miners were his champions. At a consultation of mine-owners, when a reduction of expenses was urged because of a temporary depression of the ore output, it was proposed that the miners' wages be cut to $3.50 a day. Mackay opposed this, insisting that the economies ought to be introduced some other way.

"I always got $4 a day when I worked in these mines, and when I can't pay that I'll go out of business," he said.

"But the way things are now the work isn't worth $4 a day," urged a man who was the representative of a big block of stock, but who had no practical knowledge of the mines.

"Worth it!" exclaimed Mackay, his indignation rising, "Worth it! Why, man, it's worth $4 a day to ride up and down on that wire string!" referring to the steel cable used in lowering the men to their work and hoisting them out when their shift was ended.

That settled it. Nobody ever again, in Mackay's presence, proposed to cut the miners' wages. The rate for underground work on the Comstock stood at the figure below which Mackay declared it never ought to be reduced.

Clarence Mackay, worthy son of such a father, gave a munificent permanent endowment to the Mackay School of Mines at the University of Nevada, expressing the continuing interest of the family in mining life and lore.

Another sturdy personality was James Graham Fair, possessed of the shrewdness and intentness characteristic of the Scotch-Irish strain. His mind was never idle, and in his later years he was engaged in a surprising variety of financial enterprises. A born money-maker, some called him bullion-hearted; but he was far from austere, and to the miners and the general populace on the Comstock he was "Uncle Jimmie."

James Clair Flood and William O'Brien were the other two members of the famous Bonanza quartet. Although Mackay and Fair were of Irish birth, these two were both born in New York, to which their parents had migrated from the Emerald Isle. In '49, Flood and O'Brien had worked side by side in placer-mining in the northern California diggings; and later when they were in partnership in the dispensing of liquor in San Francisco, friendly association with mining-men put them in possession of valuable information which they employed to advantage in stock operations. Becoming stockbrokers and mine owners, their ample capital stood them in good stead during the profit-eating exploration—slow groping, it seemed—in search of the Big Bonanza.

Genial "Billy" O'Brien, while not as keen an intellect as his partners, was nobody's fool. His easy affability and devil-may-care daring were assets of immense value in piling up the funds which helped to stake Mackay and Fair, and he knew mining stock gambling from soda to hock. O'Brien didn't live long to enjoy his millions, for he died in 1878.

Another colorful leader on the Comstock was John Percival Jones, who already has been mentioned as the developer of the Crown Point bonanza. He became a multi-millionaire, as did Alvinza Hayward, his associate in that undertaking. Welsh by ancestry, Jones had been brought to America at an early age. Coming to California in the gold rush, he fought in the Indian wars and served as Sheriff of Trinity County, a wild and woolly shire. In Nevada he became Superintendent of the Crown Point mine and was immensely successful and popular, as his repeated election as United States Senator attested.

Samuel L. Jones, brother of the Senator, followed him as Superintendent of the Crown Point, and a very able mining man he was. Henry M. Gorham was another of my good friends at the old Crown Point.

The great Hearst fortune derives partly from the Comstock Lode. George Hearst was there among the first in the discovery year, and retained his interest in the district, though mines in South Dakota, eastern Nevada and elsewhere later were his main concern. Marcus Daly went from the Comstock to his spectacular successes in Utah and Montana. E. J. ("Lucky") Baldwin was another who made a stake in the Comstock early. He returned to San Francisco "to mine the Comstock from the other end—the stock board." His luck was good, but he backed it with courage and sagacity.

A brilliant coterie of mining magnates and superintendents added distinction to the Comstock, men such as Isaac L. Requa, W. H. Patton, W. S. Hobart, D. B. Lyman, Robert Morrow, Edward D. Boyle, the Janin brothers, Sam Curtis, Matt Canavan, Warren Sheridan, William E. Sharon (nephew of Senator William Sharon), J. F. Egan, E. Strother, F. F.

Osbiston, Charles Forman, Z. Lyford and R. P. Keating, just to name a few, besides those already mentioned.

John P. Jones, William Sharon and James G. Fair were aggressive leaders in politics, each of them serving in the United States Senate, and to their campaigning activities I am to devote a later chapter.

In a community where everyday talk was full of knowing references to fissure-veins, drifts, stopes, cross-cuts, winzes, silver glance, silver chloride and porphyry, it was needful for a newspaper writer to be somewhat deep in mining-lore. Not only on "visiting days," but on many other occasions I was admitted to the rich workings. Tropical exploration could have been no warmer going than some of our drift-wandering, when we descended to the lower levels.

Superintendents and foremen, and many of the sturdy miners, too, were among my friends. As to the magnates—John P. Jones, Adolph Sutro, and all the great ones—it behooved me to know them well, so that "this pencil" (to use the cant phrase reporters and editors used in those days in reference to themselves) might have an opportunity to quote them upon affairs current.

Not to be forgotten are the bankers and brokers who helped to finance the mines. Outstanding among those resident in Virginia City, besides Sharon, were George T. Marye, L. P. Drexler and F. A. Tritle. Darius O. Mills, greatest banker produced by the West, who was heavily interested on the Comstock, preferred to invest in enterprises such as milling the ore and its transportation, rather than in the more speculative mine development. He and Sharon were the main owners of the Virginia and Truckee Railroad, between Reno and the Comstock.

Joseph Le Conte, the distinguished geologist, was a frequent visitor on the Comstock, as was that geologist and mighty mountaineer, Clarence King. His Government survey party labored for years, but the most comprehensive of their published reports came just in time to be too late, for the mines were petering out fast as they wound up their monumental work. Young John Hays Hammond was one of those who served in this survey under King. He was a genuine mining man, practical and sensible. The "lace-boot, tack-hammer brigade of mine experts" who invaded the Nevada wilds in after years were looked at askance by some of the Silurians.

Many improvements in milling and reducing the ores were developed on the Comstock, the pioneer in this being Almarin B. Paul. At the very first, Mexican miners often were employed, because they had experience in working silver properties, but their methods proved too crude and too slow, and their operations were on too small a scale to suit the Comstockers.

Despite a few disputes, amiable relations prevailed almost invariably between the miners' unions and the mine-owners.

The Comstock miners, in general, represented splendid types of honest manhood, and they surmounted great difficulties in their often-perilous work. The newspapers were obliged to report an appalling continued chapter of accidents. Most disastrous was the fire which broke out on April 7th, 1869, in the Yellow Jacket mine, spreading to the adjoining Crown Point and Kentuck workings. The Comstock never forgot that horror, for more than 40 men lost their lives; and its aftermath caused intense spitefulness in several political campaigns years later.

It was a harrowing duty to notify the women-folk of the loss of their men. I recall one shift-boss, simple yet kindly soul, who went with a delegation of his fellows to a humble cottage and sought to break the news by inquiring of the woman who came to the door, "Does the *Widow* Williams live here?"

All nations contributed to the 3000 miners regularly at work. Native Americans and Irish predominated, but those ancient regions of metallurgical lore, Cornwall and Saxony, also sent their mine experts and their mine laborers.

"By *Tre, Pol* and *Pen* ye may know the Cornish men," and sure enough, the payrolls of the mines bristled with names like Trevillion, Trelease, Trezona, Tregellis, Treglown, Trewhella, Trewartha, Trezise, Trevaskis, Tremayne, Treloar, Trevethan, Polmear, Pengilly, Penaluna and Penrose.

A heritage of mining skill has been handed down for countless generations in the mines of Cornwall. Of these great wanderers, the Cornish, someone has said, "Wherever a hole is sunk in the ground today—no matter in what part of the globe—you'll be sure to find a Cornishman at the bottom of it, searching for metal." They sunk many a hole in the flank of Mount Davidson.

I was always on terms of good-fellowship with the hearty Cornish folk. I loved to hear their quaint old-country talk, though I can attest that it is libel to say that they use the English language as if it did not belong to them. Still, the "Cousin Jacks" do have many startling locutions. It is alleged that one was heard to say, in regard to the misfortune of some lady acquaintance, "What's it to we, *us* don't care for she!"

Many Cornish miners, though, have astonished people by their eloquence, and some have so developed this talent as to become pulpit ministers and even cabinet ministers, charming by their discourse. They possess a strain of religious fervor, and even in rough surroundings display a fondness for books, as witness their patronage of the well-stocked Miners' Library in Virginia City. Independence, thrift, geniality, excitability, contempt for familiar dangers—these are characteristic of them. And with what zest they can sing their fellowship song, *One and All,* and their old patriotic ballad, *Shall Trelawney Die.*

After the decline of the Comstock, many of the Cornish went to Grass Valley and Nevada City in California, famous for their deep mines; some wandered to Australia and South Africa; others went back to Cornwall, and many are the pleasant messages I have had from old cronies, postmarked Redruth and Penzance.

During the lively Bonanza era on the Comstock, other contingents of miners kept green their racial traditions. The Irish, of course, with the Knights of the Red Branch, the Ancient Order of Hibernians, and such societies galore (Michael Davitt came and organized a big unit of Parnell's Land League up on the Lode); the braw Caledonians, who exulted in the games, where their men of might put the stone and tossed the caber; the French and French-Canadians, the Italians and Slavonians and Mexicans, all celebrating their own holidays in glorious care-free fashion—with many of these I was so fortunate as to foregather, welcomed into their midst, to partake of their national viands and refreshments. And with the Dutchmen I was a guest at beer-picnics and the strenuous turnerfests, "verein" they loved to display their bodily ability and agility.

A German mining expert, Philipp Deidesheimer, invented the square-set system of mine timbering early in the development of the Comstock, and it was this which really made possible the working of the richest mines. Another Teuton, Baron von Richthofen, possibly a forebear of the "Red Knight of Germany", World War ace, made a study of the geology of the Comstock Lode which proved of great value.

Only a few hundred of the miners were Germans, but many of the experts—Americans as well as Germans—had received instruction in the famous Freiberg Academy of Mines, in Saxony, which was the center of silver-mining and silver-smelting technology when the Comstock Lode was uncovered. It should be added that the Comstock developments carried these arts much farther, so that mining-men from all the world came thither to see and learn. The Comstock became the real Royal School for Miners.

CHAPTER EIGHT

Lots of Excitement

*E*xploration of the Big Bonanza treasure-vein and the proof of its astounding richness kept the Comstock camps booming. Thousands of fortune-seekers swarmed in. Despite the memory of Vigilante activities a few years before, Virginia City became the goal of reckless adventurers. Shootings and stabbings were all too frequent.

Great excitement followed the shooting of Barney Kenney— Little Barney—a gambler, by Matt Redding on April 12th, 1874, in the El Dorado saloon. Redding was himself a gambler, the arrogant king of the underworld, and he foiled prosecution by the plea of self-defense. It was true Barney had drawn his pistol on him, but a friend of Redding had thrown up his arm so that the bullet went high. Redding then drew and killed his adversary. But Barney had been a popular faro-dealer, and Redding lost his friends and his luck together. He drifted away from the Comstock, and years later died a pauper.

Provocative of endless disputes were the mining claims, and some of these squabbles over mineral locations amounted to guerilla warfare. Perhaps the most desperate battle over a claim was fought at the Waller Defeat shaft, between lower Gold Hill and Devil's Gate, on October 3rd, 1874, when several men were killed. Well I recall the excitement which ran through the region like wildfire.

This dispute arose between contending factions for control of the Justice mine, which also included the Waller Defeat shaft. The case was dragging through the courts, and in the meantime endeavor was made to supplant the Superintendent, Smith, with a new one, C. F. Kellogg. The Smith faction had about a dozen armed men at the works, both at the Waller Defeat shaft and the old Justice shaft. At dusk of the fateful evening, about twelve or fourteen heavily armed men marched down there, under William Kellogg, brother of the new Superintendent. He explained that the men were armed "in order to hold the works if they were given up," and he proceeded to parley with the forces in possession. The mine-foreman assured him there would be no trouble if he came with proper authority, and as he started back toward Gold Hill with a constable to get this (each side had some court order to show) a number of his men, impatient at the delay, got out of hand and made for the Waller Defeat shaft-house, whose garrison was promptly reinforced by about six men from the Justice shaft, a couple of hundred yards distant. The defenders called on the invaders to halt. Kellogg rushed back and warned his men not to advance, but two of them pushed past him and continued to go forward. One raised his revolver, and instantly a volley laid him and two companions low, all mortally wounded. After a pause in the firing, Kellogg called that he wanted to treat with the besieged, and was told that he could approach nearer if he came alone, but that if another attempted to follow the whole party would be fired on. As he reached the door, he was fired on and fell. Michael Cain, one of his brave men, ran up to carry him away, but received a load of buckshot in the breast and was instantly killed. The Kellogg party fired their pistols at those in the shaft-house, but with what effect was not known. Unless some of his men made a move to follow him, the killing of Kellogg was a treacherous murder.

A big crowd came down to the scene of the firing, and soon a cordon of guards was thrown around the shaft-house. They marched back and forth all night. It was the general belief that the defenders would never be taken alive. In the morning, not a man was found inside the building—all had escaped, *perhaps* before the guard was set. A regular arsenal of shotguns and pistols was discovered, and whisky demijohns. A coroner's jury found that the five victims had died from gunshot wounds inflicted by parties to them unknown, and though four men were arrested on suspicion they were finally discharged by the Grand Jury because of insufficient evidence.

It was rumored that a silent, sidling little "shotgun miner" named Dick Prentice had done most of the killing, but he was given only a perfunctory examination, and released.

The yield of gold and silver from the Comstock Lode in 1874 amounted to $22,000,000, despite all the quarreling and litigation, which tied up some of the properties. Even long-somnolent Carson City below, less than a score of miles to the southwest, awakened to new life and prosperity, because of its nearness to the treasure-vein. Not since the big Washoe Rush had western Nevada been swept by such feverish excitement. Carson, too, had its Vigilantes and lynchings, its street-duels, its Chinatown tong wars, though the little capital had quieted down decidedly since the early days when bad Sam Brown, the desperado, had strutted around the saloons boasting of his many killings, for which he was not apprehended.

Even when I went down to Carson for a space, to engage in the lively journalism of that place, I kept in close touch with the Comstock camps, and returned before many months.

CHAPTER NINE

Capital Interlude

Carson City, smallest of State capitals, was biggest in importance (in the view of elated Carsonites, anyway) at the height of the Bonanza era. It was not a suburb of Virginia City, insisted its spokesmen, who were many, but the garden and the social resort for the affluent Comstock—an oasis of civilization in the desert.

Carson lies about thirty miles south of Reno, in circular Eagle Valley. It is a beautiful homelike community adorned with flowers and tree-lined streets. The redoubtable Kit Carson had been here, and in neighboring Carson Valley, in the early '30s; settlers came about twenty years afterward, but not till 1858 was the city laid out. The founder was Abe Curry, picturesque pioneer. At first the settlement had a troubled existence, with a swarm of desperadoes to contend against, but after Sam Brown fell before the shotgun of Henry Van Sickle and after the Vigilance Committee staged a hanging or two, the peaceable element gained ascendancy.

During the meeting of the Legislature, the capital was overrun with Comstock journalists and politicians. At all times, the place was a hotbed of electioneering activity. Caucuses, county conventions and State conventions, ratification meetings and jollification meetings, kept the political pot boiling. Excitement reached its climax with the inauguration ceremonies of the veteran cattleman, "Old Broadhorns" Bradley, duly installed as Governor for a second term, with a genuinely eloquent address by Jewett Adams. One of my best friends (though he

JOHN PIPER, OF PIPER'S OPERA HOUSE, VIRGINIA CITY

PIPER'S OPERA HOUSE, VIRGINIA CITY, IN LATER YEARS

MINERS OF THE BOOM DAYS. THEY WORKED IN THE HOT STOPES
AND LEVELS OF COMSTOCK MINES

© *Behrman Collection*

MOUNT DAVIDSON FROM THE LOWER DUMP OF THE
GOULD & CURRY MINE, 1865

was a Democrat and I a Republican, in a partisan community), Adams was then Lieutenant-Governor, and later he became chief executive of Nevada by right of election. The Democrats also boasted Endless Elliott and a host of fiery speakers with limited terminal facilities, including not a few Kentucky colonels, late C. S. A. The political atmosphere was surcharged with electricity when we Republicans cheered to the echo the resounding periods of Tom Fitch and other stalwart spellbinders. Personal frailties of the candidates whose cause the orators espoused were often all too well known to the electorate, but if those in the race were "good fellows" that excused much. A certain ward statesman in his appeal for votes apologized, "Any mistake our candidate might make must be charged to his head and not to his heart!"

Candidates usually were as wildly extravagant with their own "long green" as with the public funds, if they got to them. To corral the voters they would stage wind-up rallies and burn bonfires for a week before the election, hold torchlight processions with bands "discoursing military airs," and deck the town with political banners, silken emblems of civic purity and advancement. Some candidates went wild on the banner proposition. They had banners to burn, and often did burn them after election. Explained one member of our central committee, who doubtless hailed from the East, "Banners cost money, big money, but just think what good they do in elevating the taste of the people to the white vest and silk necktie level."

Where campaign funds were being spent with such lavish hand, it was only natural for practical politicians on the other side to impute ignoble motives to the patriots who, in their careers of self-denial, were giving up their lives, their fortunes and their sacred honor, working for civic purity and the elevation of the homes of their neighbors. Many of the elective offices carried with them the appointment of only a single deputy, but some candidates appeared to have no conscientious scruples whatever about making many promises about one job to the swarming aspirants. Their rough-hewn philosophy was expounded to me by a promising young incumbent, "It's just as easy to let a friend down gently after election as to make that friend feel bad by telling him in advance he would not be It." For their part, the loyal henchmen promised themselves, "We will stick to our peerless leader forever, unless he gets defeated."

"In solid phalanx these voters stand," intoned our campaign orators, fanning the fires of political hatred between the adherents of Sharon and Sutro. Even gentlemanly Harry Mighels of the *Appeal* was wont to refer to his rival editors collectively as "the Sutronian kennel."

It was a dull year when Carson did not have at least four newspapers, serving a literate multitude of perhaps 4000—and hundreds of Virginia City and Gold Hill papers circulated there also, much too freely to suit Carson publishers. My principal journalistic activity in the capital city was not with the *Appeal* or the *Tribune,* the leaders in the field, but with struggling sheets (the *Daily News,* and later the short-lived *Herald*) trying to edge into their eminence.

The most formidable rival of the *Appeal* in those days was the *Nevada Tribune,* directed by "Deacon" R. R. Parkinson and his son E. J. Parkinson, often called Old Parkie and Parkie Junior. The Deacon somehow had taken a violent dislike to young David Sessions, a South Carolinian by birth and a Princeton alumnus, known even among the unlettered for his familiarity with the Latin and Greek classics. Sessions sometimes filled in as the "brevity and levity man" of the *Appeal,* and when Harry Mighels had to go "down below" (that is, to San Francisco) on important business, he left the young scholar in the editor's chair. Immediately a fierce quarrel flared up between him and the elder Parkinson, and when the "old man" of the *Tribune* (who was born under the British flag) was referred to as "a chance scribbler of foreign birth who shocks you by committing murder on his Sovereign's English at every breath," his rage was unbridled. As he swept around the corner in a blizzard to seek redress, he bumped right into Dave Sessions. The Deacon applied the usual epithet and then a few unusual and fancy terms of disparagement that he had thought up himself. Even though his adversary was described by his friends as "a man of fine culture and unaggressive disposition," at this provocation he visited chastisement upon the head of Old Parkie, "bloody but unbowed." Everyone was all prepared for what followed, because Ed Parkinson, the son, forthwith served public notice that he would settle with Sessions. At their next meeting, on the street, both opened fire with revolvers. In the fusillade of shots, Sessions suffered a shattered hand and Parkinson fell, wounded in the left flank. Though both wounds were severe, they were by no means mortal.

Some years later, the Parkinsons nursed a feud with Sam Davis, who, after the passing of gallant Harry Mighels, went down from the Comstock to succeed him on the *Appeal.*

Carson City, that ambitious little community, in 1874 supported thirty-six saloons, each with its sympathetic barkeepers, whose genial humor as they filled the chalice to the brim always made a man feel at ease, even if the world had gone awry. Good cheer abounded at Dick Brown's *Bank Exchange* and at Tump Winston's saloon and gaming hall, noted for its faro bank layout; at Gus Lewis' *Old Sazerac* and Vic Muller's *Headquarters,* and Mark Gaige's *Magnolia* and the *Occident* (with sumptuous keno parlors) and Henry Decker's and Dolph Shane's and Pendola's place. Lyman Frisbie's *Old Corner,* theme for song and story, inspired the local muse:

> "Thar's flounders in Frisbie's winder,
> Thar's sperrits at Frisbie's bar,
> And thar's nothing for to hinder
> A body from feasting thar."

Of similar import was a little effusion of my own, a couplet which was devised to draw patronage to the Veranda House, on the Comstock—

> "Then stay at the Verandy
> And to the mines be handy."

The Ormsby House, long the leading hotel in Carson City, was a landmark around which clustered cherished traditions. It was started by Major William Ormsby, who was slain by the Piutes in the Pyramid Lake campaign of 1860 and had a county named in his honor, as had Captain E. T. Storey, who met a like fate in that short but bloody conflict. In the middle '70s, the enlarged Ormsby House was run by George Fryer, and many distinguished guests partook of its hospitality. When a Senatorial campaign was under way, the charge to United States Senators or aspirants to that august office was always $100 for a suite of rooms and the regular corkage for wines. Senators Nye, Stewart and Sharon all paid without the quiver of an eyelid, but when Fair came along, he balked and went elsewhere, for indeed the old hotel had lost its pristine glory.

Some years after the Fryer regime, the manager of the Ormsby House was John Pantlind, who ran the place regardless of expense, inspired by the fact that he had the vast capital of Haggin

and Tevis behind him. But at last even these millionaire sportsmen withdrew from "Pant" their backing, feeling that they
would need backing themselves in order to keep up with the
lavish scale of operating losses.

Mine-host at the St. Charles Hotel in the early days was
George Tufly, that substantial citizen to whom earlier reference
has been made as one of the best-liked men in Nevada. A native
of Switzerland, "Old Tuff," as he sometimes was affectionately
termed, scaled more than 300 pounds, and his broad and manly
form in the portal of his hotel warmly welcoming the arriving
guests was a figure always to be remembered. But he gave up
the hostelry to devote his attention to banking (a warm-hearted
banker, Uncle George) and to serve as State Treasurer of
Nevada.

The Warm Springs Hotel, a mile and a half east of the city,
was another well-known resort, from early days. Picnics at
Bowers Mansion and Farmer Treadway's ranch near Carson
had a big popular appeal, usually drawing a large contingent
from the Comstock; and throngs of sports moved down from
Horntown and Slippery Gulch to take in the races on the Carson track. Most of the visitors were well-behaved, but sometimes roughs invaded the lesser saloons and even tried to stand
off the barkeepers, refusing to pay for their juniper-berry juice
and chain-lightning whisky, telling the publicans to "chalk it
up on the ice." Such defiance was met with summary chastisement with bungstarters, black bottles and other weapons ready
to hand. The even tenor of affairs was not helped any by police
officers of the Comstock coming down to celebrate and empty-
ing their shooting-irons at the ceilings.

It was after a sortie such as this that an old German taverner
explained to me, with expressive gestures indicating swift de-

parture, "Vell, I don'd exactly runned avay—I choost *go on oudt!*"

In its turn, Carson sent big delegations of the fancy to the prize fights held at select spots along the Geiger Grade. A special train carried Carsonites up to Virginia City to see Lotta, the beloved actress who had gone from the Sierra gold-camps to worldwide renown. She played at Piper's Opera House, but did not come to Carson that time. Often, as in this instance, John Piper captured the sole Nevada appearance of a celebrity. But then Carson had its theaters, too (though the Opera House was not built till some years later) and even had a company of stars headed by Mrs. D. P. Bowers, which Piper sent. The Templetons, with little Fay the bright particular star, were special favorites.

The California Minstrels proved all too popular, for they got drunk and failed to make their final scheduled appearance, though patronage at all performances was overflowing.

Lectures by Professor W. Frank Stewart, man of ores and ologies, were regular treats for the more reflective. My learned friend agreed with Napoleon that iteration is the first figure of rhetoric. For comic relief, Harry Mighels brought Josh Billings out to lecture, which reminded old-timers of that earlier Nevada lecture tour of Artemus Ward, so quaintly chronicled. At Big Creek, where the lecturer spoke from behind a drinking-bar, the saloonkeeper who was the promoter of Ward's lecture banged on the bar with his big fist at the close of every point, applauding, "Good boy from the New England States! Listen to William W. Shakespeare!"

As a member of the Chautauqua Society, I took it on myself to arrange for several lecturers to come, to enlighten "the discriminating and intellectual Carson public," as my brother journalists phrased it. In a campaign to solidify the position of Carson as the cultural capital, we promoted big spelling-bees, too, presided over by the State Superintendent of Public Instruction. In these, two schoolmarms and Governor Denver[1] and myself served as leaders. The typographical fraternity gave a good account of itself.

That was the period when Hubert Howe Bancroft was publishing his long series of histories of the Pacific Coast. Some of the early contracts, if I remember aright, called for the purchaser to take the entire series of volumes in sequence as they were published—an awkward kind of "open" contract, with no stop-order clause. A butcher in Carson, of German extraction, was persuaded on the ground of regional advancement (he was not much of a reader) that he should have Bancroft's histories, the explanation being that he could pay for them as they appeared. He could not imagine any man being able to turn out more than one or two of those big books in a year, so he thought it safe to sign the contract. But Bancroft was indefatigable and had plenty of help (I aided in assembling some Nevada material for him myself) and the bulky and costly volumes came forth with startling rapidity. Our Carson butcher protested mildly when they ran over ten, but as they began to mount up toward the thirty and nine which they attained, he became excited, and at last obstreperous. Still he respected his pledge, as attested by his autograph scrawl on the contract.

I chanced to be in his shop when Phillips, the book-publishers' agent, brought in the latest Bancroft history, shining in new calfskin. The butcher was cutting meat at the block, and as he glanced up his face was as red as rarest beefsteak. At first he demurred at accepting the proffered history, but when Phil-

[1] Frank Denver was Lieutenant-Governor in 1871-1874.

lips flashed his signature on the original contract, the Teuton took delivery.

"All right, I take it," he assented savagely. "I take your tamned pook, but see vot I do vit it—choost see vot I *do* vit it!"

He laid the history open, face upward, on the meat-block and came down with his cleaver, cutting it in two. Then with trembling eagerness he ripped off page after page, spread them down on the block, slammed a handful of liver into them, feverishly wrapped the pages around it, enclosed the whole mess with butcher-paper and thrust it into the hands of the horrified book-agent.

"Dot's vot I do vit your tamned story-pook," he bellowed, as Phillips shrank through the butcher-shop door.

Somehow, even when I see a particularly savage book-review, I am apt to regard it as pretty mild after all, remembering the violence of that literary criticism with the cleaver.

In the social life of the community, the volunteer fire companies took a prominent place, and firemen's balls were gala affairs. Each of the companies—the Currys, the Swifts, the Warrens—was independent. Unlike Virginia City and Gold Hill, Carson City had no chief engineer to direct the engines at fires and "to suppress any trouble that might arise," as the newspapers had it. Sometimes the last engine to arrive at a blaze could get no water, for the cisterns in the vicinity were being drawn on by engines already on the ground. The keen rivalry between the fire laddies, which this chronicle will note again, resulted in several free fights at fires, where fists and spanners were wielded with notable effect.

An effort had been made, early in Carson's history, to elect Colonel Abe Curry, city father, as chief of the fire department, but some of the companies balked, and so the Curry Engine

Company swore that if Abe couldn't be fire chief (which they considered the foremost place in any community) nobody should be chief, and they stuck to it.

Abe Curry was generous to a fault. The consequence was that at some times he did not have as much money as he did at others. Several fortunes passed through his hands. Once the Curry Engine Company asked him to advance them money when it was hardly convenient for him to do so. A circus arrived in Carson that day and as the proprietor was heard to say that he did not like the outlook for making expenses, Curry offered him $700 for the privilege of running the show that day, saying that all he cleared above expenses should go to the Curry Engine Company.

The offer was accepted, and such rustling and hustling was never seen there before. Tickets were peddled by the firemen and their wives and sweethearts, the men being called together for the drive by the fire bell, just as if there had been a house burning. The Indians and Chinese were induced to attend by sweeping reductions. To use Farmer Treadway's expression, "the country was canvassed for miles around."

But in the long run the circus deal proved not very satisfactory, for after all the trouble, when Curry counted up he found they had made only half a dollar. Next day Abe sent the engine company a check for $300, but the profit on his circus speculation he kept as a pocket-piece until his dying day.

A series of circuses came to Carson afterward. Most notable perhaps was the Montgomery Queen Circus and California Caravan, "a giant among dwarfs," which also "made" Virginia City and other Nevada towns. Presenting the "aggregated wonders of the prolific earth," Queen announced on arrival, "Although I have tripled my attractions and quadrupled my expenses, there will be no raise in the price of admission—charging the same price as the ordinary little shows charge." It is sorrowful to record that this "peripatetic coliseum and great moral spectacle" was wrecked not long afterward on the rocks of bankruptcy.

The circus folk had reason to remember the Washoe zephyrs that swooped down through Eagle Valley and sometimes made naught of the canvas cities. Mark Twain, when he wrote about Carson, celebrated these giant winds, which blew high and blew low, and left our streets and alleys looking like the ribbed sands of the seashore. Mark, it may be recalled, described a typical zephyr as carrying "a dust-drift about the size of the United States set up edgewise."

High winds at times made all the more hazardous the fires which have been mentioned. Several of the blazes were incendiary, and the identity of some of the firebugs was more than suspected. While I was in Carson, talk of lynchings was rife, but the editors pleaded with the aroused citizenry not to be hasty, lest their city should lose the Capitol and perhaps the State Prison—for as a matter of fact a new Penitentiary was started near Reno, though it was never finished. The legal hanging of a murderer, James Murphy, about this time, gave pause to threats of necktie parties. But a Vigilance Committee, the "601," was formed, and many people supposed it to be a regular secret organization with grips and signals, outside and inside sentinels, grand officers and regalia. Some speculation was hazarded as to what "601" meant. Whatever its significance, it meant business. A few months after the Vigilantes organized, a crowd of men one night awakened Tom Burt, a criminal whose bad record was known, and took him to the graveyard and hanged him. On his breast was a sheet of paper bearing the inscription "601."

Questionable characters were warned to steer wide of Carson, "where the rope not the woodbine twineth."

All of which has scant bearing on the fact that I had sold my share in the little *Herald*, fast-fading upstairs neighbor of the *Appeal*, and had returned to the nearby Comstock, just then reveling to the full in its gleesome games.

CHAPTER TEN

A Sporting Coterie

A royal family of sports, those old-timers in Nevada. Joyously they entered into every pastime from pedro to gunfighting, and each was willing to bet his bottom dollar to back his fancy.

Politics, of course, was the greatest breeder of excitement—we're coming to that. "Bucking the tiger" was a close second.

Of prize-fighters and wrestlers—local lights and importations—the camp had a bruising bevy. There was a whole series of slashing fights between Jimmy Trevillian and Patsey Hogan, both weighing in around 140 pounds. In the third of these, near the Mound House on the old Carson road, in 1874, Trevillian had Hogan bested in the 7th round when a spectator bellowed that Jimmy had a piece of iron in his glove. The referee found that Trevillian's seconds had placed a wad of oakum a couple of inches long in his hand because it had swollen; and with that disclosure the mob stormed the ring, pulling up the stakes. The referee came back and declared that Hogan had won the fight on a foul, though there was a bitter dispute as to the purse. Pistols were drawn but the referee, in the phrase of the day, "failed to be killed."

A couple of years later, local Jimmy worsted Two-handed Sullivan from Australia. They fought according to the then-new rules of the London prize-ring.

Memorable also was the ring battle waged by Jack Hallinan of Virginia City *versus* Billy Lynn of Eureka, the local lad walloping out a victory in 19 rounds. That was a real grudge fight.

As gory a battle as any I saw in Nevada was the mill on the Steamboat Springs road, in which Dublin Pete Lawlor beat Jack Askew (alias "Skewers"). It was Ireland against Cornwall, and the big crowd yelled itself hoarse throughout the 65 rounds. Prizefighting at that time was under legal ban, though many fights were held, regardless. When both bruisers were indicted, Skewers decamped, and he was never seen on the Comstock thereafter. Dublin Pete, arrested, was released on bond. His sureties were his backers, Dick Paddock and Tom Hughes, then conducting a saloon and cockpit; and when, later, these notables were killed in a gun-fight with officer McDonald, Pete felt himself no longer under obligation to linger around, and thoughtfully jumped the country.

Not to be overlooked, when naming the exponents of the manly art around Virginia City and Gold Hill, are Bing Williams, Harry Maynard, Bill Davis, Red-handed Mike (O'Connor), The Lancashire Lad, Cockney Charley and Tom Kean, who often presided as master-of-ceremonies. To the Comstock, too, wandered the gypsy fighter, Jem Mace, master of the modern science of boxing, and he taught the boys his craft. My percentage of hits was not high when I was permitted to put on the gloves with this elusive genius, and the old-timer considerately "pulled" his punches in my direction. John L. Sullivan came later in all his glory, affable and affluent. We became "cronies in one night." Modestly I admit besting the Boston Boy in a contest—but not in boxing, and that is another story. At this time John L. Sullivan was not lecturing upon the evil character of his antagonist and ultimate conqueror, John Barleycorn. Instead, he was an active champion, in the ring and at the bar. You may imagine the splash when he hit the Comstock!

The Cornishmen loved wrestling, and fierce were the contests in which they struggled—wrestling in canvas jackets, in accordance with the usage of their native county.

Rifle-shooting and pistol-shooting matches served to keep eyes and trigger-fingers fit, and naturally were immensely popular. The shoots held by the Emmet Guards, Sarsfield Guards, Montgomery Guards, and other militia units—dominantly Irish, as their names bespoke—were closely contested. As lieutenant of the Sarsfields, I often took part in competition on their rifle-range at American Flat.

On Sundays and holidays a group of my friends and I used to practice at shooting dimes in the air, with pistols which had hair-triggers. We got the idea from Captain Bogardus, the world champion wing shot, who came to Piper's Opera House to give an exhibition of his skill. Having familiarity with guns and pistols from earliest youth, I became quite expert, and this probably saved my life on at least one occasion. Steve Gillis, though, could always beat me.[1]

Sports now under interdict were freely held. The Comstock applauded bear fights, bear-and-bull fights and similar contests, on all of which liberal bets were placed. Some of the bears were grizzlies. In one battle I saw a bulldog defeat two wildcats.

During a dog-and-bear fight in Carson one night, bruin after a couple of rounds broke his chain, turned from his adversary and chased the managers of the show twice around the hall. The laughing spectators, all in the comparative security of the gallery above, cheered the bear lustily but offered to bet on the managers in the race. The scared humans

[1] Brutus Blinkenberry of Gold Hill told of "practicing his regular two hours a day at shooting out humming-birds' eyes and picking off gnats' heels on the fly."

scurried up pillars to safety. Another time, on the old Alhambra Theater stage in Virginia City, a grizzly cub chased the bear-baiting promoter up the scenery, wrecking several Streets in New York.

Jim Orndorff added variety by chasing coyotes with greyhounds on Forty-Mile Desert. No pink coats were in evidence when his Virginia City Alkali and Sagebrush Sporting Club spurred across the waste, whooping like madmen.

Cock-fighting was a regular institution, the "mains" being established mostly in saloons. Some of the most exciting chicken arguments were between the long-winded birds of Jack Hallinan and those of Alex Chapelle—representing respectively the finest feathered champions of Nevada and Michigan. Alex Chapelle had brought out a score of choice birds from Detroit, and he might have won if he had taken his time, but his chickens were not accustomed to the rarefied atmosphere of that mountainous region, so Chapelle went broke at the rate of a thousand on each fight. But I must say he was as game as his chickens, for he took his medicine like a man and never kicked.

Cruel as it is, the sport brings out the nobility of absolute gameness. My old friend, Colonel K. B. Brown, who knew a thing or two about how to place the gaff so that it would do good service, used to discourse to me with native eloquence upon the admirable qualities shown by the fighting birds.

"The gamecock is a gentleman; he is the aristocrat of his race," he exclaimed one day. "There is a pride in the bearing of blue-blooded poultry that marks them as the equal of the best of us. When you meet a bird like that big fellow there, from the Philippines, you instinctively realize that you are in the presence of one of the noblest works of nature. You've heard about that hapless human to whom a yellow primrose by the brook a yellow primrose was and nothing more, or words to that effect? Well, that's the way with most people about gamecocks. All roosters look alike to them.

"Really, I'm sorry for such people; their education is so much neglected. Now just think of classing Hallinan's magnificent birds with the Leghorns and Plymouth Rocks and Cochins that are in Neighbor Smith's back-yard!" cried the Colonel, appalled at the thought of such stupendous presumption.

"Look at the haughty glint of that white fellow's eye," he continued, pointing to the fowl dubbed *Conquistador*, "and note the wicked way in which his indomitable spirit blazes up once in a while. Why, he's as proud as any Spanish grandee. There's no such thing as his quitting if he ever gets into the ring. He'd fight a buzz-saw and give it the first hack. You might find a bird that could beat him, for the day of defeat must finally come to the best; but nothing could scare this chicken off an inch of his ground. You might kill him, but you couldn't whip him.

"This gamecock and I were utter strangers this morning, but when Jack Hallinan introduced us and by his manner showed that he thought I was all right, the bird took to me at once. That's the difference between anything that is well bred and the thing that has a yellow streak. Self-respect is the first ingredient of respectability and it is the crowning attribute of gentility. With this characteristic of personal dignity goes the frank demeanor that disdains to suspect anything low on the part of a companion.

"There he stands, a veritable feathered gladiator, proud of his past and confident of his future. He was bred a warrior and he does not shrink from the steel. He looks you in the eye as if to say, 'What would you with me? If you come in

JOHN MACKAY, "BOSS OF THE COMSTOCK"

A VISITING FIREMAN, CHIEF DAVID SCANNELL, OF SAN FRANCISCO,
ON VISIT TO VIRGINIA CITY.
(CHIEF K. B. BROWN OF VIRGINIA CITY WAS THUS ARRAYED.)

"YOUNG AMERICA" FIRE ENGINE, VIRGINIA CITY, NEVADA

peace I am your friend; if you seek a battle, draw and defend yourself.'

"I love to think that such as he represents the true American character—gently disposed to his friends, honest in his pride of birth, honoring his ancestry by maintaining the glory of his family name, and going to his final reward with the satisfaction of one who has always performed his duty under all circumstances. That's why I say that the gamecock is a gentleman."

CHAPTER ELEVEN

Needles, the Comstock Tragedian

*Q*uaintest and queerest of sporting characters—yes, and most pathetic—was Needles. "The Comstock Tragedian" he was called by everybody.

He would make the round of the saloons, a wandering minstrel, singing many a scrap of balladry—some old, some new, and one bit original with himself, ending plaintively

"Before you now you behold
Needles, the Comstock Tragedian."

After singing his song he recited a poem of his—he called it THE BLIND BOY's LAMENT, and said he wrote it himself. Dan De Quille made a sketch of Needles in that character. It shows Needles as he appeared during one of his fat spells.

Comstockers thought that Needles was an entertainer that beat them all. He used to do all kinds of character acting, *al fresco,* as Al Hayman [1] would call it. He was never on the regular stage, that I know of, except to play the lean apothecary in ROMEO AND JULIET for Lawrence Barrett once, and at another time to play the Ghost for John McCullough's HAMLET— that was in Piper's Opera House. On those occasions he was billed under his true name of George Cogill, for he was a

[1] A theatrical manager in San Francisco in the early days.

brother of The Cogills, then known all over the world as minstrels and sketch-artists.

Needles could have had a regular engagement, but he could do better on the outside. He could go into a saloon any day or night, sing a song, tell a story or give a recitation, and take up a collection of two or three dollars. Then he got all the drink he wanted besides. None of the regular engagements offered to Needles included an allowance for budge, and so he deemed it wise to reject them.

When Needles was broke and hungry, he was wont to recoup his fortunes by engaging in spectacular "games" which drew the attention of all the sporting fraternity. I remember the first time Needles appeared under the management of Jim Orndorff, of the Delta Saloon. It was one of Jim's "flowery" plays—just such as the camp was always expecting.

Jim matched Needles against an Unknown, who was backed by Bill Gibson, for a race for $100 a side and drinks for the crowd. What kind of a race do you suppose it was? Well, I'll tell you, for you'd never guess. It was a race through four joints of stovepipe.

The boys around town, of course, bet their money on Needles, for he was a big favorite with all, and we didn't think it possible for any galoot to come from Carson, where Gibson had his Unknown staked out, and beat our Needles through four joints of stovepipe. It was arranged that the match should take place in the Delta keno parlors, and Billy Robinson and Original Ike sold pools on the event for a month in advance. The time for the contest came on, and the Unknown showed up slick and slim. Gibson brought his man to the scratch in first-class condition. Just before time for the gladiators to step into the arena, if I may borrow from the poets long enough to express it that way, somebody who had money up on the race, asked: "Where's Needles?"

There were a hundred hearts that sank down to zero, for our home champion had disappeared.

"Oh, never mind about him," chirped Orndorff, though he looked mighty pale around the gills. "Don't you worry about Needles. He's been training for three weeks; hasn't eaten enough to keep a canary alive, and for two days I have forbidden food altogether. He has been living on our rarefied ozone. I left him in his dressing-room not thirty minutes ago. He was just putting another hole in his cinch-strap. You'll see him on time as thin as a rail and—"

"Here comes Needles!" shouted somebody on the outside of the crowd.

The men fell back right and left and in stalked Needles like King Tarquin in his pride. You ought to have seen him. He was togged out from head to foot in gala attire—plug hat, swallow-tail coat, doeskin trousers, patent-leather pumps, a "dude" cane and eyeglasses. He was drunk as a lord, and was dressed like one.

"What do you mean by this kind of a deal?" sternly demanded Jim Orndorff.

"My name is Normal—"

"Yes, I suppose it is," blurted Orndorff, before Needles could go any further. "I suppose your name is Normal or something like that, and I suppose my name is Dennis. Needles, you have betrayed me. You have been drinking."

"M'lord—*hic*—I cannot deny—*hic*—th' soff impeachm'n'," responded Needles with a majestic wave of the hand. "I have taken a drop for my stomach's sake, as Senator John Percival Jones of Gold Hill would say to Colonel Timothy Dempsey. Colonel Orndorff, I have sinned and I 'serve punishment. Let the sentence of—*hic*—court fall upon m'contrite head. I throw myself at your feet and cry mercy. See me here, m'lord, kneelin'—"

"Oh, get up," snorted Orndorff. "Get up and shuck those duds quick. If you haven't done worse than drinking you may save your bacon yet."

With tears in his eyes, Needles thanked his magnanimous benefactor. Steadying himself against the gas-pipe railing that ran around the reception room of the keno parlor, he took off his coat and then his vest.

What do you think? You may hardly credit it, but it's true. Needles had been eating. He was swelled up like a toad. The "suckers" who had bet on him tried to hedge, but it was too late.

"Ride him on a rail!" clamored one outraged citizen.

"Tar and feather him," shouted another.

"Lynch him! Lynch him!" yelled the infuriated mob.

But Jim Orndorff's voice rose clear and calm above the clamor. "Give the boy a run for his life," he pleaded. "Let him start in the race. Maybe he has a chance yet. If he loses, let the consequences of righteous indignation be his fate."

"That's fair! that's fair!" chimed the crowd which a moment before was thirsting for his gore. "Give Needles another chance for his life. Maybe he can win yet!"

"Grease me and let me try," whimpered Needles, who had been subdued to tears.

He was soon stripped and greased, and the word for the start was given. The first two feet in the stovepipe Needles was ahead, but his fatal fault of eating just at the wrong time proved his ruin. He stuck in the pipe like a fat shoat in a picket fence. The other fellow spun through in hollow fashion and took "the stuff."

That was Needles' last star engagement. He was rescued by the police and fled to Bodie. Ben Lackey, who helped him to get away, was beaten for Chief of Police at the next election.

"In Bodie," Needles confided to me later, "I had an attack of pneumonia and came perty damn near croakin'. They give me up for dead for a while, and the undertaker came in to measure me. I'll bet my entire capital that feller collected his bill from the county for the coffin that I never used. I would have died if it hadn't been for a gambler who took a likin' to me. After I got well the boys were goin' to give me a benefit, but the light air didn't agree with me and I had to leave.

"At Bridgeport I fell in with a banjo player and we started to take in Sonora and other California camps. We bought a donkey for two dollars, and puttin' a load on him commenced our professional tour. After three days' trampin' we reached the summit, where we made a camp in the snow and came near freezin', because we had neglected to take our blanket coats and buffalo robes with us. Linen dusters and summer pants will do well enough for the valleys, but they hain't the proper thing to tackle the mountains in. The snow was twenty feet deep in some places. But that wasn't the worst of it. When we got up in the mornin', cold and hungry, we found that the donkey had eaten all our grub and had chawed off his lariat and gone. That left us sixty-five miles from any house or settlement, without even a two-dollar donkey for breakfast. We were hungry when we slid down into the valley, you bet, but I soon recuperated and struck for the railroad—and here I am."

Needles was always on the go. After he drifted back from Bodie, one day in Virginia City he came to me and begged, "Lemme have a half. I want to go to New York."

"You can't get to New York on a half," said I.

"Can't I?" said he. "You jest try me, and see."

Well, I lent him the half, and next day I got a postal-card from Winnemucca saying he was there safe and sound. Next I heard from him at Elko, then Salt Lake, then Chicago, and finally I got a card from New York, telling me he had seen the Fifth Avenue Hotel and had spent a week in the Tombs.

It took him some time to get there, of course; but he did it. He did not ride under trains, but in them. He would go into a train and before the conductor would have time to yank him out, he would do a turn for the passengers and make himself "solid," so somebody would let him hide under the seat. He was so slim he could crawl into a hole that would squeeze a cat. If it came to the worst and he was found out, the passengers often would take up a collection and pay his fare, so as to have him along to make fun for them.

When Needles got back he told me he was only put off eighty-three times. He kept a diary and recorded all his evictions. I asked him what he had wanted to borrow that half for, when it appeared, from his own story, that he didn't need it.

"Oh, that wasn't for traveling expenses," he confided. "That was simply to buy postal-cards with, so I could do the elegant and let you know how I was gittin' on."

You were likely to find Needles in a haystack when he was not the guest of some county, arrested for "fragrancy." He had no regular abode.

As there was then no community chest or other charitable arrangement, every man about town was supposed to do his civic duty by supporting at least one person who couldn't support himself. Arthur McEwen finally chose Needles, the Tragedian, for his special charge, leaving Sleepy, the Opium Smoker, for me. After that, so long as we sojourned in the mining districts, two of Nevada's unworthy needy received the support which McEwen insisted was their due. In hard times, the community had appeals for "the worthy needy ones," but he argued me into a different philosophy. He pleaded for the *unworthy* needy ones.

"My way is to help the undeserving poor, because the deserving poor have all the rest of the world working for them," said McEwen, and he practiced what he preached.

The last time I saw Needles was on Kearny street in San Francisco. Poor Needles, the lad was looking a trifle old. Why, he had gray hairs in his head. It didn't seem more than a year or two since he was a tall, slim sapling of a boy with a tow head and a freckled nose, around the Comstock.

When I saw him he was looking a little the worse for wear. "Jest blew in from Arizony," he said. "Hard time, poor country; bad jails; no accommodations for gentlemen at the police stations."

Of course he worked me for a half. When Needles went for an old Comstocker, he always "touched." He caught me on that once-familiar song of his:

> "Oh, I've been a great star in my time,
> Although I'm now but a seedy one;
> I was known, when fresh in my prime,
> As Needles, the Comstock Tragedian."

CHAPTER TWELVE

Race of a Fire-Engine

*R*aces through stovepipes were mere preliminaries, compared to some of the exciting main events staged in old Nevada. One thriller was an endurance contest by a fire-engine down at Carson City during the early days, and this seems a good place to tell about it.

The inspiration for the match was Abe Curry, inveterate gambler. Not that Abe was a card-sharp, but he was willing to take a chance on almost anything, like most pioneer mining men. They're used to putting everything to the hazard.

He and old Alva Gould were the original locators of the Gould & Curry claim at Virginia City, and owners of that famous mine. Mark Twain says that Curry owned two-thirds of it, and sold his property for twenty-five hundred dollars, and an old plug horse that ate up his value in provender in seventeen days. Four years later the mine's stock-market value was more than $7,000,000.

But Uncle Abe, as he used to be called, was not bitter about that, and he was not always unlucky. When he did win he just "scooped" the gang. He won fifteen horses from Ed Sweeney on Grant's first election, and twice as many watches and six-shooters from other fellows around town. He won a horse and buggy on the weight of a pig that was running loose in the street, and a house and lot on the number of beans in a glass jar. He would bet on any proposition, from the number of straws in a hay-stack to the height of a flagstaff, or the length of the parson's sermon the coming Sunday.

Sometimes he took what looked like the worst of the game, but he always depended on his luck to pull him through, which it frequently did.

It was after he had gone over to found Carson City that Abe Curry became the backer of a fire-engine. He bought the old Knickerbocker engine of San Francisco, which had come originally from Boston around the Horn in 1849, and took it to Carson where he presented it to a fire company, and the old machine was rechristened Curry Engine in his honor. The engine, driven by manual power, did good work there for many years.

Carson, as the capital city, got so proud that it thought it ought to have a *steam* fire-engine, so one was bought and christened the S. T. Swift Engine, after Sheriff Shubael Swift, who made himself the most popular man in the county by having the hanging of a murderer take place in a little valley just on the edge of Carson City, so that the people could stand around on the surrounding hills and see the performance as if they were in an amphitheater.

Gus Lewis was elected foreman of the steam-engine, and frequently used to josh Abe for being foreman of a hand-engine that was years behind the times.

"One thing let me tell you, Gus—my engine has a record, and that's something yours hasn't got," retorted Abe one day.

"Oh, that's nothin'," came back Gus. "She kin make a record any time she wants to. You jest wait till she is called into active service, and see her spin."

"I'll bet ye a hundred dollars ye can't make her run twelve hours."

"It's a whack! I'll take all such bets as that," snapped Gus.

"I want some o' the chicken pie," said Sheriff Swift when he heard that Curry was on the bet.

So Abe bet him a hundred. All the other members of the Swift Engine Company wanted their share of "the chicken pie," and Abe accommodated them. He put up all his bank-account the first day, and then they crowded him into gambling his horses and watches and revolvers and such-like truck. They couldn't bluff out Uncle Abe on any proposition, and he took everything that was offered.

The time for the trial found Carson in a blaze of excitement. Half of Genoa came down to see the fun; Empire fairly turned out in mass; and the sports on the Comstock, when they learned of the contest, crowded over to lay their money on the line. Colonel K. B. Brown led the delegation.

The bet was that water should pass through the engine for twelve straight hours. Essey and Shear were the engineers for the Swift outfit, and as they were as proud of the engine as Gus Lewis was, they had the machine in good shape. It was 6 o'clock in the evening when it started, and it was to go till 6 o'clock the next morning. To make a sure thing of it, the engineers allowed the machine to run very slowly, and kept up all the steam the safety-valve would allow. For firing up they used pitch, bacon and coal. The water was let run through an open butt back in the cistern, without any pressure on the water-gauge.

There was not a sleepy eye in Carson that night. Everybody was out at the pumping match. There sat Abe Curry on one side of the machine and Gus Lewis on the other. They were surrounded by many of their friends, and though the best of feeling existed between them they looked like warriors bivouacking on the battlefield in order to be ready to renew the struggle at early dawn.

About midnight Gus sent one of his understrappers to say: "Mebbe you'd like to bet $150 more that she won't run twenty-four hours."

"That's jest what I wanted to bet in the first place," said Abe.

"Put up," said Gus.

H. S. Mason, the original stakeholder, was found in the crowd, and after Abe had rustled a few minutes the money was added to the other pile.

The bars around town were doing a land-office business, and Curry's friends were telling how sorry they were that Abe had made such a foolish bet, but of course if he was going to throw his money away they might as well get a chance as anybody else. About half after 2 o'clock somebody came into the Sazerac saloon and yelled:

"She's beginning to weaken!"

All rushed out and sure enough the little engine was showing signs of distress. She was coughing badly. The rich fuel had filled the boiler flues with soot, and the slow rate at which the engine was going had given them no chance to clean themselves out. The machine shook like a man with the chills-and-fever. The engineers saw what the trouble was, but it was too late, and a little after 3 the engine stopped stock-still—literally choked to death.

Of course Curry carved the watermelon, to use a beautiful simile from the sunny South. He bought all the champagne behind George Fryer's bar and turned the Corbett House dining-room into an oyster grotto. Everybody congratulated Curry and he spent two days giving back the watches and six-shooters he had won.

Did the steam-engine ever redeem its reputation? Why, it proved a perfect gem. "Frequently it ran from thirty to forty hours at a fire without making a skip," claimed a local historian, but this praise may be attributed somewhat to exalted civic pride. Anyway, it could throw two streams of water over the Capitol dome.

CHAPTER THIRTEEN

The Turf

*T*he rugged terrain of the Comstock region, set mostly on end, did not encourage horse-racing. There was scarce level land enough for a racetrack, but finally a smooth flat a couple of miles north of Virginia City was discovered by Jim Orndorff and Jack Magee, partners in the Delta Saloon, and it became a great Sabbath-breaking resort. Not only horse-racing was held there, but also many of the bull-fights, fox hunts, dog-and-panther fights and coursing events which enlivened the program of sports.

Most of the horses which competed came from the stables of Dayton and Silver City, and though thousands of dollars changed hands, the racing was lamentably slow for such a speed-loving camp. Some of the exiled Kentucky gentlemen sojourning there were first to protest; and it was decided to import some blooded California racers and put on a contest marked by real celerity. A couple of running horses, thought to be well-matched, were brought up, though some of the sports shook their heads doubtfully as to the effect of the great altitude on the speedsters.

Enter now the conspirators. Perry and Birdsell, partners in a livery stable during those early days, contrived by an absurdly low bid to secure the keep of those race-horses. They gained the confidence of the handler, plied him with liquor red and white, and on a bright moonlight night just about a week before the day appointed for the big race they drank him into insensibility. Then they led out the horses from their stalls, over to the track. Perry rode one horse, an iron gray, Birdsell rode the other, a bay; and starting from the grandstand they went around the track as fast as whip and spur could urge the steeds. The gray won by three lengths.

"To make it sure," suggested Perry, "let's change riders."

After a rest, they shifted each to the other mount and then tore around again; but the result was the same; the gray won decisively.

The moon that night was high in the sky, flooding the flat with light. It was almost like day. Fearfully they looked around to see if they had been followed and watched; but they discovered no snoopers.

They would have been less at ease if they knew that one of the sporting coterie, as if by instinct, had sensed their plan, and was watching through a field-glass from a shadowed summit nearby. Tom Peasley, it was, report said later: certainly he or some betting ally had learned of the secret trial heats.

Perry and Birdsell chuckled to themselves about the dead sure thing proposition ready for them. Never such a set-up to haul in the suckers, confided Birdsell to his partner, as they returned the race-horses to their stalls, grooming them so that they showed no signs of their midnight runs when the heavy-eyed handler looked at them in the morning.

Betting was at fever heat on the Comstock as the day of the race drew near; pools were selling in every saloon and gambling-hall. The conspirators mortgaged everything they had right up to the hilt and plunged into the pool with about $20,000.

Mile heats were to be run, best three out of five, to decide which horse was faster. They were run off next Sunday, before several thousand wild-eyed spectators.

Though the bay horse unexpectedly won the first heat handily, Perry and Birdsell refused to be ruffled; but when the bay led the gray to the finish in the second heat, their supreme confidence wilted. "True to form," muttered they with deep-chested sighs of relief when the gray captured the next heat.

They were themselves again; but only for a brief respite, for—the bay horse won the next and deciding heat! There was a swirl of angry men by the judges' stand, as the bay streaked under the wire. Gun-barrels glinted ominously, and Perry and Birdsell tried to shake themselves clear so that they could shoot it out. Each thought himself foxed by the other; and Tom Peasley, who had snooped in on the trial heats and had egged his cronies to put up every dollar they could scrape, was suspected of the grand double-cross, and just escaped being lynched.

When quiet was restored in a few days the secret leaked out, and Perry and Birdsell and the rest became reconciled to their loss. The handler of the race-horses had out-smarted them. Though deep in his cups, he had prepared for the trial heats that night by loading the feet of the bay horse, inside the shoes, with plates of lead, heavy enough to slow him down considerably: sufficient to deceive the local clockers.

A raft of money represented the take of the city sports who were behind this little stratagem. But these flush gentry fell in love with the wide open ways of Virginia City and Gold Hill; they tarried a few days. At the Washoe Club they stacked up against some of the best poker-players of the mining-camps; then tried to recoup at Tom Buckner's farobank layout. When they departed sadly for the big city, they had to borrow money to make the trip. So that those race-winnings never left the Comstock!

Besides the track north of Virginia City, often called the Association course, there was a racetrack at Carson City which saw much better running and trotting, and somewhat later yet another at Reno which was the scene of a spirited racing-meeting annually at the time of the State Fair.

Some mighty fast horses were raised on the Carson Valley ranch of Henry Fred Dangberg, one of the earliest settlers.

For a long period, Theodore Winters reigned as monarch of the turf in Nevada. But his sovereignty was challenged by that brilliant and erratic Comstock attorney, Charlie Bryan, who had made a fortune through mining litigation and proceeded to dissipate it on "the sport of kings." His horses consistently took the dust of those from the Winters stable, and Bryan went around with a haunted worried look.

He purchased the speedy Emigrant Maid in California, and trudged over the Sierra leading her all the way, in an endeavor to keep secret his new acquisition; but he was spotted, and the news spread like wildfire in the sporting world. Winters learned at once, and he imported a blooded racehorse which beat the Maid by lengths.

Then Bryan bought the noted black colt Lodi; Winters countered by purchasing Norfolk, Kentucky stallion, eldest son of the illustrious blind horse Lexington. It is asserted that Norfolk never felt whip nor spur, and never lost a heat. The horse was brought out from St. Louis, and won several races straight running in California. It was there, at San Jose, that Norfolk met Lodi. On the night before the race, Charlie Bryan slept in the stall near his race-horse, with a shotgun beside him. His mind held hallucinations as to evil plots against his entry, and during the race he had to be placed under restraint. Again the Winters horse won, and the distressed condition of poor Bryan became more marked—and a brilliant career closed in shadow, without even the solace of a victory on the turf over his arch-rival. Norfolk beat Lodi three times, the last contest at Sacramento setting up a world's record for the three-mile race—5:27½, with the losing horse only two seconds slower.

There were hordes of wild horses wandering Nevada's sagebrush plains in those days, and they were hunted—mostly for their hides. Sheep and cattle were run on the ranges, and superior horsemanship prevailed amongst the range-riders. We often saw this displayed when buckaroos swirled into camp; but my real acquaintance with Wild West riding came when I went sheep-herding with Dan Wheeler into California and the Northwest.

Some of my happiest vacation days were those spent sheep-herding with Dan, who was a pioneer stockman of Nevada. We would drive the sheep past Pyramid Lake over into California in Honey Lake Valley, northward by Klamath Falls (then Linkville) and into the Rogue River Valley, where we would sell the sheep.

"It makes me tired to hear people talking about Arabs and Indians and Mexicans managing horses better than free white American citizens. My idea is that the American lays over the rest of the world in horsemanship, the same as in everything else," old Curly Bill Garhart used to say. Perhaps he was right.

John Best McKissick of Susanville, up in Honey Lake Valley, whom I met when traveling with Dan, was the finest horseman of his class that I ever saw, and no Indian ever could compare with him in managing a cayuse. He didn't pretend to be a horse-tamer. He wouldn't have tamed horses if he could. He preferred them wild, and he could ride anything that wore hair. It used to be the custom to have riding tournaments up in Honey Lake Valley, but John Best won so many prizes that the others got tired. They didn't like to bar him off, so they just gave up the contests altogether.

It was only child's play for him to do all the tricks which the Mexicans think are so difficult. One of these is to bury a rooster in the sand, leaving only the head exposed. The test is for the horseman to ride at full tilt and as he passes, he has to reach, and catching the head, pull the chicken out of the sand. Lots of riders get hard tumbles in trying this, but John Best McKissick never had any such bad luck and he never missed.

He would even go further than anybody else would think of attempting. I have seen him ride a raw bronco, right off the range, and pick up five dimes in succession placed ten feet apart on the racetrack.

With the riata there was not a man on the continent that could match him. Nobody who ever saw him rope a steer would bet against him when rodeo time came and the young men gathered in to try their skill.

It was on one of the trips to the Northwest, after disposing of our sheep at Medford, that I continued on to Olympia, where I had been as a boy. And that recalls that it was there I saw the Blue Mare race, and I can't refrain from telling the story.

Olympia enjoyed a big boom in horse-racing, during which time the Blue Mare was the favorite in all the pools. Trotting races were almost unknown. Cy Mulkey expressed the common opinion when he said: "I don't go a red on them track-pounders that go banging round the course as if they would tear the ground up and then don't make the mile inside of two minutes after all."

The Blue Mare was a really good animal, though not thoroughbred. His endurance was something remarkable. I have seen him win three races in a day. Nobody knew how the Blue Mare got that name, for the animal was a bay gelding that belonged to the Shelton family. Some oddities of nomenclature may be explained, but this was a riddle to which no one ever offered a satisfactory solution.[1]

I knew a highly esteemed shepherd dog whose name was Robert Burns. She was the property of Dan Wheeler, and was the favorite daughter of Dan's old dog Bango, that had the reputation of being the best sheep-dog that ever crossed the Siskiyou mountains. The way in which Robert Burns got her name is readily told. She had the misfortune to be born without a tail, and as a natural consequence was called Bob. As she grew in age, wisdom and dignity it was recognized as a manifest injustice that so good a dog should have so short a name, and therefore it was lengthened to Robert. An enthusiastic Scotchman, in Wheeler's employ, in honor both of the dog and the poet, completed the name by adding Burns, thus making it Robert Burns.

The Blue Mare got his name simply from a freak of fancy on the part of his principal owner, Levi Shelton, for he wasn't blue and he wasn't a mare. The Blue Mare had won so many times that he was practically excluded from ordinary races and it was only when some new candidate for racing honors came to the front that the old favorite was given an opportunity to show his qualities.

It was generally conceded that the horse that could beat the

[1] A Chinook Jargon word, of French origin, is Le-Blau, "a sorrel horse, chestnut-colored." (Shaw's Chinook Lexicon, p. 35.)

Blue Mare would be able to win the western half of Washington. Several horses had been brought from Victoria to contend against the home champion, but one by one they had gone back to their island home crestfallen.

Similar fates had befallen the racers from Oregon. Even California had sent its blooded representatives, and they, too, met with defeat.

Charley Granger was proprietor of the stage line between Olympia and Monticello. He had been instrumental in bringing a number of fast horses against the Blue Mare, and all of them had lost.

One day Granger stood in front of the Postoffice and as the stage came down Main street he said to Postmaster Munson: "There's a broken down old stage horse that can beat the Blue Mare all holler."

Munson's breast swelled with local pride as he said: "I'll go you a year's salary that he can't." Olympia was then a fourth-rate office and the salary was not very big.

Granger's banter was soon carried to the Sheltons. The Sheltons are a large family, and they are sports and bloods to the backbone. Levi Shelton was one of two brothers, but which one he was nobody ever could tell, as they were twins and looked exactly alike. He was a fighter from the ground up.

The preliminaries for the race were soon completed and $1,000 a side put up in the safe of the County Treasurer.

It was the boast of the Sheltons that the Blue Mare was always in condition—that he didn't require any training.

Just as soon as the race was arranged Granger took his steed out of the team, christened him the Stage Horse and began to put him through a course of sprouts. I tell you, there was a big difference in his looks in the next week. His fetlocks were trimmed off and he was rubbed down and fed eggs until you could see your face in his coat as in a looking-glass.

I believe the Sheltons caught up the Blue Mare off the grass and fed him some shelled oats once a day just to give him wind, but I'm not sure about that.

Anyway, the time for the race came on, and the whole county went to see it.

On the track excitement ran high. There was no limit to the gambling. After men got up all their money they staked their farms, for the Blue Mare was to bring them out all right.

Most of the strangers and a few horsey-looking sharpers were backing the Stage Horse. He appeared in elegant shape, and the jockey on top was dressed in regulation racing toggery, velvet breeches, patent-leather boots and all.

The Blue Mare was not without his admirers, though his paunch looked pretty big. One Webfoot chap came near being knocked down on account of a jocular remark about "the plow-horse country-jake outfit", for the Blue Mare's rider was a tow-headed Shelton boy, who wore a checked gingham shirt, blue drilling overalls and buckskin moccasins covered with beads.

Mart Shelton had to explain several times about a suspicious looking lump on the Blue Mare's left side. One of his ribs was broken when he was a colt, and it had gradually turned as he got older, until it seemed to be sticking right into his entrails. It had never seemed to hurt the old horse, however, and the Sheltons had never thought of having an operation performed.

The judges' box held Governor Terry, United States Judge Hewitt and Indian Superintendent McKinney. Colonel John Miller Murphy of the *Standard* and Major E. T. Gunn of the *Transcript* acted as timekeepers.

The horses were called up, and at the second trial got a good sendoff, for jockeying was not allowed so much then as nowadays.

It was a two-mile race—twice around the track—and the yell which greeted the start was enough to scare the ordinary horse out of his skin. The Stage Horse had the pole.

"Go it, Old Blue!" "Hold 'em tight, Stagey!" "Go it, Overalls!" "Go it, Breeches!" and such enthusiastic calls rent the air as the racers reached the first quarter, neck and neck. Then the Blue Mare began to lag behind, and when the stretch was reached, the Stage Horse was twenty yards to the good. Down they came past the grand stand, Velvet Breeches leading Overalls so far that it looked hopeless.

"Never mind," said Mart Shelton, "just wait till the Blue Mare gets his second wind."

"Two to one on the Stage Horse!" yelled Granger.

No takers.

"Five to one! Ten to one!" came next in rapid succession.

Still no takers.

By this time the horses had neared the backstretch and it was seen that the rider of the Stage Horse was holding up so as to give Old Blue a chance for an interesting finish and to let the people have the value of their money in sport, even if they did lose their bets.

They turned into the straightaway for the last struggle. The Shelton boy had lost his big straw hat in the beginning of the race, and as he stood up in his stirrups and gave the yell of the Shelton clan, his long tow hair streamed back on the air like a flag of truce.

Down they came, thundering along, almost hidden by their own dust. The backers of the Stage Horse cheered as they saw him forge ahead.

Again the Shelton yell was heard, and it was echoed at the foot of the grand stand, where a hundred Sheltons stood to welcome their old horse to victory or defeat.

The Blue Mare recognized the slogan of his people. He pricked up his ears, straightened himself out and made a fierce struggle for the mastery. At twenty yards from the wire the horses were nose and nose, both riders whipping, spurring and yelling like mad.

They dashed past the judges, and the quarter-stretch crowd jammed in behind them.

"Which has won?" was the shout. Nobody could tell, but ere they could think an accident happened which still further increased the excitement.

Before the Blue Mare could be stopped he had run against a hitching-post near his stable, striking on his left side. The post struck the broken rib and snapped it off, forcing the jagged ends into the old horse's very heart. He fell and died instantly.

The judges rang the bell. The rider of the Blue Mare hobbled up with his saddle on his arm. Holding up his hand in salute he said: "My horse is dead."

After a moment's consultation Governor Terry, speaking for the judges, declared, "The race is given to the Blue Mare by a head. Time—well, we can't give any time. Major Gunn and Colonel Murphy were so interested in the race that they forgot to look at their watches."

CHAPTER FOURTEEN

A Battle of Titans

*H*orse-racing was not the only sport of kings—that is, mining kings. Most of their thrills came right out of their titanic tussles with the forces of nature, and with ambitious competitors for fortune's favor.

In the financial rivalry for control of the Comstock, the Bonanza firm of Mackay, Fair, Flood and O'Brien were pitted against William Sharon and his associates of the Bank of California, generally referred to as "the Bank Crowd." Sharon, as has been told, had come to Nevada as confidential agent of the Bank, at the behest of its cashier, the meteoric Ralston. Notable for his tenacity of purpose, Sharon not only guided the participation of the Bank in the development of the Comstock but also augmented his personal wealth by shrewd and fortunate deals, so that this slight little man of great determination became one of the richest millionaires in the West. Before the rise of the Bonanza firm, he was hailed as the king of the Comstock, with sway over the destinies of most of its mills and mines and other enterprises.

A struggle for mastery was to be expected. Sharon, archrival of the Bonanza group, was reported to have said, in derision, that Flood and O'Brien were nothing more than "bit-whisky sellers," and to have prophesied that he would make John Mackay "pack his blanket back over the Geiger Grade."

The story goes that O'Brien, with native belligerence, countered with the prediction that some fine day he would be selling his bit-whisky over the counter of the Bank of California. Mackay contented himself with the quiet observation that he was able to pack his blanket over any grade, as he had often proved, but that Bill Sharon could hardly pack his roll a hundred yards up-grade without stopping for breath.

When the Bank of California was founded in 1864, D. O. Mills and William C. Ralston were its leading stockholders. Mills for a time was President. Ralston was Cashier. A man of vision, public spirit and sanguine temperament, he interested the bank in the constructive enterprises characteristic of a new country, and by the time he became the bank's President, when Mills resigned in 1873, Ralston was financial dictator of most of California and Nevada. As I have said, it was he who had sent Sharon to the Comstock, and the bank became top-heavily interested in mining shares and mine development; the milling of ores; supplying water, timber and fuel to the mines and the Comstock communities; and in the railroad linking the Comstock with the transcontinental line.

The Bonanza firm fought monopoly by starting its own milling company, and, with millions in ready cash, prepared to organize a bank—the Nevada Bank—to offset the influence of the rival faction. Of a sudden, in the summer of 1875, a severe selling movement struck the mining stock-market; all shares slid dizzily, as even the Bonanza shares were thrown overboard. Comstock securities depreciated $60,000,000 in less than a week.

On August 26th, 1875, the Bank of California closed its doors. Some ascribe this to the Bonanza group, holding heavy liabilities against it, catching the Bank Crowd napping and contriving its downfall. Amidst the terrific excitement in San

Francisco that day, Mackay and Fair were in the Bank, and the story goes that O'Brien, mindful of his boast, came in and placed a fat demijohn of whisky on the counter and set out some glasses; but he got no further with his gloat, for Mackay bounced him from the place, warning him that the state of public opinion was such that a play of this kind might result in a serious outbreak adverse to their interests.

Next day the Bank directors met, excluding Ralston; and his abdication was demanded when it was found that the Bank's funds were almost depleted and that his personal indebtedness to the institution ran over $4,000,000. Ralston, as soon as he signed his resignation, repaired to North Beach, where he was in the habit of swimming frequently. A sturdy swimmer, he went far out. Suddenly he was seen struggling in the water. Before a boat could reach him, he was dead. His friends said he died of a stroke; his enemies that he had committed suicide.

Sentiment softened the judgment upon him who had so tragically over-reached himself. Tom Fitch, pronouncing the eulogy at his funeral, recounted his benefactions and his public service in fulsome metaphor: "Commerce commemorates his deeds with her whitening sails and her laden wharves. There are churches whose heaven-kissing spires chronicle his donations . . . He was the supporter of art; science leaned on him while her vision swept infinity. The footsteps of progress have been sandaled with his silver. He was the life-blood of enterprise; he was the vigor of all progress; he was the epitome and representative of all that was broadening and expansive and uplifting in the life of California."

The suspension of the Bank of California was followed by the closing of the stock exchange in San Francisco; by paralysis of business there and on the Comstock, where intense

apprehension prevailed.[1]   The financial structure of the West
was shaken, but D. O. Mills and William Sharon saved it from
collapse by re-establishing the Bank, raising a fund of almost
$8,000,000 for the purpose.   Mills, honored for his unswerving
integrity, served as President until the institution had recovered
its strength and standing.   The Bank of California re-opened
on October 2nd.

Two days later, the new Nevada Bank of San Francisco
opened for business, under the sway of the Bonanza group; and
it became dominant in the financial affairs of the State whose
name it bore.   The Bank of California, though still influential,
never again controlled the destinies of the Comstock.   These
two great financial institutions, while keen rivals, did not engage in bitter warfare.   Business conditions, and especially
labor conditions, throughout California and Nevada became
too much disturbed to encourage that.

In the midst of the troublous times, on October 26th, 1875,
a mighty fire swept Virginia City.   I remember that conflagration, for in it I lost everything I owned, including a trunkful
of personal keepsakes, and my special pride, a pair of new
gum-boots.   But this fire brought about far more disastrous
results, for it destroyed two thousand dwellings and many
public buildings.   It was my fate to be in the middle of flaming San Francisco in 1906 and the great Berkeley fire in 1923,
in which eight hundred houses burned, but the intensity of
that mining-camp blaze lingers in my memory as the fiercest
of all.   Mount Davidson seemed bursting in volcanic eruption.

The fire had started in a small one-story lodging house on A
Street kept by a woman named Kate Shay, well but not favorably known as Crazy Kate, and the flames spread with as-

[1] The streets of Virginia City were filled that night with an excited crowd.   A riot
was imminent; the military were called out, with two companies under arms.

tounding rapidity. Only by heroic efforts were the mines saved, though many mills and hoisting-works went up in smoke.

Offices of the Virginia City *Chronicle* and *Territorial Enterprise* were utterly destroyed. Their staffs were hospitably received at the Gold Hill *News* plant, across the Divide, and for several weeks the three newspapers were published from that one humming office. Rivalries and bickerings were laid aside in a flood of good feeling that swept the Comstock, as its people started hopefully on the comeback trail. I worked as a compositor in that office to help get those papers out (that was just before my Comstock reportorial days), having only recently returned from Carson City.

Even after this disastrous fire, Virginia City came back strong, and rebuilt more substantially than before. The city's pride was the International Hotel, where all the principal figures of Comstock life foregathered and where most of the mining deals and intrigues were contrived. The hotel, which was of six stories, was sumptuously furnished with mahogany furniture, ceiling-high mirrors and magnificent chandeliers.[1] Not so fine, but comfortable and commodious, was the new Fredrick House nearby, where I took up my residence, in the very heart of the life and activity of the Comstock community.

[1] The International Hotel in Virginia City had one of the very first elevators west of the Mississippi River.

CHAPTER FIFTEEN

100 Saloons

*7*he dawn of the Centennial Year, 1876, was celebrated in gallant style by the Comstock, which took full advantage of the patriotic anniversary to justify a lighthearted turning-away from memories of fire and panic. It was a prolonged New Year's jubilation.

"There was a deal of drinking on the Comstock," wrote Arthur McEwen, "but it was not all drinking . . ." The word of protest, he felt, was necessary to correct a popular legend.

No, not all, but more than enough. By authentic count in 1876 there were exactly 100 retail liquor dealers in Virginia City; 37 in Gold Hill; 7 in Silver City—a grand total of 144 in the Comstock sector. Ten wholesale liquor dealers and 5 breweries helped out. The Delta, the Silver Palace, El Dorado, Palace, Capitol, the Sawdust Corner—these were among the best-known of the places of refreshment in Virginia. Spiro's, with ancient Spiro Vucovich as proprietor, was another pioneer place. Dan O'Connell—Taffy Dan—whose place was near the *Enterprise* office, was a genial host, a favorite with me.

Some of the bars were well-conducted, others were riotous and disorderly houses. As in everything else, their virtue depended upon the people who ran them. I can think of few more snug, comfortable places than some of these old-time taverns, and their proprietors were respectable and respected.

Jim Orndorff of the Delta Saloon was alderman of the Second Ward.

Many of the important civic meetings were held in saloons in early days; and on Sundays, as has been noted, they were sometimes the scene of divine services, before the churches were built.

These saloons were often very elaborate affairs. Witness this advertisement of The Tiger, Joseph Mendes, proprietor, over at Eureka (I don't know if it says truth, I never was in it myself—it probably was a pretty tough place): "This saloon has been fitted up with a view to comfort, unsurpassed by any similar establishment in Nevada. To a stranger it is a perfect mystery. Up stairs and down, turn as you will, you always find yourself before a bar, supplied with the choicest brands of Wines, Liquors and Cigars. Experienced and attentive bar-keepers are always on hand to serve the patrons of the House. San Jose Fredericksburg Beer constantly on draught. Also English Porter, German Wine, St. Louis Beer, Milwaukee Beer, and the celebrated Culmbach Beer on tap."

A roisterer sued in Virginia City for defective sidewalks, which had caused a grievous bodily injury to him on his spree. The defendants objected that the man was drunk. The judge ruled in favor of the plaintiff, handing down the sage opinion that a drunken man is entitled to good sidewalks as much as a sober man, and needs them a great deal more.

There were many gentlemanly drinkers. In fact, the loss of politeness in drinking was one of the distressing signs of retrogression on the Pacific Coast, especially among younger people.

In the old days mellow drinkers who had lived their allotted three score and ten were not infrequent. They took their liquor with all the courtesies and ceremonies which the importance of that function warranted. This was illustrated by the demeanor of Patrick Harrington, whom I visited on the 104th anniversary of his birth. His granddaughter, a gray-haired matron, brought in the necessary ingredients and with great dignity and precision he brewed an aromatic drink. Naturally I asked whether he had always been addicted to the use of stimulants.

"Oh, no; one time I swore off for fifty years," replied the hearty old fellow, with a sigh of regret.

This reminded me of the story of Brutus Blinkenberry of Gold Hill, who groaned when his wife accused him of being drunk twenty-seven nights in the preceding month, and who, when sharply interrogated by his spouse, explained that by his groans he was expressing sorrow for missing those other three nights.

When the pioneers came to California and Nevada, they brought with them the drinking habits of their old homes, and the result was a composite code of etiquette touching this important social problem. Then there were intermingled the stately manners of the Castilians as they survived transplanting from old Spain.

Unhappily, many of these customs gradually disappeared, for with the rising generation the main object appeared to be to gulp down a drink and get out as soon as possible.

The free luncheon, so much disparaged by those who had no idea of the social object it was intended to accomplish, was treated with disdain by those callow drinkers. They ate, to be sure, but it was with a rush that forbade digestion, even, much less politeness. Harry Mighels in a historic controversy with General John Kittrell declared that the free luncheon originated from the charming social customs of the Blue Grass State, and explained that "from this grew the habit of Ken-

INTERNATIONAL HOTEL, VIRGINIA CITY, SAID TO HAVE BEEN THE FIRST
BUILDING WEST OF THE MISSISSIPPI RIVER WITH AN ELEVATOR!

ALONG C STREET, VIRGINIA CITY, 1877. INTERNATIONAL HOTEL IN CENTER

tucky gentlemen carrying canes with big crooks that could be hooked over the arm, thus leaving both hands untrammeled for operations at the free-lunch counter."

It was in San Francisco, though, that the free-lunch really was first developed as an institution, and soon its influence pervaded the entire West. So far as my experience went, there were few men worth the knowing on the Comstock who did not understand how to get their money's worth in a decent way at a free-luncheon. But tenderfoots constantly invading the cocktail route were likely to outrage the finer feelings of old-timers by their crude East-of-the-Rockies ways. They seemed not to realize that they must never seem hungry or in a hurry when enjoying the barkeep's hospitality at the free-lunch counter.

A Comstock Chesterfield once confidentially undertook to instruct a group of newcomers in the approved procedure.

"Having approached the counter with the easy dignity of a man of the world," he said, "you must look over the dainties with a critical eye, and after marking for your own certain choice bits, you saunter carelessly toward the bar and order your favorite tipple, motioning for the attendant to hand it to you at the side-board. There are several reasons for this, but the most important is that it gives you more time to devote to discussing the viands, and time is the essence of the ceremony. Make it a point never to go to a free-luncheon alone, for you ought to remember that when companions tarry long at the board each gives countenance to the other.

"Usually, I take pains to associate myself with a Kentucky gent, or at least with a man from Missouri, at such a time. It may seem like a small thing to the unreflecting, but a man's early bringing up may unfit him for social companionship. My liking for the gentlemen from Kentucky is not based on any personal peculiarities, but grows out of the fact that they as a class comprehend the delicate points of the game. Supposing there is a salad or some other fine piece of the caterer's art before you and you want to be helped a second time, you can see at once that for you to back up your plate and ladle out your own rations would be raw work. That's where your side partner comes in. He divines your preference and at once assumes the role of host, hinting that he would like to hire that cook if his friend, the barkeep, hadn't a prior claim. Of course you yield to the pressing invitation of your fellow-feaster, and you in turn steer his plate to the viands of which you know him to be fond, even though he may be backward for a moment or two. So you pass the buck from one to the other until you get all you want, and the barkeep, hearing you praise his layout in such wholesouled manner, won't be able to find it in his heart to kick because you have depleted the larder and left nothing worth mentioning for his regular cash customers. I have made a study of barkeeps, and I know that they feel like I do in matters of this kind, and all the world knows that if there is anything in life that I hate more than another it is a bungling novice showing off what he doesn't know about etiquette at a free-lunch counter."

My old friend, Colonel K. B. Brown, used to denounce those who were breaking down the drinking traditions which had been a-building for a century.

"Yesterday," he said to me at the Silver Palace, "I was shocked to see three young men, one after the other march into a drinking-place where I was leisurely enjoying a flagon of native burgundy, and take their liquor raw, grab a bite from the sideboard and escape without so much as a word of friendly greeting to any one. Even to the bartender they muttered but one word, and that was 'Straight.' The movement made by these young men as they tossed off the liquor was like that of the stage-actor representing a Russian drinking vodka. Now, I have sampled that same vodka, and I must say that I don't blame a Russian or anybody else for getting rid of such a vile decoction as quickly as possible, but it is an insult to good American liquor to treat it that way. Understand, I do not particularly object to the monobibe habit of these young men. That is all right when the proper ceremonies are observed, but the sullen solitaire is what is wrecking the country and making its drinking habits a reproach to civilization. To enjoy a drink properly one must mix the ingredients himself or at least he must take an interest in the mystic rite if performed by another. Then there is the grateful aroma that arises from the blending process which may not be enjoyed by the man in such a hurry that he never stops to exchange the compliments of the day with fellow-mortals.

"Seldom are heard the gracious salutations of yore," he mourned, "even among friends, and scarcely at all among mere drinking companions. There was a time when, if gentlemen touched glasses in a public resort, it was with almost as much recognition of the dues of hospitality as if they were responding to toasts at a banquet of wine. But these elegant and urbane gentilities are fading away and in their place have come the incivilities of sodden, lonesome guzzling. I feel it my duty to protest, before the gracious and elevating institutions of the country are obliterated by this sweeping wave of retrogression."

CHAPTER SIXTEEN

Gentry of the Green Cloth

"*B*ucking the tiger" was an amusement everyone could try on the Comstock. All kinds of games were running, and all hands played—faro, roulette, euchre, keno, poker, pedro.

There were many high-toned professional gamblers who held the respect of the community and enjoyed the confidence of their fellow citizens, just as if they had been in any other line of business.

Bill Gibson, owner of a saloon and a faro bank layout, was known as a man who never turned a dishonest card, and when he was elected to the State Senate his neighbors learned for the first time that his name was really William De Witt Clinton Gibson—but everybody continued to call him Bill. As a legislator he justified the trust reposed in him by the people, for when several other members were "caved down the bank" and lobbyists tried to swerve him from his pledge, he replied simply: "Gentlemen, I gave my word of honor as a gambler that I would support this measure, and by the Eternal I'll keep my promise, if I'm the only man to vote that way."

And he did.

Big Bill, who ran his square faro bank at Gold Hill, won plentifully and contributed generously to the churches and charitable institutions. A polished gentleman, he was as chivalrous as John Oakhurst.

Joe Stewart was another gambler whose word was good without endorsement at the Nevada Bank or the Bank of California for any amount that his game might require, day or night, to meet reverses.

To these may be added, as of equal standing, Billy Dormer, Tom Buckner, Tom Dimond, Jim Orndorff, Jack Magee, Miles Goodman, Jesse Bright, Tump Winston, and their dealers. Ramon Montenegro, a courtly Californian of Castilian lineage, was a gambler who devoted friendly attention to my own education, revealing to me all the card-sharpers' tricks of which to beware.

The man of sporting proclivities who was eager to bet on another man's game found what he was looking for on every corner. The gaudy roulette wheel spun around and around, the little ball flying in the opposite direction, and the croupier sang in his monotone, "Git yer money down, boys—35 to 1 on the numbers; even money on the colors, the high, and the odd numbers. Git yer money down while the ball rolls." And then the little ball slowed up and dropped with a click into one of the numbered notches, the croupier raked in his winnings and occasionally paid out a stack of chips to a winner, and again the wheel spun.

One of our foremost gambling characters was Doughnut Bill, otherwise Sweetcake William. This sagebrush flower toiled not, and was wont to spin only from one faro table to another. Bill never did a day's work in his life, and it was tiring him out. He had a languid air, when he was called to answer one day in the court of Judge Cox of Virginia City.

"You are charged with assault and battery," said his Honor, "in having belted a man over the head at the Diamond Grotto Saloon last night."

"Jesso," calmly replied William, stroking a dyed mustache

with a hand burdened with rings. "Ye see, Jedge, I walked back to the game an' took out a twenty in two-bit chips. I bet five on the four an' six to win an' coppered the queen to take the eight with two an' a half. Then I put down two on the ace straight, fur I was bound to make a scratch, bein' down to my seams, as it were, with the hash-man an' the lan'lady. The five on the four an' six was raked in. I got away with my bet on the queen an' eight an' looked aroun' to see how the ace was gittin' along, when I see a stiff walkin' away with it fur a sleeper. I didn't say nuthin' but took it outen his fist all in good natur, an' win a ten by copperin' the jack. By this time the deal was nearly out, an' the deuce, trey, nine, seven, eight an' ten-spot was cases. 'Copper the odd an' take the even,' sez I, layin' down all I had—jest twenty-eight big dollars. Well, yer Honor—"

"My good fellow," interrupted the Judge, "you are talking Greek to me. I know nothing of this jargon."

"What's that, Jedge?" asked William, slightly puzzled.

"I say, my good fellow, that this hasn't anything to do with your case of assault and battery. You gamblers are becoming too turbulent altogether. I have a good mind to make an example of you, sir. It would be well for men of your class to remember that you are allowed to carry on your immoral trade merely upon sufferance. When civilization, sir, advances somewhat in these Western outposts, the country will not be mortified by the spectacles of legalized vice which now disgrace the State of Nevada and render it so difficult a task to keep the rising generation from following the evil examples which are constantly before their eyes. Proceed, sir, but drop your professional slang and remember that this Court knows nothing about the game of faro or any other gambling device."

"Oh, ye don't?" said William. "P'r'aps ye don't call to mind the night you an' me snatched a fifteen-dollar sleeper when a drunk didn't sabe enough to pick up a split on a bet o' thirty. P'r'aps ye don't remember when I staked you at three this mornin' over in the Dew Drop Inn? P'r'aps you and Jake Small ain't snacks in ropin' in snoozers? P'r'aps—"

"Silence!" roared the Court, glaring at the grinning crowd of hangers-on, outside the rail. "There seems to be nothing in this case, William. You leave the Court to infer that you were being cheated and you lifted the stiff under the ear. You're discharged."

Of faro, the familiar saying was, "The bank will clean you out if you stay with it," but still there were plenty of players and some of them were graybeards. The play was high, and there was no bidding for players. Faro is a thinking, as well as a losing game, and the men who deal it know that silence is golden. Every drop of the cards means win or lose in faro, and the cases were soberly sized up before the bet was made.

Keen students of human nature were these gentry of the green cloth, and they had dramatic opportunities to exercise their faculties of discernment.

"I make no pretense to being much of a palmistry expert in the modern acceptance of that phrase, but I can tell whether a man is a thief or not as soon as I see him handle his chips at a faro game," said my picturesque friend Colonel K. B. Brown, who, before holding the exalted position of chief of the Virginia City fire department, won social and financial standing in the Comstock community as a high-roller in front of and behind the faro layout.

"You'd be surprised to know how many men are subject to temptation that way," added the Colonel, "and only the dealer and the look-out get an insight into this phase of human character. You see, most of the players are busy with their own play, and so have no chance to think of what others are doing, for which reason they miss the little episodes that are noted by the men behind the box.

"Now, you must understand that I do not accuse every man of being a thief just because he picks up a 'sleeper' once in a while, for that is part of the game, as it helps to even up what he is likely to lose in a similar way; that is, by forgetting some of his stacks and letting them go by default on a dead card, which makes them lawful prey by right of discovery to the first man who detects their orphan condition. When I speak of such temptations I refer to the way some people have of systematically trying to separate fellow-players from their checks.

"Close observation in this regard once proved of value to me, for it saved me a snug fraction of my bank-roll, and nobody ever knew how I got onto the combination. It happened along in the '70s when I was dealing in Dick Brown's Silver State saloon near the divide between Virginia and Gold Hill. I was running the night shift, and had just relieved Long Brown, the day man, when I saw one of the leading stock-brokers of the place take a seat and pay in for $50 worth of checks. He was not a frequent visitor at our place, but as I had placed a small section of my stock account with his firm, he probably thought that reciprocity demanded that he should bestow on us part of his patronage. I had never watched him closely, but there was something about the shape of his hands and his way of clutching his checks that I didn't like; almost his first motion aroused my suspicion, and from that moment I kept a close scrutiny on his doings. The movement that caused me to think he was not all right was when he touched a stack of reds that were heeled from the nine—taking the seven to win. At first he only jumbled the checks as he placed another stack

of exactly the same color and value heeled from the ten for
the eight to win. With careless ease he straightened up the
checks and gently tapped them as if with the hand of an
owner. After the next turn he again touched them, as if by
accident, this time knocking off the copper and letting the bet
go straight for both cards. It was a swift but easy movement
by which he shoved that stack of checks between the nine and
eight, and from there to the four on the other side of the board.

" 'What became of my bet on the nine?' roared a young fellow called Ike Furst, a few moments later; but nobody seemed
able to say, except to intimate that he had switched and lost
on some other card or that he was 'sinking' on himself.

"My broker friend won as if pursued by a demon of good
luck, yet once more I saw him chase Ike's checks into his pile
in the same ingenious way. The change was so gradual that
only a person posted on the scheme could detect it. Just before
midnight he 'whipsawed' me, and as I paid both his red stacks,
I shoved them over to Ike, telling him that they were his,
which statement he accepted without knowing or caring to ask
why.

"The broker looked up, caught the wink in my right eye
under the down-turned brim, and cashed in.

"Next day when I asked to have my account transferred to
a rival establishment, he only smiled and said 'Certainly.' Ten
days later the big brokers of San Francisco sent the Sheriff
after him and I was about the only stock-buyer in town who
didn't get pinched. It wasn't so very much—only about $30,-
000—but it was worth saving, and for this I had to thank my
ability to watch one man while dealing faro bank for a dozen
others."

Everybody gambled. Even the bankers and big mining men
were not excepted, their favorite retreat being the sumptuous

Washoe Club, renowned for its all-night poker games. A story was current on the Comstock as to how a mysterious stranger came to try to queer William Sharon with W. C. Ralston. Sharon it will be recalled, was manager of the agency of the Bank of California at Virginia City and Gold Hill, while Ralston was chief of the great bank in San Francisco.

"I can tell you that Bill Sharon is a desperate gambler," ventured the stranger.

"What does he play?" asked Ralston.

"Poker."

"How high?"

"The sky's the limit. I've seen him bet $10,000 on two pair before the draw."

"Hoyle says the time to play two pair, if you're going to play them at all, is before the draw, so I guess Sharon's method is sound. But what I want to know is this: Does he *win*?"

"Well, yes, I'll say he does."

"Always?"

"I never knew him to quit loser."

"That's all; thank you," and Ralston bowed the visitor out.

The stakes were generally high, the play was devilish fast—yet some there were who got no thrill from poker on the Comstock.

When I called upon him one day, in my capacity as mining reporter, I noted that John Mackay was glum. He neither scowled nor smiled.

I turned to leave the room, but he motioned to the pile of reports on his table that told of yesterday's mine developments.

Mechanically I looked over the papers, made a few minor notations, and was about to go when he got up and went to the rear of his office and looked out of the window which gave a view of Six-Mile Canyon and Sugar Loaf Hill, with Forty-Mile Desert in the distance.

Mackay always was quiet, reticent. But his smile was perfectly beautiful, and usually he was on good terms with himself and the world.

This morning I sympathized with him in his evident loneliness, and I longed to tell him. The two great mines he was at that time developing—the Con. Virginia and the California—were producing bullion at the rate of a million a month. His was the lion's share. Besides, he owned the controlling interest in the Union Mill and Mining Company, the Virginia and Gold Hill Water Company, a Flume and Lumber Company, and so on. His income was probably $250,000 a month—three millions a year.

"You seem depressed, Mr. Mackay," I ventured. "Is anything the matter? Is there anything I can do to help out?"

"No, thank you, my boy. Not a thing. That's the trouble. I wish there was something you or anybody could do for me. But there isn't. Last night I was playing poker at the Washoe Club, and it was a stiff game, with the luck that I didn't want all coming my way. Every time I drew I got my hand—three jacks, king full, pat flushes—then I opened on three aces, and I played them for the last before the draw, but a plunger sitting to my left was holding four queens and betting like a cyclone, while each of the others was raising the pot as fast as it came to him. Finally it was my last say and I just called, showing down four aces.

"Of course, I won the pot. But I got no thrill.

"I measured the value of the great stacks of red, blue and yellow chips which were in front of the players, and it seemed that with my run of luck that money was about to be mine.

"Then all of a sudden came the chilling thought: What of

it? Even if I should win every cent in sight it would not make the slightest difference to me!

"'Leave me out boys,' I said, 'I'm through! When I can't enjoy winning at poker there's no more fun in anything.'"

The players gathered up the checks in the pot and adding them to Mackay's previous winnings, had the "banker" redeem them and piled the gold in front of Mackay's empty chair.

Next day he was notified to call and get his money. But he declined. He didn't want it. "Keep it," he said.

Half of the Mackay money the players divided among themselves. The other half they gave to the charity fund of the county.

At the end of the year when Mackay sent in his usual contribution, the secretary commented, "This is your second contribution."

"Never mind, don't tell anybody," said Mackay.

There were many legends of the desperate play engaged in by some of the plungers of the lesser order. Pizen Switch, for instance, had a "game man with a game leg." Two Sacramento gamblers dropped into town one night and engaged the local talent, including the man with the wooden leg, in a game of poker. They won all his money, whereupon he took off the wooden leg and pawned it to them for $100, which was lost. An ardent courter of Lady Luck, the next night he "dug up" and paid for his wooden leg, resumed play in the poker game, and before morning had corralled most of the money on the table.

It used to be quite a joke to tell a stranger, "You know, pardner, in Nevada if you haven't ace, face nor trump, you've got a right to ask for a new deal." It was all right to ask— but try and get it.

The spirit of gambling pervaded the entire community. **A**

great library association of San Francisco started a lottery to finance its undertaking, and many of the tickets were sold in Virginia City. When the Nevada legislature passed a law legalizing a lottery to raise funds for the orphans' home and an insane asylum, the *Territorial Enterprise,* the leading journal of the State, mildly condoned the adoption of the statute on the ground that the people were evidently inclined to take a chance for their coin in one form or another, and pointed out that if they did not have an opportunity to patronize a home venture they would send their money to California for a like investment. "And besides, we have institutions of our own that need help," the editor concluded, thus clinching in public approval the establishment of the lottery.

So that there was ample precedent for the recent laws enacted in Nevada making gambling "a wide-open proposition."

CHAPTER SEVENTEEN

Staging

*L*ong after the coming of the railroad, the stage-driver stood ace-high in Nevada. Atop his Concord coach, cracking his long whip over the leaders of his prancing six-horse team, he was a figure that appealed to the public fancy. Drivers such as Hank Monk, Curly Bill Garhart, Bill McFarland, Big Jake and Bill Mooney were popular heroes, not to be toppled from their eminence despite the frequent stoppages of stages by outlaws who "had the drop on them" from out in the sage.

"There never was any stage service in the world," Hubert Howe Bancroft assures us, "more complete than that between Placerville and Virginia City. A sprinkled road, over which dashed six fine, sleek horses before an elegant Concord coach, the lines in the hands of an expert driver, whose light hat, linen duster, and lemon-colored gloves betokened a good salary and an exacting company, and who timed his grooms and his passengers by a heavy gold chronometer watch, held carelessly, if conspicuously, on the tips of his fingers—these were some of its features."

The transcontinental railroad made obsolete this stage route across the Sierras between Placerville and Virginia City; but the most renowned driver on that road, Hank Monk, continued in service with Jim Benton's stageline which operated on the scenic route between Carson and Lake Tahoe. Hank it was who drove Horace Greeley on a mad ride over to old Hangtown—as Placerville then usually was called—to make a campaign speech. It is a story a-thousand-times-told, in variant form, but all agreeing that the dashing driver, while scaring the great man almost to death, and heedless of all commands and prayers to stop, kept assuring his jouncing passenger, "Keep your seat, Horace, I'll have you there on time!" It was a memorable phrase which long passed current on both sides of the Sierra, where many firmly believed Hank made Horace famous by insisting he keep his seat. Probably the most spirited and humorous account of that ride (though not the most accurate as to route) is by Artemus Ward, who reveled in the comic spirit of the mountain mining-camps, especially Virginia City, which he discovered to be "paved with silver."

When on the road, Hank Monk was wont to mend his clothing with copper harness-rivets in lieu of buttons. The legend is that a San Francisco clothing manufacturer, Levi Strauss, about 1872 learned of the success of Hank's ingenious method; certain it is that he made a fortune in copper-riveted overalls.[1]

Hank Monk was a chum of mine at Carson City. I can see him now, in his travel-worn suit of corduroy,[2] beneath his battered old Stetson. Immensely popular, he was well known to Mark Twain, Bret Harte and a host of other notables, most of whom he drove over the Sierra route. His true moniker was Henry James Monk, but few knew that. The poise of our noble coachman might have hinted (to an historian) lineal descent from George Monk, Duke of Albemarle, king-maker.

[1] By Western cowboys, overalls are often termed "Levis."
[2] Hank Monk was judiciously appareled in corduroy of the true tobacco-juice tint.

Hank remained in harness almost till the day of his death—more than 30 years of skilful stage-driving. I remember how heart-broken the veteran was when he had the first stage upset of his long career. Hank was hurrying from Glenbrook, on Lake Tahoe, to Carson City, trying to make a train-connection. Just east of Saint's Rest the stage overturned, spilling the driver and the dozen passengers, of whom eight were on top of the coach. Providentially, no one was seriously injured; but Hank was never the same jovial fellow again, and he died not long afterward.

Mark Twain in Roughing It gave a sarcastic account of their high mightinesses, the stage-drivers. And they captivated Robert Louis Stevenson when he visited California, as you may read in Silverado Squatters.

The famous whips of Nevada were men of supreme skill and endurance. One of the most expert was little "Sagebrush," otherwise John Burnett. "Big Jake," christened Jacob Putnam, when he gave over the ribbons set up a faro bank layout on the Comstock and prospered. "Big John" Littlefield, Charlie Livermore and Baldy Green were other drivers of distinction. Baldy, by the way, figures largely in the next chapter.

Richard Gelatt had a stage-line of his own between Carson and Genoa. Bill Mooney, jovial Irishman, and "Curly Bill" Garhart were proprietors of livery stables in Virginia City after they left off staging, and they furnished resplendent turn-outs for an appreciative public, as did the Lukes in Virginia (later in Reno) and Simon Ogg in Gold Hill. "Curly Bill" was of herculean strength. When young John Mackay was trudging to the mines, "Curly Bill" gave him a lift—a service remembered in a munificent manner by the Mackays when in his declining years Bill needed kindly aid.

HANK MONK, MOST FAMOUS OF STAGE-DRIVERS

STATE PRISON AT WARM SPRINGS, NEAR CARSON CITY, 1865

STAGES LEAVING WELLS-FARGO OFFICE, VIRGINIA CITY

The stage-driver was not far behind the prospector in opening up new territory. More than thirty regular stage-lines were in operation in Nevada even as late as 1880, most of them leading from points on the railroad to interior camps, many of which now have disappeared utterly.

Wells, Fargo & Company bulked big in carrying express, for years holding a virtual monopoly, transporting all the bullion and much of the mail. Government post-offices were not at once established in many of the outlying mining camps, but at rates only about ten cents above the usual postal rates Wells, Fargo & Company in early days would deliver a letter entrusted to them, almost anywhere. Their shotgun-messengers often were regular companions of the stage-drivers when convoying treasure.

Not only did the earliest stage-drivers have to fight off Indians and bandits. There were other dire tribulations. In emergency all the men passengers were called out to aid the horses make the heaviest grades, and on several occasions stages were blown over by the fierce wind-blasts of the Sierran winters. Runaways on the steep winding grades added to the perils. Ned Boyle, Superintendent of the Alta mine at Gold Hill, showed a cool head and a steady hand while returning by stage from Paradise. The stage struck a big rock, jouncing the driver off the seat, and the horses ran away. Boyle, inside the coach, sized up the situation and leaning out shot one of the leaders dead, with a revolver. This brought the other animals to a stop, just as a sharp angle in the road was reached. Boyle's action saved the lives of all aboard. His son, Emmet Boyle, served with distinction as Governor of Nevada.

The most famous, or infamous, grade, and one which tested the nerve of the early stage-drivers, was the Geiger Grade, just below Virginia City on the way to and from Reno. After the railroad came to the Comstock, staging over this picturesque route was discontinued, but the road was well maintained— as it is today. But never was it notable for safety, and my greatest thrill came when an old Indian squaw arose suddenly beside the road and frightened my horses so that they dashed wildly down the Geiger Grade, dragging behind them the careening carriage, with myself and my fair companion, Ella Bishop. Tugging at the reins, more by luck than good guiding I brought the trembling horses to a stop—not only saving my own life, but best of all, that of the lovely lady who became my wife.

CHAPTER EIGHTEEN

Knights of the Road

*I*n the early days, stage-robbing was one of the most active industries on the east side of the Sierra Nevada. Not exactly a legitimate business, still it was looked on with easy tolerance even by leading citizens.

Strange stories were whispered as to some of those worthies. The stage company had to make good any loss, and on more than one occasion merchants were suspected of having tipped off their friends the road agents when they were going to send large amounts of coin by Wells-Fargo's stages through the mountains or across the desert. The holdups came off as scheduled, and the crooked merchants divided the profits with their allies.

The profits were high and the risk, while great, not as big as it would have been without friendly juries. The identity of many of the foremost knights of the road was well known in the communities in which they moved, but the difficulty was to secure convicting evidence against them if and when they came to trial.

Risk for the road agents became greater when the express company placed "messengers" on the stages to defend the property they were carrying. These shotgun messengers at one time were instructed to carry their guns with their muzzles resting on their toes—they did not *dare* fall asleep! One-legged shotgun messengers were scarce as one-armed stage drivers. Not that there were not some of these, either.

I used to know a stage-owner named Preston whose wagons were stopped so many times up in Montana that Wells-Fargo threatened to take their business away from him and start an opposition line. This made him so angry that he called his drivers together and told them that they were a pack of cowards, and said he'd like to see anybody stop *him*. That was before shotgun messengers were common and every driver was supposed to look out for himself. Preston said he intended to drive the mountain section of the line himself for a while and they'd see how easy it was for a man with sand in his craw to stand off the road agents.

That night he made his word good. He drove out of Helena in an old-fashioned mud-wagon, with a shotgun resting across his lap and two passengers in behind.

About seven hours later one of the passengers drove the wagon back to town. The money-box was gone and Preston was lying in the bottom of the wagon with both of his hands literally shot off at the wrist. He refused to throw up his hands when told to. The last time I saw Preston he had two brand-new wooden hands, with black kid gloves on them. They looked well enough, but were not good for much except dress parade.

When the messengers went on the box, some of the road agents turned their activities elsewhere. One of the most notorious, Big Jack Davis, decided on a bold stroke: he and his masked gang held up a Central Pacific express train near Verdi, a few miles west of Reno, and escaped with $40,000, yielded by the strong box of Wells, Fargo & Company. Sam Davis always insisted this was the first train-holdup in history. It won Davis nationwide notoriety. (Jack I mean, not Sam— they were no relation.)

In the penitentiary Jack pleaded as his excuse that he became crazy for want of money to work his mine. He sought to levy other assessments on the public, for when he was at large, about seven years after the Verdi robbery, he and two pals made a bold attempt to rob the Eureka and Tybo stage at Willows station, forty miles south of Eureka. The three desperadoes one evening captured the station, tied up the hostler, and lay in wait for the stage. As it drove up they cried out to Jimmy Blair and Eugene Brown, the express messengers, demanding surrender. Blair jumped to the ground, and as he reached it received the fire of two shotguns. He replied to the fire, grappling with one of the robbers, while Brown, who had stayed on the box, planted a charge of buckshot in the follow's back. Brown was wounded in the leg by a pistol bullet from one of the highwaymen at the rear of the stage. The fire was returned, and the pair of bandits still able to ride threw themselves on their horses and streaked off into the sage, making good their escape. The wounded robber was Jack Davis, and he died on the road into Eureka. He was buried in the county graveyard, and not a mourner attended his funeral. In appearance, Davis was meek and placid; he might have been taken for a professor or a clergyman.

Bullion from the Comstock mines was often carried out by big six-horse teams. Mackay and Fair sent out every night such a team with all the bullion it could draw—this particular bullion being about 55% gold and 45% silver. Small bars had been used in earlier days, but the mine owners by the mid-'70s were sending it out in big bars such as a man could hardly lift. This made it difficult for the road agents to get away with the treasure, and many of the sports on the Comstock felt that the stratagem amounted almost to a swindle of the stage robbers who, in this instance, had the sympathy of the public.

A desperate fellow named Clement Lee blew into Virginia

City with three companions—no one knew much about them —and they started a big faro layout. The establishment was well supplied with money; like as not, it had been won at the point of shotguns somewhere far off in the sage.

Not content with the big rake-off at their faro joint, the quartet of sharpers soon set out for bigger stakes. The custom then was to close up the games at high twelve on Saturday night. They closed duly when the clock behind the bar in the adjoining saloon showed "hands up," and they made sure that they were seen by the loungers in the place. Then they crept below, where horses were tethered, and spurred hotfoot down the Geiger Grade in the dark. They rode at a terrific pace through Dead Man's Gulch, where a slip on one of the turns would have hurled horse and rider to eternity. But their time had not come, and they made the distance to the valley below faster than it had ever been covered. There they had four fresh horses staked out in a grove of cottonwoods. They shifted saddles to the new mounts, threw some drinks into their own thirsty throats, and then started off again into the starlit night, pulling up finally on the road at a bend they knew well, a couple of miles from Reno, on the route to Honey Lake.

They had calculated their schedule to a nicety. Soon the Reno stage came careening through the night, its six horses making it spin along at a great rate. The four bandits sprang into the road; Clem Lee cried to the driver to stop, but so fast were the horses going that he could not pull up short (some say he didn't try, but whipped them up instead) and Clem had barely time to spring aside to avoid the coach. As it was, one of the wheels grazed the light overcoat he was wearing, and ground into it a long yellow mark. Clem shot one of the foremost horses as he turned, and the others piled up on the body of their dead leader.

The stage was stopped, but a deputy sheriff on the box had pulled a gun and sent a bullet through Clem's partner, Dick, killing him instantly. The sheriff was rudely disarmed, and as the passengers were ordered out and ranged in line, Thomas, the driver, threw down the box. While the plunder was being gathered, one of the robbers went up to the sheriff and threatened to kill him, but Clem Lee prevented that. He ordered all the victims back into the stage, and waved it on its way with his menacing gun.

The three gamblers buried their dead partner hurriedly in a grave scooped amidst the sage; mounted their horses, dashed back to the cottonwoods, changed horses and spurred up the Geiger Grade to Virginia City—and were in bed before nine o'clock in the morning. Nobody would suspect them, they felt assured, for even if their absence was observed, it would be thought impossible for them to have made the trip to and from the scene of the holdup. They could not have done it without the relays of horses, and then only by galloping like mad.

One seemingly insignificant detail gave them away. A woman passenger had looked out with startled gaze when the command came to halt, and had seen the wheel graze the pistol-arm of Clem Lee as he sprang aside. "Look for a man with a wheel-mark burned into the right sleeve of his light overcoat," she had said, "no brush ever made could take that out!"

So on C street in Virginia, when a young man of the town came strolling along in a light overcoat, the police looked for the telltale mark. It was there, and he was apprehended. He protested and proved his innocence; but his coat, he said, had been lent to Clem Lee that night. Clem and his companions, one of them the wayward son of a Washington millionaire, were arrested and sent to prison.

The knights of the road were no respecters of persons. Hank Monk, the most famous stage-driver in the country, was stopped just like the rest.

One lone highwayman, recalling perhaps the Boston Tea-Party, had his face painted red like an Indian when he stopped a stage up Bodie way, but it was in excellent English that he ordered the driver to throw out the strongbox.

Speaking of holdups, I call to mind a catchy bit of frontier balladry called *Baldy Green,* which used to be the most popular song on the Comstock. Charley Reed's *Chicken Tamale* and Daniels' *Razzle Dazzle* couldn't compare.

K. B. Brown used to laugh and stamp his feet when he heard Charley Rhoades play the banjo and sing it. "Everybody stamped their feet in those days," explained "K. B." in reminiscent strain. "That was before the dudes had introduced the custom of clapping. You can bet your life that anybody would have been tarred and feathered or ridden out of town on a rail just as quickly for clapping his hands as he would for wearing a swallow-tail coat. Old Judge Mesick and Jonas Seely and Colonel Bob Taylor and Jase Baldwin and Rollin Daggett, all used to sit together in John Piper's old Opera House, and whenever Rhoades would come out and sing *Baldy Green* they'd hit on the benches in front of them with their six-shooters and call 'Bully!' until Piper would try to give them back their money to get them to stop.

"I'll always believe that Rhoades wrote *Baldy Green* himself, though I understand Hank Donnelly, Superintendent of the Eureka Con. mine tried to prove that Alf Doten did. The way the song came to be written was that Wells-Fargo's stages were being robbed nearly every day, just as if Milton Sharp or

Black Bart had been there, and their high-toned driver, Baldy
Green, seemed to be the favorite with the road agents. Anyway, they stopped him oftener than any of the others.

Some suspicious people used to say that Baldy was in with
the play and gave the boys the right tip, but that was all josh.
Everybody who knew Baldy protested that it wasn't so, but
it made him madder to tell it on him than if it really was true.

One of the exciting events in Baldy's much-interrupted
career is immortalized in the song:

BALDY GREEN

I'll tell you all a story,
    And I'll tell it in a song
And I hope that it will please you,
    For it won't detain you long;
'Tis about one of the old boys
    So gallus and so fine,
Who used to carry mails
    On the Pioneer Line.

He was the greatest favor-ite
    That ever yet was seen,
He was known about Virginny
    By the name of Baldy Green.
Oh, he swung a whip so gracefully,
    For he was bound to shine—
For he was a high-toned driver
    On the Pioneer Line.

Now, as he was driving out one night,
    As lively as a coon,
He saw three men jump in the road
    By the pale light of the moon;
Two sprang for the leaders,
    While one his shotgun cocks,
Saying, "Baldy, we hate to trouble you,
    But just pass us out the box."

When Baldy heard them say these words
  He opened wide his eyes;
He didn't know what in the world to do,
  For it took him by surprise.
Then he reached into the boot,
  Saying, "Take it, sirs, with pleasure,"
So out into the middle of the road
  Went Wells & Fargo's treasure.

Now, when they got the treasure-box
  They seemed quite satisfied,
For the man who held the leaders
  Then politely stepped aside,
Saying, "Baldy, we've got what we want,
  So drive along your team,"
And he made the quickest time
  To Silver City ever seen.

Don't say greenbacks to Baldy now,
  It makes him feel so sore;
He'd traveled the road many a time,
  But was never stopped before.
Oh, the chances they were three to one
  And shotguns were the game,
And if you'd a-been in Baldy's place
  You'd a-shelled her out the same.

The passage, "He made the quickest time to Silver City ever seen," was sung very rapidly, and you must understand that the line in the song about Baldy never being stopped before was sarcasm. That's what hurt him.

Poor Baldy! He had hard luck in his latter day. He got to be a common rancher out near Winnemucca, where he could see nothing but cattle, cattle, cattle, from one month's end to another. It paid, of course, but just think what a letdown it was. And that wasn't all. The last time I heard of Baldy he was a Justice of the Peace, and they were threatening to send him to the Legislature.

CHAPTER NINETEEN

Nickanora, "The Spanish King"

*T*he Wells-Fargo people closed up some of their mountain offices, it is alleged, because when a stage was robbed a jury couldn't be found in any of the outlying communities which would convict the highwaymen. The reason suggested may have been only a bluff. But they came pretty near doing the same thing out in White Pine once. It was during the reign of Nickanora, who, according to my idea, was the king stage-robber of Nevada.

His true name was Nicanor Rodrigues, but of course the Missourians and others on the frontier could never get their tongues around anything like that, so they called him Nicka-nora, or more generally Nick, for short. He was a handsome young fellow, who was born among the mountains of old Spain. His father held some kind of a government position —was an army officer, I think—and started Nick out early with a few hundred pesos and his wits to make his way in the world.

Nobody knows what brought Nick to California, but he used to tell about when he lived in Rome, Paris and the City of Mexico. He was only sixteen years old when he was captured along with a stage-robbing outfit in Tuolumne County in California, and sent to the penitentiary for ten years.

He was soon pardoned on account of his youth, and went to Nevada, where he made his greatest record.

Nick was a many-sided personality, for he was a polished man-of-the-world as well as a debonair bandit. His favorite amusement was to give game dinners, at which he would preside with all the grace of a Chauncey Depew or a Ward McAllister. He didn't lack for guests, either, for he patronized the best French restaurants in Virginia City, Pioche and the other towns he favored with his visits. One such sumptuous spread he gave in Pioche at Hamilton's restaurant. Many "big guns" of Nevada dined with Nick, because a game dinner with plenty of champagne is always hard to refuse.

The woman who lived with him came from a patriarchal Mormon family and worshiped him.

While Nick was great on stopping stage coaches either by proxy or in person, he preferred to go to the fountain-head, and that was why he bothered the quartz mills so much. His first operation in Nevada, so far as I know, was when he got into the Imperial Mill at Gold Hill, and snaked the hot amalgam right out of the retorts. Colonel Gray was superintendent of Imperial then. Nick would laugh till he'd cry, they say, telling about how the Colonel took on over the loss. He never thought of suspecting Nick and his Mexican assistants.

It is believed by old settlers that every mill in Nevada at one time or another paid tribute to Nick. He had a regularly organized band, and was recognized as a kind of king among them. His share of the spoil must have amounted to hundreds of thousands. Nobody ever will know how much it was, for at first the mills were hardly ever watched, and the pans and retorts could have been robbed seven days in the week and nobody be the wiser.

Soon after the Imperial robbery, Nick got a wheelbarrow-load of unretorted bullion from the Pacific Mill in lower Gold Hill, and buried it just outside the Silver City graveyard. When he got time, he turned it into neat bars and sold them.

He came near being caught in one of his exploits, which he went into simply as a flyer. That was when they used to "stage it" over the Geiger Grade. One evening he saw three bricks loaded into the boot of the stage for Reno. They were from the Ophir upper workings and nearly all-gold. Nick at once bought a ticket for Reno, and got up beside Baldy Green, the driver. Between Steamboat Springs and Reno he managed to drop those bricks out of the boot of the stage. When he got to Reno he hired a buggy, and, going back over the road, picked them up—no one had come along—and drove for Gold Hill.

Of course the bullion was quickly missed, and as soon as it was light enough to see, a Washoe County constable went out to look for it. He got onto the buggy-tracks in a minute, and followed them right to the door of a big assay office in Slippery Gulch. The boy who slept in the office said the bricks were left there by a stranger who wanted them run into small bars.

No arrests were made, and they tried to keep the matter quiet, hoping that the mysterious stranger would come back; but Nick was too smart for that. He heard that the bullion had been recovered by the stage company, and lay low. He was arrested several times on suspicion in Virginia City, but they were never able to prove anything. He got tired of being watched and went out to the White Pine country, in eastern Nevada. Soon after he got there the Shermantown mill was robbed of a sack of unretorted bullion. Nick was arrested, but he was acquitted because Judge Jesse Pitzer defended him.

After that the stages were stopped nearly every week. Gilmer & Saulsbury owned the stage line and carried Wells-Fargo's express. Nick and his crowd got so they didn't care so much for big bars of bullion because they were hard to handle. They preferred to take the stages coming in with coin.

They got away with cash belonging to the Nevada State Bank at Pioche. Colonel Henry I. Thornton, later a big lawyer in San Francisco, was one of the principal owners. Colonel J. W. Wright, the manager, wanted to get $2,000 in silver into Pioche, and he concluded to have it sent by mail instead of by express, as it was cheaper. Nickanora and his crowd stopped the stage two miles from Pioche at 9 o'clock at night, robbed all the passengers, broke open the treasure-box, which was nearly empty, then cut open the mail sacks and got Colonel Wright's $2,000. Some people used to say that Nickanora got the tip on the silver bundle from the San Francisco end of the stage-line, although I never took much stock in that story. Nick was arrested, but was acquitted, as he had a dozen witnesses to prove an alibi.

In less than a month the stage was stopped again. Nick, who by this time had earned for himself the title of "the Spanish King," did not wait to be arrested, but took refuge in the mountains. After weeks of fruitless search the officers gave up hope of finding him.

One day he sent word to the express company that he would like to compromise. He said he was tired of being hunted like a wild beast, and thought he could offer an arrangement that would be satisfactory to all. Colonel W. W. Bishop was at that time attorney for the stage company, and as they were as much interested as anybody in having the depredations stopped, Colonel Bishop, as their attorney, was chosen ambassador to visit Nickanora's court, wherever it might be located. Billy Bishop used to tell us about that adventure:

"A young Mexican acted as my guide. We left Pioche on burros at midnight and went over Spring Mountain. Taking a long sweep to the right we soon struck a rugged ravine and started up it. I could see armed Mexicans behind every clump of sagebrush. We passed safely through the defile until we reached a grove of stunted pines. These, we found, hid the entrance to a natural cave or tunnel, which ran into the side of the mountain.

"Our burros were tied behind the trees, and torches were furnished to us by an old woman who emerged from the darkness of the cavern. After going about seventy-five yards into the tunnel my guide whistled, and seven or eight big fellows came cautiously out from behind the rocks and advanced to meet us. Without a word they seized a large flat stone, which looked like a part of the floor of the tunnel and moving it aside disclosed a lower chamber, oval in shape and about the size of an ordinary church.

"A ladder was thrust up, and following my guide downward I found myself in the presence of Nickanora and some dozen or so of his most trusted friends, several women being of the number.

"Nick was very brief. He said all he wanted was to be left alone. If the stage line and the express company would let up on him and not prosccute him he would protect their property until one side or the other should see fit to terminate the contract, in which case fair notice should be given. I was authorized to act, and at once accepted his terms."

It used to be said, too, that the express company paid him a salary of $2,000 a month besides. Be that as it may, Nickanora soon made his appearance in Pioche, and going directly to Wells-Fargo's office, said to Colonel B. F. Sides, the agent: "If I can prevent it, your stages shall never be stopped so long as you are agent here."

The Spanish King kept his word, but finally Sides left and was succeeded as agent by one Siebert. Within a few days Nickanora called on him and said: "I am extremely regretful, *Señor,* but I am no longer able to take care of your treasure-boxes. You must protect your own property."

With that he withdrew, and his crowd began robbing stages again in their old-fashioned, vigorous manner.

Nickanora was arrested and put in jail. He was indicted and his bail was put so high that even he couldn't give the bond. He saw conviction and the State Prison staring him in the face, so he got desperate. Joe Hoag was jailer under Sheriff Wes Travis, and had charge of the prisoners. One day three of them managed to get their cells open, and when Hoag went in to make his inspection that night one of them knocked him down with an iron bar. He was not knocked senseless, so he pulled his pistol and fired, but missed, and the next blow of the bar settled the business. Joe was not killed, but he was insensible for several hours, and it took him a long time to get over it.

One of the fellows who got out with Nick was a big French-man named Eugene Billieu, who was awaiting trial for murder. The other was a common horsethief, who was called Yank. I never did know his name.

Though the whole community was up in arms against them, they escaped by stealing some fine horses in Spring Valley and riding to the ranch of James Maxwell, a big Mormon, at the headwaters of the Sevier river in Utah. Maxwell formerly lived in Pioche, but had to leave because he killed a man over a mining-claim.

After a week's rest at Maxwell's, Nickanora and the French- man returned to within twelve miles of Pioche, where they robbed the stage and stole a band of horses from C. H. Light. With this plunder they got to Utah, and the three started for Mexico. Yank's body was found fifty miles from the Mormon's ranch, and the big Frenchman's remains were discovered by a party of prospectors not far from the same spot. Nick had done for them both.

The Spanish King was lost from sight for some time. Rewards were offered for him dead or alive, but so far as I know nobody tried to win them.

The last time he was heard from was when a miner who used to work in Pioche returned from Sinaloa, Mexico, in 1888. He said he saw a man whom he thought was Nickanora, though he was not sure, who called himself Don Felipe Castro Estrada. He was a regular mogul on his own *rancho* in the mountains and possessed more horses than any other man within fifty miles.

CHAPTER TWENTY

Bad-Men

*I*t was a current saying that the first thirty graves in Virginia City were those of men who died violent deaths. While we may not credit this, it was not unusual to see "Shot" or "Stabbed" or "Murdered" inscribed upon the tombstones and head-boards along the Comstock Lode.

Already I have stressed the fact that in the '70s almost all adult males there went armed—which led to a high order of courtesy, except among those looking for trouble.

One of the cardinal points of politeness in old Nevada was to throw up your hands right quick when the other fellow got the drop on you. He didn't have to say a word. The man covered knew what he meant, all right. All this about "Hands up!" or words to that effect is stage stuff. When men are in dead earnest they use few words, and usually are too intent to say anything.

It is legendary that one of the simple head-boards over a lone Comstock grave read,

"He had sand in his craw,
But was slow on the draw,
So we planted him under the daisies."

On the frontier, it was unforgivable, being slow on the draw!

Before coming to the Comstock I had been among the in-nocent bystanders at a number of shootings—in Olympia,

Washington, for instance, when young Howe shot Kendall. Boone Helm, most desperate of the bad-men of the Northwest, I had seen led captive in irons. I saw in action those pioneer editors, John Miller Murphy and E. T. Gunn, both quick on the trigger; and at Roseburg, Oregon, I had met Bud Thompson and the Gale brothers, who had hard-earned reputations for like alacrity. When Thompson shook his head you could hear the bullet rattle which was lodged within.

When I was up on Puget Sound as interpreter on the Indian Reservations, Old Toke, friend and chieftain, gave me *"Klale Kelini Ta-mah-no-us"* which may be translated "black kick-back necromancy," 'and which (he averred) punishes severely anyone seeking to do me any injury. It did seem to aid me in my Comstock adventures.

In later days I knew Wyatt Earp and Bat Masterson, but not during their active careers as gun-fighters. In a professional capacity I met Chris Evans and George Sontag, the railroad bandits, besides an all-around assortment of fellows with itchy trigger-fingers.

The Comstock had more than its share of bad-men, even though it boasted no ruffians of epic fame such as Jesse James, Billy the Kid, or Slade. Henry Plummer, leader of the notorious "Border Legion" fled to Carson in early days and was hidden by Billy Mayfield, a professional gambler. Jack Blackburn, sheriff—to distinguish him from his deputies he was called High Sheriff—accosted Mayfield, who admitted that Plummer had been in his cabin, but had made good his escape.[1]

When Blackburn found himself foiled, he rushed the gambler with fury. Mayfield stood his ground, stabbed the

---

[1] Only for the time, though, for he was strung up by the Vigilantes in Montana a few years later.

high sheriff to death with his bowie-knife, and escaped from the saloon in which the affray occurred, only to be captured soon afterward.

Before Nevada had a State Prison of its own, Abe Curry kept the prisoners on contract. He impounded them in the big stone house at the Carson Warm Springs which became the State Prison, the Legislature buying it from him for that purpose. One of the first prisoners entrusted to Curry's care was Billy Mayfield. One night Mayfield told Curry he had a bad headache, and asked that he shouldn't be wakened next morning very early, as he wanted to sleep it off.

"All right, Billy," said Abe. "You just sleep as long as you want to, and nobody shall disturb you."

That evening Mayfield slipped his chains, which had already been filed, and got out, while Abe and his cronies were engaged in a tight poker game. Mayfield later said, "It was a king full against a queen full. I decided that if I couldn't go out on that hand, I couldn't go out at all!" Before he went he stuffed up his bunk so that it looked as if a man was in it. When Fred Turner, the guard, went around to lock him up late at night he called to the prisoner, but receiving no answer supposed he was asleep and bolted the door.

In the morning Abe rode up to town on the horse-car railroad which he had built for the accommodation of the legislators. Somebody met him and said, "Well, you played merry perdition last night, didn't you, letting Mayfield escape?"

"No, sir; he didn't escape," retorted Curry.

"Yes, he did."

"Bet ye a hundred dollars that he didn't," said Curry, always ready for a wager. The bet was taken and the men started back to the prison, two miles away.

"You just come with me and I'll show you," said Abe.

"Come, Bill, get up," he continued, going into the cell and shaking the form under the blankets which he supposed was Mayfield. Of course he lost his bet and got laughed at besides. But nobody laughed while he was looking. Not much! It would have been little less than suicide to have done that.

Mayfield was never caught. It was general knowledge that he was hidden in a house near Huffaker's, in Washoe County, for a long time after his escape; but the new sheriff, in gratitude, perhaps, to the man who had vacated a place for him, went there and searched the house without seeing him. Mayfield was shot down in Idaho a couple of years later after a dispute over a card game. Thus ended the career of audacious Billy Mayfield, but not till after he had sent a humorous account of his escape to the *Territorial Enterprise,* which printed it for the edification of its laughter-loving public.

Stone walls do not a prison make—not one that holds always impervious to drill and file. So porous were the walls, so frequent the escapes from Nevada jails that scofflaws suggested that it would be a good plan to strengthen the jails with new coats of whitewash.

In 1871 came the "big break" at the State Prison, when 29 blood-guilty convicts escaped. All able-bodied men in Carson sprang to arms to aid the warden and the guards, and the militia was called out. For months the desperate fugitives were hunted down, through Nevada and California.

Another jailbreak which caused a sensation, I recall, was some years later, when five of Sheriff Williamson's prisoners broke from the county jail at Virginia City. The ringleader was "Red Mike" Langan, under charges of murdering Pat Leonard, whom he had knifed to death on C street as the climax of an old feud. Red Mike was notoriously quarrelsome, having served time for assault and battery on several occasions; and a few years before he had shot one Maxey at the Delta Saloon. Another participant in the break was Mark Brown, horse-fancier, who had stolen an equipage in Six-Mile Canyon; and with him and Red Mike went three men held on burglary charges.

These burglars could break *out* as well as in, for they made a hole under a window in the south wall of the jail, prying out the bricks with a crowbar fashioned from a brace taken from an iron bedstead. A significant fact was that Red Mike had helped Pete Burke build the Court-house, and knew not only every weak point of the jail, which was part of it, but the exact materials used. He knew that the mortar was worthless, and could be crumbled to sand in the hand. All he needed was an opportunity when he was not watched. That chance came, and he went—and the other four rogues with him—through a three-foot wall in about half an hour.

Rough-and-ready justice was meted out at times. In 1871, a ruffian named Perkins (alias Heffernan) who had shot a man in Virginia City for some fancied insult was captured by Vigilantes and hanged. When the body swung clear, a fusillade of shots was fired into it. Exciting moments were those for the mother of Maude Adams, and for McKee Rankin, who were playing at Piper's Opera House at that time!

Public executions with due process of law were usually conducted with great ceremony, before large crowds. One of the most pitiful spectacles I recall was the hanging whereat a craven culprit was hurried from this life, near Virginia City. This condemned man had somehow gained the impression that he could not legally be hanged after sunset. The time for his execution was late in the day, and by every kind of subterfuge he sought to delay proceedings. Finally, when he gained sanction for "more last words," he launched into a ghastly kind of filibuster, talking against time—till the sun went down. The sheriff tried to break in and stop the flow of halfwit oratory, but to no avail; and finally the trap was sprung in the midst of a long periodic sentence, as the late sun was gilding the heights.

As newspapermen, we watched the stories of killings develop. Word went around that one man would shoot another on sight, and usually (not to give the lie to popular report) he would try to make good his boast, though oft beaten to the draw. Men fought to the death for almost any trivial reason, or for no reason at all.

An interesting dispute occurred at a dance at American Flat—a man being shot during the row, though that didn't stop the dance. The cause of the dispute: "Which was the head of the hall—next to the fiddler or next to the big crack in the floor?"

The case came duly to trial.

"Which side won the fight?" asked the old Judge, leaning forward intently.

"Next to the music," was the response.

"Decision affirmed by this court. Defendants dismissed. Call the next case."

Many of the slayings were in hot blood during the course of poker games, and the pleas of self-defense and justifiable homicide were usually sufficient to "spring" the survivors of such slashings and shootings.

An event which caused great popular tumult was the shooting of two popular sportsmen, Tom Hughes and Dick Paddock, in a battle with Robert McDonald, a policeman, in the Delta Saloon, Virginia City, in the early morning of January 2nd, 1877. Both had more than one drink too many that night, and the verdict was that McDonald had inflicted the mortal wounds in self-defense and in line of duty. He was given a reward.

Dick Paddock had a reputation as a fighter, but Tom Hughes had once been a constable and was not so belligerent, and his friends declared he was killed while trying to act as peace-maker. Paddock had survived a street-duel with the noted Farmer Peel, though in that fight he had been wounded in the breast and in the right hand. Hughes and Paddock were saloon-men of local note, proprietors of a cock-pit, and members of the Montgomery Guard, a militia organization made up largely of Irishmen. I remember the big funeral accorded Hughes, a lieutenant in the Montgomery Guard, which turned out in full dress and numbers; and Paddock, who lingered a few days longer, was given like honors, though a private. The Sarsfield Guard and Emmet Guard sent platoons to the Hughes funeral; Knickerbocker Engine Company was in attendance *en masse,* and all the other fire-engine companies were represented. The procession was headed by Rippingham's Band, playing the dead-march from *Saul.*

One editor—names on request—had a bitter quarrel with another, who was a consumptive. In the fight which followed, the latter's left lung was pierced by a bullet. The remarkable part of it was that upon his recovery, he was entirely cured of consumption. His example is not likely to be followed by many, but this was thoroughly effective in his case.

Mark Twain, in ROUGHING IT, presents spirited and accurate details about some of the early killers on the Comstock. Sam Brown, Farmer Peel and Tom Peasley were among the most notorious. Brown, who had slain fifteen men, was a great swaggerer; Dan De Quille described him by saying that he walked into a saloon "one side at a time." Langford Peel, called "Farmer," was mild-mannered but dangerous. Jim

Cartter was a fighter who never retreated a millimeter in a quarrel, and he had the reputation of killing several men, all of them in fair fight.

Among the crew of gun-fighters on the Comstock, some were gallant men who fought only when battles were forced upon them by busy searchers after trouble. In my estimation, Pete Fitzgerald, whom I knew well, was the most intrepid. Captain Ed Byrne, Tom Fillebrown and Leslie Blackburn (who had four notches on his walnut pistol-butt) were not averse to gunplay. Blue Dick, Rattlesnake Dick, Red-Handed Mike, Cut-Mouth Burke and Mike McGowan, "the Man-Eater," were other well-known fighters, but of a lower order.

Quite a lot of notoriety was won by the "shotgun miner," Prentice, who was reputed to have been the principal factor in the fatal shooting of five men at the Waller Defeat Shaft. He had shot from cover, so no one was sure. Prentice had thought to enjoy renown as a "chief," but the Comstock hardly felt that he had killed his men in fair fight, and he was shunned. Later on, I shall tell about Arthur McEwen's encounter with him. When Prentice edged into an altercation in which Eugene Markey, the wrestler, was engaged in the Delta Saloon, and drew a pistol to shoot him, Markey kicked the weapon out of his hand. They tumbled over each other on the floor for possession of the gun, but the strong fellow got it and shot Prentice in the arm. Many were disappointed when the wound proved slight, and it was not until about ten years later that Waller Defeat Prentice, as he was called, met a persistently-sought fate in a dispute over a trivial sum which he declared was due him from Jerry Mulligan, a rancher in Six-Mile Canyon. Jerry was a quiet, peace-loving fellow, but when the aggressor made threats against his life and visited his house to collect by force, the rancher let him have the contents of both barrels of a shotgun, and the coroner's jury failed to consider the deed blame-worthy.

In like manner, when Sam Brown was shot by Henry Van Sickle, a rancher at Genoa whom he wantonly had fired on, the coroner's jury brought in the verdict that Brown had come to his death from "a just dispensation of an all-wise Providence," or in other words, "Served him right!"

One Gossen, mortally wounded in Pioche by a gun-fighter named Casey, in his will left $5000 "to the man who kills Casey." This manslaughtering brave was duly shot dead by Jim Levy, whom he had needlessly affronted. Levy got the $5000, but it did him no good, for he set up as a fighting "chief" on his own account, and was killed in a brawl.[1]

Mike McGowan was called "the Man-Eater" in no mere metaphorical sense. Mayhem was his specialty. When aroused to cannibalistic frenzy, he sought to bite ears, nose or fingers from his antagonist. Most of the others had the fighting instincts of gamesters, but not Mike.

Some of those killers had a warped sense of humor. One day, with a committee from the State Legislature, I was being ushered through the State Prison at Carson. A big Irishman, Hon. J. F. Egan, was in the party. We came upon a little shifty-eyed, black-haired fellow who was apparently a trusty, for he was watering some flowers in the garden. The warden spoke to him, "Say, Domenico, tell these gentlemen what you did to get in here." The gardener shrugged his narrow shoulders, "Oh not'ing—not'ing," he protested.

"But you must have done *something* to get in here."

"Oh, not'ing—not'ing," repeated Domenico.

---

[1] In Deadwood, tough South Dakota camp, in 1874, "Jim Levy was the top-notcher of them all, except Wild Bill. Jim was killed down in New Mexico by Milligan, whose claim Jim had iumped." (See Wilstach, "Wild Bill Hickok," p. 268.)

"Come on, now," prodded the warden, "what *did* you do?"

"Oh, not'ing," replied Domenico, with a sly glance from his snapping black eyes at Egan, "jus' kill t'ree Irishmen."

Deeming it my duty to report in the newspapers which I served the full details of various shooting affrays, I found myself sometimes walking the streets under sentence of death. One who had threatened me was confronted before the International Hotel one night.

"I understand you say you're going to shoot me on sight," said I, as evenly as I could. He noticed my motion, and protested hurriedly, "I haven't got a gun on me." "Well, get your gun and come shooting," I said. The crowd waited around with me, expecting some excitement, but the blusterer didn't show up.

When I wrote some frank denunciation of the off-color political activities of a "peace" officer at Virginia City, he also gave out the stereotyped message that he would "shoot on sight." Upon entering a place of public entertainment one evening I came upon the threatener in the act of raising a whisky glass to his lips. Self-defence prompted my move. I shot the glass out of his hand, then quickly asked if he wanted any more. He was reaching for the ceiling as he admitted sufficiency.

A few others who objected to the ventilation of their shooting affrays were going to clean up on me, the offending editor, but never got around to it. Yet let me admit the anxious, uncomfortable feeling induced by such threats, uttered by irresponsible rascals with nervous trigger-fingers.

Many a "bad man from Bodie" would come into Virginia or Gold Hill and proceed to unlimber his artillery in a frontal attack; and Candelaria, Eureka, Pioche and other camps sent their embattled contingents.   Their local pride was monumental.

I recall when an ornery stranger reeled into a C street saloon, and pounding the bar with his six-shooter until the glasses danced, announced: "I'm a roarin' ripsnorter from a hoorah camp, an' I can't be stepped on. I'm an angel from Paradise Valley, an' a bad one, an' when I flop my wings there's a tornado loose. I'm a tough customer to clean up after. Give me some of your meanest whisky, a whole lot of it, that tastes like bumble-bee stings pickled in vitriol. I swallered a cyclone for breakfast, a powder-mill for lunch, and haven't begun to cough yet. Don't crowd me!"   The visitor having delivered himself of this gasconade, the bartender busied himself hunting for some fusel oil, while rubbing the glass with red pepper.   One by one the loungers near the stove quietly slid out of the side door, and when the bad-man turned around, the place was empty.

CHAPTER TWENTY-ONE

Some Fighting Editors

*A*s Alf Doten told me on my first assignment as a Comstock reporter, "licking the editor" was a favorite pastime of the people, especially of bad-men who were not anxious to have their shooting and cutting affairs made part of the permanent record.

It was not absolutely necessary for an editor to fight as well as write, but at least he must show a willingness to defend himself in a manly way and stand on his rights, no matter what the result, or else his usefulness in journalism would be impaired to the verge of nothingness. In other words, he might as well walk the grade, first as last, since his days were likely to be few and full of trouble.

Brave as a lion, Dan De Quille was modest to the point of bashfulness. His intrepid soul was disclosed when, after Farmer Peel had accomplished one of his many killings, and the Virginia City *Enterprise* contained an accurate account of the affray, Dan braved the anger of the man-slayer. Hearing that Peel was threatening vengeance, Dan sought the gunfighter and found him in his favorite saloon.

"I hear you are looking for me," said Dan.

Peel saw at a glance that the tall, slender reporter was not afraid of him, and replied that he was nettled at the plain words of the account of the shooting, but that after reading it over a second time he found that in the main it was accurate and so he had decided that there were no grounds for complaint. Whatever were his failings, and notwithstanding the general belief that bullies are cowards, Peel was really a brave man, and in Dan De Quille he recognized an equal in the only realm of which he had any conception.

That episode established Dan's reputation for intrepidity, and won the respect not only of Farmer Peel, but of all his kind. They knew that if Dan wrote up their affrays they would get even-handed justice.

At another time, Dan took a knife from a bad-man who objected to having his exploits mentioned in the public press. If Dan had killed the scoundrel he would not have been arrested.

Dan De Quille used to laugh at the tribulations of a "local" editor—city editor, we call him now in the big places.

"How often it happens," wrote Dan, "that some one—generally Mr. Jenkins—comes to the hungry, itemless 'local' with 'Oh, such a rich joke!' on his friend Slasher, a man with whom you (the 'local') have not the slightest acquaintance. Jenkins is very anxious—persistently so—to have you get off his great joke on Slasher. He assures you over and over that he and Slasher are the greatest friends alive, and that he wouldn't for the world say or do a thing to hurt Slasher's feelings—why, Slasher regular dotes on him, and he does the same by Slasher.

"The item will tickle Slasher when he sees it—he is such a jolly dog, this Slasher: so good-natured and fond of a joke. Jenkins is sorry you don't know Slasher; he is sure you would like him, and he will introduce you to Slasher the first opportunity.

"Finally Jenkins tells you the immense joke on Slasher and

laughs—oh, how he laughs. He knows Slasher, and can see him in his mind's eye, and all the circumstances attendant upon the joke are vividly impressed upon his mind. It is a rich thing as he sees it, but to you it has no point, and your make-believe laugh is a sorry effort.

"You are at last coaxed into making a promise to publish the joke, as you are assured that the jolly dog, Slasher, has some inkling of the matter and will rather expect to see himself in print. You make a note of the outlines of the joke, and for the remainder of the day are quite miserable every time you see the same. You don't see how you are to make anything readable out of the flimsy skeleton furnished you. You find in reality the man Jenkins has thrown upon your shoulders nearly the whole responsibility of getting up the joke.

"However, the man so much doted upon by Slasher has given you liberty to color the thing up; in fact, said to you several times: 'Color it up! color it up! Damn it, you know how to do these things!' You write up the joke and do 'color it up' with a vengeance. Finally, you make a passable thing of it.

"Next morning you seat yourself in the sanctum and look over the paper. You come to the joke, and as you read it in the big, clear type, it seems to loom up, and looks a great deal bolder than it did in manuscript. You begin to think you may have added a trifle too much color, yet the thing is rather funny and you laugh—laugh just a little, for at the moment there comes a rap at the door—a regular shower of thundering raps.

"You are somewhat startled, but by an effort recover your equanimity, and in a cheerful tone say: 'Come in.'

"The door opens and in comes a huge, broad-shouldered, black-whiskered, six-footer—striding in tremendous boots that have soles two inches thick and tops that reach above his knees.

He wears a very slouchy slouched hat, and has awful arms and hands. The giant eyes you over.

" 'My name,' he cries, in thunder tones, 'is Slasher!'

"He might have saved himself the trouble of speaking. You knew the moment you heard the knock at the door that Slasher was coming, and you knew the moment the boots and whiskers marched towards you that Slasher had come—Slasher in all the awfulness and grandeur of his wrath.

" 'My name is Slasher, and I want to know what in the name of hell this means? This, sir—*this!*' pointing with his big hairy forefinger to that 'great joke.'

"You cough and try to make out you don't see just what he is pointing out.

" 'Did you write this?' still pointing at the great joke on him, given you by his bosom friend, Jenkins.

"You finally say you did publish the thing—it is only a *thing* now—at the earnest solicitation of his most intimate and particular friend, Joshua P. Jenkins, Esq.

" 'Him! Jenkins? That damned ass! That squirt! That sneaking, impertinent, bladder-headed puppy! Jenkins? Why, the sneaking low-lived pimple! I'll mash him the first time I meet him; I'll spread his nose all over his face. As for you, sir, you ought to have had better sense. By thunder, I ought to pull your nose! I've half a mind to pull it, anyhow!' but, after eyeing you a moment, he gives a snort, turns on his heel, and departs. . . .

"Thus you make the acquaintance of that jolly dog Slasher, and all without the cold formality of the introduction promised you by his bosom friend, Jenkins."

Sometimes the editor had a hankering to deal out chastisement himself. Major John Dennis, when publishing a sheet in Tuscarora, had a row with a man on the street. His opponent, old Rockafellow, was locked up on a charge of disturbing the peace and using vulgar language, and Dennis, going to the jail, put up his bail-money, forty dollars, for the satisfaction of getting him out where he could lick him. He secured his enemy's liberation and as an aftermath got soundly thrashed himself. Next morning in the justice court the victor failed to show up, and his bail was declared forfeited.

One of the famous street-battles in Virginia City was that in which Denis McCarthy worsted T. B. O'Brien, henchman of Kearney, and president of the Workingmen's Party on the Comstock.

A tall, light-haired Scot, just my age, became my intimate friend and companion in Comstock journalism. Arthur McEwen was his name. He had worked as a manual laborer on railroad construction in California, at a time of financial stress—and later delivered with success a lecture on "Hard and Easy Shoveling." Craving adventure, he wandered to Nevada; and it was not long before he had a taste of the adventure he sought.

It was in Gold Hill, and McEwen had just arrived in camp. He had come up to the mountains to be associate editor of the Gold Hill *News*. He was young and jolly and regularly "one of the boys," as anybody had to be to get along in those diggings.

One morning he went into Donovan's saloon to get his usual stiffener, to which every patron of the house was entitled free of charge. The theory was that a man who spent his money in a saloon had a right to at least one cocktail to start the day with. Some took advantage of this, of course, and went to twelve or thirteen saloons for their morning nips, but as a general thing, I think, the respectable ones didn't extend their routes to more than seven places.

Arthur McEwen, then, went in after his "matutinal tipple," as Doughnut Bill used to call it. As he was waiting for the barkeeper to dissolve the sugar, a quiet-acting, little dried-up-looking fellow, in a faded brown suit of clothes, sidled up to him and said:

"Hello, Mac, old boy. How do ye open up this mornin'?"

McEwen did not let on to hear him, but the other fellow didn't mind that, but in an off-hand way remarked:

"Gimme a cocktail, too, barkeep. I guess I'll drink with Mac."

"I guess you won't," snorted out the bristling editor. "I pick my companions as a general thing, and when I want you to drink with me, I'll ask you.

"See here!" said McEwen, turning to the barkeeper. "What makes you let a bum like this lie around your place to insult gentlemen when they come in for a drink?

"Get out of here," he fairly shrieked, turning to the intruder again. "Get out of here, right quick, or I'll bust your jaw and throw you out."

The quiet little fellow turned on his heel, like a man who had been misunderstood, and walked over to the stove, where he stood blinking out of his beady black eyes, in a wicked sort of way. It would be hard to say which was the more surprised, the barkeeper or the little fellow who invited himself into McEwen's company.

"As for me," said K. B. Brown, who told me of the incident, "I nearly fainted. It fairly took my breath away, and the Napoleon solitary that I was in two cards of doing got so confused in my head that I lost it, and I've never got that near since. I believe certain I'd have made it that time, for I had the diamonds and hearts all benched, and the jack of spades and the seven of clubs were the only ones covered in the discard and were not troubling me very—

"What's that? Oh, yes; about the rest of the story. You

must really excuse me, but I've tried a thousand times to work that game of solitary out in my head, but I couldn't do it.

"Well, the barkeeper and I told the gang what McEwen had done, and we all agreed that he ought to have some kind of recognition, and so a collection was taken up. When I set a tin bucket of dollars on the pine box he used for an editorial table he looked up, and quickly asked:

" 'What's this?'

" 'Oh, just a little tribute from some of us boys,' says I kind of careless-like.

" 'What on?' says he.

" 'We want to show that we recognize merit,' says I.

" 'How? Explain,' says he.

" 'Well,' says I, 'when a man comes raw into the camp and bluffs out the boss killer of the diggings the first clatter out of the box, we put it up that he's a good one and we want to make ourselves solid. Hence these Carson stove-lids, as my friend Senator Jones calls 'em. I'm appointed a committee of one to deliver the tin.'

" 'But what have I to do with all this? What have I done?' he asks again.

" 'Your modesty becomes you as much as your bravery,' says I, for the young ink-slinger was establishing himself higher in my opinion every minute.

" 'This morning,' says I, 'What you did over in Donovan's saloon, you know, when you showed your nerve like that; when you wouldn't let Prentice drink with you, you know, and—'

"But he wouldn't let me finish what I was saying.

" 'What!' he demanded, 'Was that Prentice I was talking to and threatening to smash in the jaw? Is it possible that is the man I have heard so much about? How did he know me, I'd like to know?'

" 'Yes,' says I, 'that was him. That was Prentice. He knows everybody, and that was his way of introducing himself. He felt, of course, you'd be proud to meet him.'

" 'But that's not Waller Defeat Prentice,' he says, aghast. 'Not the fellow that killed five men when they tried to capture Waller Defeat Shaft, and him inside loaded up with shotguns and six-shooters and bowie knives?'

" 'The same.'

"You just ought to have seen McEwen then. It was not easy for me to keep him from rushing out to hunt up Prentice and maybe beg his pardon.

" 'Don't do it,' says I. 'Don't do it. It'll be a dead give-away, and you'll never hear the last of it. Now you've got your reputation established as a fighter, keep it. You can't imagine what it will be worth to you. Just gaze on this bucket of dollars,' and I gouged up a handful of the castings. 'That's the first installment. You can't tell how many more will come.

" 'Look at you now. Don't you notice how much attention is paid to you? There's not a man in Gold Hill asked to drink oftener than you. If you want to be elected Constable you can get it as slick as a whistle, and two years from now you can be solid for Sheriff or Congressman.'

"My speech had the desired effect, and wringing my hand in thankful enthusiasm, he said:

" 'Colonel, I'll take your advice. I'll stick it out on that line. I never shot a pistol more than a dozen times in my life, but I'll learn how. I only know how to box a little, but I'll take lessons from Bill Davis and go into training as a general all-around fighter, though it's terribly against the grain, Colonel— terribly against the grain, I assure you.'

" 'But the bucket,' says I, 'the bucket belongs to Fatty's oyster-stand, and I promised to return it. If you'll empty the silver into your coal scuttle or waste basket, so I can get the bucket, I'll feel a thousand times obliged.'

" 'Oh, hang the bucket,' says he, 'take it away as fast as you please, and the dollars, too, for all I care, only don't give me away on the fighting proposition. Don't you do it, or, by thunder, I'll make you think I'm not so easily scared as I look.'

"Don't you know, I hope I may be starved alive if I ever made a winning while those dollars lasted—not one. I never picked up a white splitter. And there sat Caribou George right there in the old Sawdust Corner playing raw faro-bank from soda to hock, coppering me every time and stacking up reds and blues so high he couldn't see over 'em.

"What about Prentice? Well, he kind of dropped the subject. He said he didn't want to have anything to do with a man who didn't know enough to be afraid of the boss of Gold Hill."

And what about McEwen? He served well as an editor of the Virginia City *Chronicle*. He became known as one of the ablest, most fearless writers in America. But his writings raised up a host of powerful enemies. He was honored by their hatred. He earned their dislike by denouncing their evil methods. Those who were most intimately associated with Arthur McEwen know that in all his dealings with public men and public affairs he submitted every proposition to the touchstone of truth. If misinformed or misled in any way he had the courage to acknowledge the error and make amends. It takes a strong, just man to do that.

McEwen's ability received recognition in the greatest world of newspaper work, not only on the Pacific Coast, but throughout the country. In journals of national importance he more than held his own in contests with the strongest publicists. In truth he wielded a claymore, and sent many a discomfited opponent reeling from the arena of debate.

"Laying the rod on many deserving backs," *Arthur Mc-Ewen's Letter* startled San Francisco in the mid-'90s. "I can at least put men as they really are beside the statues which they have erected to themselves, or had erected in their honor by dishonorable hands," he promised in his first issue. "In this sense the *Letter* will be 'personal'—intensely so." Certainly it was.

The *Letter* grew in popularity, and at one time Arthur Mc-Ewen, Frank Lane, Bob Davis and myself busied ourselves with its publication in the old *Star* office on Montgomery Street, of which the guiding genius was Jim Barry, as genial as he was gifted. Perhaps I should explain that this Frank was Franklin K. Lane, later Secretary of the Interior, and this Bob was *the* Bob Davis—Robert Hobart Davis in the biographical dictionaries. Sam Davis and Joe Goodman were there at the same time. Joe Leggett was a frequent visitor. Ambrose Bierce dropped in occasionally until he and McEwen had a fierce set-to.

A chance word of disparagement started this warfare which was carried on between Ambrose Bierce and Arthur McEwen. There never was anything fiercer in Western journalism—those two brilliant men, at it hammer and tongs. Nothing was too bitter for them to say of each other.

San Francisco was thus in 1895 treated to "personal journalism" of the vanishing frontier type, with the antagonists acknowledged champions in their craft.

After a few slighting references to his erstwhile friend, which went unnoticed, Ambrose Bierce in his "Prattle " column in the *Examiner* made a frontal attack upon Arthur McEwen, terming him "one whom Providence has for some mysterious purpose permitted to wear a clean shirt and know how to spell."

Bierce hailed McEwen as a "distinguished illogician, inaccessible to the contagion of truth and logic."

Under the provocation of this attack, McEwen was stirred to reply. However, he did not respond in print for several weeks, apparently busying himself with the compilation of select vituperation against the man whom he called the "Bully of the Press."

When Arthur McEwen replied in his famous *Letter* he winnowed the soul of Ambrose Bierce over the coals:

"None have admired more than myself his extraordinary skill with the pen. He has wit and a satanic humor, as well as a rare command of language. But being hard and little, it is impossible for him to expand, or to enter into the thoughts or feelings of others. His highest aim now, seemingly, is to insult, and if he can frame his insult in an ingenious phrase his ambition is satisfied. . . . He is most at home when breaking butterflies on the wheel, when torturing poor poetasters and feeble scribblers of prose, who but for him would remain unheard of."

Bierce waved the controversy aside: "There are more interesting subjects than this literary pouter-pigeon, but I cannot forbear to add that in his four-column exposition of my unimportance he gave himself a deal of needless though congenial trouble."

Neither of these free-lancers was the winner—both were necessarily losers in an interchange like that. It was particularly deplored by such as myself, a warm friend of each of them. But writing of this kind was the stock-in-trade of Ambrose Bierce especially. These unveiled aspersions were written by the contending champions in their professional character. They were printed mainly for the edification of the public. There was no reason why they should not have said these things to each other eye to eye, or written them in private letters, except that they made "good copy," and that was what Arthur and Ambrose wanted, apparently.

One would have thought that after this exchange of insultingly open letters, it would have been a case of "pistols in the morning," but there was no duel. This despite the fact that both were of known personal bravery. Arthur McEwen, that braw Scot, with his Comstock upbringing, was entirely fearless; and Ambrose Bierce, who always retained his military bearing, had served with gallantry as an officer in the Civil War.

It is not often recalled that Ambrose Bierce had been a mining engineer in Nevada—out White Pine way; and, like Mark Twain, he really began his writing career in the Sagebrush land. He was a man of charming manners; and, as I knew him, genial rather than bitter. In this instance, the style was not altogether the man.

CHAPTER TWENTY-TWO

Sagebrush Journalism

*7*he early history of Nevada journalism sparkles with brilliant names. There were giants in those days who were intellectually the peers of the best in the profession. Their writings were quoted north, south, east and west. In editorial utterance they were outspoken, vigorous, free, sometimes fierce, almost savage. With a boundless prodigality they scattered gems of thought and shafts of wit through their columns, lending life and color to the current history of their sagebrush plains and ore-bearing crags and canyons.

To call the roll would be to summon memories of some of the best writers the West has produced—Mark Twain, Dan De Quille, Harry Mighels, Rollin Daggett, Joe Goodman, Sam Davis, Denis McCarthy, Arthur McEwen.

The story of journalism in Nevada begins with the *Territorial Enterprise*. It was started in Genoa in 1858, was moved to Carson in 1859, and to Virginia City in 1860, where it gave up the ghost in January, 1893. The passing of such a notable paper as the *Enterprise* caused widespread comment throughout the country. The leading journals of the United States published sympathetic and stirring obituaries. Its loss was felt everywhere. The Society of Pacific Coast Pioneers flew its flag at half-mast.

The *Enterprise* died with its boots on. Like a brave old sport whose luck had gone to seed, the *Enterprise* met its fate with the stolidity of a gunfighter. The valedictory did not contain a whine or a whimper. "For sufficient reasons we stop," was all the editor said.

Nothing could be more characteristic. The paper was published in a community of speculators and its proprietors ever knew that its existence was a gamble—that it depended on the cast of a die, the discovery of a "true fissure" vein, the pinching out of a quartz stringer or the development of a bonanza.

Attempt was made to revive the *Enterprise,* but it ran only sporadically, and its paling flame flickered and went out—forever.

Aside from the political exigencies which precluded its future successful publication in Nevada, the depression of the silver market, the diminished output of the mines and the consequent dwindling of Storey County's population settled the fate of this veteran paper.

Fabulous stories are told of the financial success which attended the publication of the *Enterprise* in early days. It is said that when Joe Goodman and Denis McCarthy were owners, during the flush times of the Comstock excitement, the paper earned a clear profit of $1,000 a day, and that the proprietors didn't keep any books, but conducted their business on a strictly cash basis and carried their dividends home in water buckets at the close of each week—this in a town of less than 30,000 inhabitants. At that time it was a bigger publication than any boasted by San Francisco.

The death of the *Enterprise* recalled a peculiar passage in the career of a man named Jernegan, one of its founders, over at Genoa. At that time most of what is now Nevada was called Carson County, Utah. Genoa, which was a Mormon settlement, began to languish in 1860 and the paper was moved to Carson City, which had suddenly sprung into prominence as a freight-team center. It was at Carson, some months before the paper was moved to Virginia City, that Jernegan lost his interest in the establishment on account of his inferior financial ability. He had been the controlling spirit at the beginning and the loss stung him to the quick. He seemed to think that he had been wronged, though his dispossession was simply a business transaction where the officers of the law were called on to do their duty. Vowing vengeance he started out to kill the paper by abusing Alfred James, his former partner. This plan proved futile, but he swore that he would get even. His time came at last. On his deathbed out in White Pine County, near where Barney made his historic remark about it being "a wild night on Treasure Hill," Jernegan left a legacy of malediction—it was all he had to leave anybody—for the *Enterprise*. "I call on God to curse the *Enterprise* and all, dead or alive, who robbed me," he wrote in his leather-covered diary, which was found in the cabin where he died, "and I also call down the curses of the Great Jehovah on Nevada by quarter-sections and subdivisions." That was in 1881. It took a long time for him to get his play in operation, but his system seemed to get working at last.

The Virginia City *Chronicle* and the Gold Hill *News* were wellnigh as famous as the *Enterprise*. I worked on all of them, first as compositor or foreman, later in reportorial and editorial capacities, so that I was fellow to almost all the strong personalities who made up Comstock journalism.

Some of the names chosen for early Nevada newspapers were striking and apt. In the realm of journalistic nomenclature W. J. Forbes was easily first, because he had many chances to show his skill. In Eureka the Forbes paper was called *The Cupel,* which name had a significance understood by everybody in the community. Eureka was a camp in which all the ores required smelting, and in order to make a test the assayer was compelled to make use of the *cupel,* a little receptacle of bone-ash in which the precious metals, mixed with the base metals, were placed and subjected to a high degree of heat. The cupel absorbed or eliminated the base metals, leaving on top a shining button of pure gold and silver, ready for weighing and showing accurately the value of the ore. It would be difficult to select a name more appropriate for a true newspaper—one that fills the requirements of the profession, which is in honor bound to show forth the truth and to cast away the mixtures of prejudice and misrepresentation.

When Forbes moved to Virginia City and invaded a field already occupied, he candidly recognized that he was not attempting to fill a long-felt want, and with grim humor styled his paper *The Trespass.* At Battle Mountain he had another little sheet which he called *The Measure for Measure.* I'm coming back to Forbes later—he's an interesting subject.

John Dormer made a happy stroke in naming his Candelaria paper the *True Fissure.* This paper also (for a few months I was John Dormer's right bower on it) was in a mining-camp, and the name was intended to convey the thought that the Northern Belle, the Lucky B and the other mines of Candelaria and Pickhandle Gulch were in fact located on a true fissure-vein, which was the hope of every camp in Nevada which aspired to rival the Comstock Lode. John Dormer had a rich fund of humor. He wrote asking "exchanges" to send him two copies of their newspapers—"one for our own use, and one to be stolen."

The *New Endowment* was another odd title, and *The Old*

Pah-Ute (first called *The Old Pah-Utah*) harked back to the aboriginal days of the country.

The queerest of all the names chosen for newspapers in Nevada was possibly that of the Waubuska *Mangler*. The paper was supposed to have been published in Waubuska, in Lyon County, but as a matter of fact, it never had any existence outside the Carson *Appeal* office. There was never any paper published at Waubuska, but the *Appeal* imagined one and located it there. For some years the *Appeal* pretended to reprint savage editorials credited to the *Mangler,* whose editor it frequently took to task as "a disgrace to journalism."

The controversies between the *Mangler* and its contemporaries were continued for years and with such a show of plausibility that some people to this day still regard the Waubuska *Mangler* as one of the liveliest sheets ever published in the arid West. When the *Appeal* got tired of keeping the fictitious newspaper before the public it announced that the editor, on account of ill-health, had closed up his office and gone east. It re-published a valedictory containing these statements and supplemented it with a story that the publisher had really slid out between suns to avoid a grand jury indictment. Nothing more was heard of the spectral *Mangler* after that and the real cause of its suspension is still a matter of speculation.

The Nevada newspapers had little use for managing editors and copyreaders in those days. Every reporter wrote what he pleased and hung the copy on the "hook." The printer set it as written, and it went through that way. But, as has been hinted, the man who wrote an article was personally responsible for the statements and sentiments it contained. If a person who was criticised didn't like an item he could always find out who wrote it by asking at the editorial rooms, and the author was supposed to back it up or back down, as the case might be. In any event, nobody else was called on to fight his battles.

As explained in the life of Mark Twain by Albert Bigelow Paine, the first instruction given by Joe Goodman to a reporter was never to write, "It is reported," or "We are informed," or anything like that, but to find out the facts and then give them as actual happenings. That was one good reason for the infrequency of retractions in the Nevada newspapers. It didn't pay to make mistakes in a country where every man was his own judge as to whether his dignity had been offended.

For years Joseph T. Goodman was a commanding figure in Nevada journalism. He did more to form the high spirit of the press in that region than any other man of the profession. His temperament led him to the classical form, however, and he never entered controversies unless forced to by unavoidable conditions. Once in, he bore himself so that the contender might well beware of another such contest.

In poesy, he was the rival of his Comstock contemporary, Daggett. And not only was Goodman a writer of distinction—he became an archeologist of recognized standing.

Charles C. Goodwin, journalist, jurist, poet, sage—all these titles are due the man whose pen was dipped in sunshine and whose heart contained the quality which turned all experiences to good. That he was imposed on by thousands of battered wrecks of humanity speaks no worse for him than that his generous nature sometimes yielded to the temptation to help the undeserving. Perhaps he shared the opinion of Arthur McEwen, that of all the people in the world the undeserving poor most merit our assistance, as the deserving poor are sure to find somebody anyway who will succor them in good time.

I do not think my statement can be challenged when I say that Charlie Goodwin wrote more editorial matter in his lifetime than any other editor in the United States. For over half a century, on the Comstock and later in Salt Lake City as the editor of the *Tribune,* his was a steady output. When in harness he seemed to have no idea of anything but work. He wanted no days off, cared for no vacations, but kept up the same steady, unfaltering pace, until past 80.

Rollin Mallory Daggett dearly loved a fight. The roar of battle was music to his ears; the smell of burning powder was incense to his nostrils. "The thunder of the captains and the shouting" delighted his intrepid soul. He was ever eager for the fray, and never lowered his lance in the presence of the enemy. Yet, in moments of peace, he was as gentle as anyone could wish. So strangely were the qualities mixed in him that while his foes dreaded him for his vitriolic attack, his friends loved him for his warm heart and his charm. When un-challenged by adverse criticism, or if not roused by opposition to some cherished belief or pet theory, he was the embodiment of elegant courtesy. But when stirred he was dangerous to any who had the temerity to confront him. He was the Cyrano de Bergerac of Comstock journalism. Like the orig-inal Cyrano, he was a gifted poet. A politician also, for he served in Congress, and as United States Minister to Hawaii.

Fred Hart, who was said to be a cousin of Bret Harte, was editor of the *Enterprise* for a time, and wrote a book of lies about the Sazerac Lying Club, one of the most flourishing insti-tutions ever in Austin, Nevada, leaving an influence still felt in the community, and an example fondly emulated by many now alive. Fred was then in the prime of his fun-making. The name of his club, it needs no old-timer to remind us, was derived from that of a popular brandy.

A talented crew, that *Enterprise* staff. The book-keeper, Henry Cohen, usually wrote the theatrical criticisms! His outlook on affairs was quaint and queer. He was talking about a prominent man who was declared by one of his companions to be anything but wise. "Judge Aude's mind is a howling wilderness," said his friend. "Worse than that," amended Cohen, "his mind is a regular Death Valley. If an idea ever got in there it would perish of loneliness."

More editor than writer was Denis McCarthy. His sense of news-value was unerring. His decisions were instantaneous, yet in sizing up the relative importance of current events, or different phases of the prevailing sensation, he was able to put his finger on the point of paramount interest, and he had the mechanical skill of a finished printer which enabled him to play it up for all it was worth. With deftness he would strip whole paragraphs from a correspondent's long-winded letter, add a word here and there and produce an article of symmetry and sequence, worthy of a place in the columns of Dana's New York *Sun*. Anything that he ever read was stamped upon his brain for all time. His mind was like a photographer's plate and retained every impression. He was one of those rare men who seem never to have found the time to be educated and yet know everything. Brave as a lion, he was always ready to back up any assertion and his *Chronicle* was long one of the leading newspapers of the West.

In earlier years he had been Joe Goodman's partner on the *Enterprise*.

Alf Doten of the Gold Hill *News* bore an honorable part in Nevada journalism. While he sought to produce a neat and workmanlike sheet, and succeeded admirably, he always recognized the primacy of news in the making of a paper, and did what few proprietors would do these days—that is, cut out column after column of advertisements to make room for good live news.

Your friend,
Alf. Doten.

ALF DOTEN, PROPRIETOR OF THE GOLD HILL "NEWS"

AT ENTRANCE OF SUTRO TUNNEL

Doten was a pioneer of pioneers, and when confidential during some friendly evening of talk, would draw from an inner sanctum of the office an old tin cup, battered and worn, together with a tin plate and knife and fork that had seen much use. The knife and fork (the latter of the primitive three-pronged kind) had wooden handles, but these handles were silver-mounted. Around the upper edge of the old tin cup there was also a band of sterling silver, and the venerable plate had been enriched in the same manner. Alf had carried these relics around the Horn and through the "gold rush" of '49.

Edward W. Townsend, afterward the widely known author of CHIMMEY FADDEN and writer of the Major Max papers in the New York *Sun,* had his first newspaper detail on the Gold Hill *News.* It was an assignment to go down the road and meet a party of about twenty officers and prisoners who were driving from Carson, the officers having in custody a notorious Chinese murderer, Ah Chouey, who, while on his way to the State Prison had bribed another Chinaman to take his place. Together with the Chinese were a couple of deputy sheriffs and a lawyer, who were supposed to have connived at the substitution, but the accusation was never established. Ned Townsend interviewed all the principals, wrote a graphic account of the affair, and got it over in time for the evening issue of the *News,* beating all rivals. This gave him a good start, and he never stopped. He became a leader in metropolitan journalism, and a member of Congress, from New Jersey.

The Michelson family of Virginia City, noted for brain-power, produced two sparkling writers, Charles and Miriam. Charlie Michelson, with whom I worked in San Francisco, went to New York as managing editor for one of the big Hearst newspapers, and now holds a position of vast influence as director of publicity for the Democratic Party, with headquarters at Washington. His sister Miriam ranks high as novelist and dramatic critic. S. Michelson, pioneer Comstock merchant, was the father of these two and four others— all brilliant. Bessie married my well-loved friend, Arthur McEwen. Most renowned of all was Albert, who went from Nevada to the United States Naval Academy, became a wizard in mathematics, physics and electricity, and astounded the world by his measurement of light-waves.

It was in 1875 when Sam Davis struck the Comstock Lode, and although he and I were always rivals in journalism, we were good friends most of the time.

Sam Davis' reputation as a practical joker laid him under the danger of reprisals. He wrote a play, produced locally, which lampooned a score of prominent citizens, among them being Judge Rising, Jim Orndorff, Jason Baldwin, Judge Knox and others, so they resolved to get even.

In Storey County, which includes Virginia City and Gold Hill and the entire Comstock Lode district, the ancient custom used to be to elect a barber as coroner. It was the unwritten law of the community, and no one thought of running for that office except he be a tonsorial artist, as they called themselves. Orndorff suggested to Sam that he ought to be appointed deputy coroner, and in that way get the first scoop on the news of the frequent killings of the camp. An election was coming on and Sam induced R. T. Brodek, the barber who shaved him and cut his hair, to enter the race for coroner, promising the support of the paper on which he was working, upon the pledge that he should be appointed deputy coroner if Brodek were successful. Brodek was agreeable and Sam went out and made the campaign of his life. Brodek the Barber was elected, and early the next morning Sam was on hand to get his certificate of appointment as deputy coroner.

"All right," said Brodek, "just get your lawyer to write out the certificate and I'll sign it."

After that Brodek dodged Sam for about a week, for he heard that Sam was on the war-path with blood in his eye. Finally Sam rounded him up. He had cooled down, so no gore was spilled; but, getting Brodek in a corner, he hissed through his teeth: "Consarn your ornery picture, Brodek! You knew that the laws of Nevada don't permit the appointment of a deputy coroner in this county, and you realized it all the time I was spending my money to elect you to your miserable office."

Thus Sam lost his chance of getting scoops on interesting tragedies. That was only his first attempt at job-chasing; not disheartened, later Sam corralled high State offices and became official historian of Nevada. He was long editor of the Carson City *Appeal*.

One of Sam's cruelest jokes was on old Doc Benton, proprietor of the Carson-to-Tahoe stage line, who at the time had divers debts outstanding, to the *Appeal* editor amongst others. When Benton was about to return to Carson from Sacramento, the *Appeal* featured a story that he had made very heavy winnings at the horse-races in the other capital city and was to arrive next evening with all the coin. Hank Monk drove him in with a flourish, on the box of one of his own stages. When he 'lighted he was met by a mammoth delegation—he beamed, till he discovered that he gazed into the expectant faces of all his creditors. Doc Benton "passed." He had brought scarce enough with him to ante in a first-class poker game.

Sam Davis in his early years published a book of humorous stories of unusual originality, a copy of which fell into the hands of Bill Nye, who was at the time in the height of his popularity as a humorist. Nye, Davis claimed, at once proceeded to "appropriate" the stories, or at least the ideas, without attempt to disguise the fact that they were borrowed, acting on the doctrine enunciated by Charles Lamb that an author has a right to claim his own wherever he finds it, and Nye claimed everything he saw and liked. Bill was touring California at the time the alleged stolen property was running through the press under the title of BALED HAY, and met Davis, who had known him when both were working on newspapers in Nebraska.

"You have a lot of gall to take my stuff and publish it that way," said Sam.

"You had a lot of gall to write it before I had time to get to it, as I certainly would if you hadn't butted in," replied Bill, and the incident was closed.

The story THE FIRST PIANO IN CAMP was one of Sam's best, and it contained reference to the admonition posted up near the instrument: "Don't shoot the player; he's doing his best!" Which has been attributed to many another—maybe Bill Nye among them—but it was Sam's.

Owners of rival sheets in Carson, Sam Davis and I had the usual personal difficulties then expected under such circumstances. Having sold out my newspaper, the *Index,* and gone to Kansas City for a few months, I deemed it wise to devote considerable time there to developing my knowledge of the Queensberry art so that I might have some chance with Sam if and when we met—for I was going back. To tell truth, I had serious misgivings, for I had witnessed Sam on several occasions—one tussle in particular when he downed Dave Crosby and held him down until he begged to be released.

On my return to the West, when about to hunt up my sometime friend, he met me on the street and almost knocked me over—but in a different way than expected—by rushing up with arms extended: "God bless you, Wells! How are you?"

Big hearted, generous, impetuous, witty and withal sentimental in the best sense of the word, Sam Davis at last laid himself down in his own well-loved sagebrush land, with the fragrant sagebrush above his pillow. May he rest in peace.

Sam's younger brother, Robert Hobart Davis—"Bob" Davis to all the world—served his apprenticeship as compositor on the Carson *Appeal* and as reporter on San Francisco newspapers, where we worked together. Going to New York he became editor of the Munsey magazines, bringing out O. Henry and a host of other stars of the literary firmament. His books and plays are legion, but perhaps his most famous work is the ode, I AM THE PRINTING PRESS, widely imitated.

Bob is celebrated as the most far-traveled newspaper correspondent in the world. More than 200,000 miles he has covered on his roving assignment for the New York *Sun,* to see everything and present his racy yarns in BOB DAVIS RECALLS. As he wrote me, "Next to a being pursued by the sheriff, I am the swiftest moving bird that roams the plain."

Sam Davis married the widow of Harry Mighels, herself an able newspaper manager.

The fine play of Harry Mighels' wit was the delight of old-time readers of the Carson *Appeal*. If McEwen's weapon was the broadsword, then it would be appropriate to assign the rapier to Mighels. His "blade was both sword and shield," and woe betide the luckless man who risked a taste of its shrewd metal. But he was not vindictive. After running a poor fellow through (speaking journalistically), he disdained to dance on the corpse, as some of his contemporaries would do, but allowed the rites of decent burial to the fragments of even his most implacable foe. There was another pleasing phase of his personality disclosed in his intermittent columns of gossip, and reprinted later as SAGEBRUSH LEAVES.

His editorials were original, spontaneous, brand new, with the unmistakable stamp of genius upon them, and minted from the brain of a scholar and a gentleman. One would look over his little one-horse country paper with wonder and surprise to find such a cultivated writer presiding over it. It was like "finding money in ashes," to use one of his own expressions. His extraordinary work, however, made him known and quoted all over the Union and during a political campaign he commanded the highest salary ever paid a Western editorial writer in those days.

C. C. Powning (Christopher Columbus he was christened and "Clum" he was called) was a prominent figure in the newspaper world of the sagebrush country for many years. Beginning as a printer's apprentice he grew up in the business and by hard knocks and perseverence acquired a valuable property in the *Nevada State Journal* at Reno. His untimely death cut short a career that had much promise.

Robert L. Fulton of the Reno *Gazette* was that rare combination so seldom seen in a printing office, namely a writer of ability and a financier of still greater ability. Everything he touched sprouted gold, and, finding that running a newspaper was not necessary to his success, he abandoned the profession, but still always retained a hankering for the smell of printer's ink and roller composition.

The coming of Henry G. Shaw to the Comstock was a notable acquisition to the ranks of Nevada journalism. He was filled with the ideals and the acquirements of metropolitan journalism, having served on the best Eastern papers. A facile writer and a polished gentleman he inspired all with whom he came in contact with a desire for maintaining the best traditions of the profession. He was editor of the *Enterprise* for some time, and subsequently entered the Government service in San Francisco.

Who shall speak the fitting words in memory of another pioneer Nevada editor whom I have already mentioned—W. J. Forbes? His own worst enemy, that lamentable fact is invariably brought out by his biographers. Doubtless it serves a useful purpose, and the custom need not be departed from even here among these words of appreciation. But he was bright with the undeniable brightness of unquenchable genius. How else could he have borne himself so well and so long under the self-imposed burden of self-indulgence? Old timers still laugh about his quips and fancies. Writing under the pen-name of "Semblens," he touched on every subject known to man, and his shafts so often hit the mark that he became popular with all classes of readers.

This man simply could not keep out of a printing office. Journalism was his natural element. Quick at repartee, trained in the use of a rich and variegated vocabulary that contained every known expression of disapprobation, his bitter words often left scars that were slow to heal. After flaying a man and hanging his hide on the fence he would say, "Thus far we have been mild," and would give his victim another basting. Some marks of hatred followed him beyond the bourne, and commenting on this exhibition of malice, a friendly hand penned these words: "The enemies of Forbes seem to take comfort from the report that he was suffering from softening of the brain. There was nothing in his latest work to indicate such a condition. Be that as it may, he was a noble soul, misguided in some respects, mayhap, but he was faulted mostly by persons whom fate had munificently forefended against any such fate as they ascribe to him."

Forbes declared that he would rather be the possessor of a handful of battered type and a rattletrap press, with a power to say his mind as he pleased, than to be the owner of any other business establishment, no matter what the financial returns, and he proved it by deserting a prosperous business to return to an editorial position, from which he was only able to eke out a bare existence.

It was in White Pine County that he found his newspaper would not pay, and he remarked editorially that "of twenty men, nineteen patronized the saloon and one the newspaper, and he was going with the crowd." He started his saloon and it was probably the only paying business he ever engaged in, but in the midst of his prosperity he sold out and, drifting back to journalism, soon lost all the profit he had made from the liquor business.

His witty sallies came to be copied all over the United States, and probably the most quoted of all, and one which has been credited to many different sources, was his thrust at Governor Nye, who secured the appropriation of $75,000 for the building of a dam and sawmill to manufacture lumber for the Piute Indians, all of which was expended with no tangible results. Forbes said that Governor Nye had "a dam by a mill site, but no mill by a damn sight."

He tried to run a Gentile newspaper in Salt Lake City, throwing down the gauntlet to the Mormons; but he picked it up again. Returning to Nevada he started a journal already referred to, *Measure for Measure,* at Battle Mountain. It was a wonderful paper, but did not pay, and a friend found him on the morning of October 30th, 1875, lying stiff and cold across his shabby bed. He had fought a fight against odds all his life, was one of the brightest writers the West had ever seen, but he lacked the faculty of making and saving money, and lived in communities where his mental superiority was more envied than appreciated. Ten years before his death, with a prophetic pen he wrote:

"Death cannot be a matter of much moment to an editor— no thirty days' notice required by law—it is the local incident of a moment, a few days as advertised on the fourth page, a few calls by subscribers not in arrears. A short, quick breath— then the subscription paper for burial expenses."

Forbes's final resting place is Coloma, California, where he lies buried beside his wife. He had been a pioneer editor in that oldest of the gold towns before going to Nevada.

Not all the drinking ended in tragedy. On the Gold Hill *News* we had a lovable convivial associate editor, who was sent out to Winnemucca on a detail, and who fell prey to the red likker of that budding community. He wired for money to get home on, but on its receipt dissipated it as before, and when he sobered up a little, desperately made an appeal for more funds. Alf Doten, the proprietor, wired the station agent at Winnemucca and requested that the errant one be sent home by freight, C. O. D. It was done.

Jim Townsend was another unique specimen, by all odds the most original writer and versatile liar that the west coast, or any other coast, ever produced. He it was, and not Jim Gillis, who was the original of Bret Harte's TRUTHFUL JAMES. He began his journalistic career in Mono County, California, with the Mono *Index* and wound it up in Carson City, where so many newspapers lie buried. He kept the West laughing for years with quaint sayings which he set up from the case as they came into his mind. They never saw manuscript. He simply set the type when he felt like expressing an idea, and worried himself almost to death because he could not set the type as fast as he could think.

To read his paper you would think that it was published in a city of ten thousand inhabitants. He had a mayor and a city council, whose proceedings he reported once a week, although they never existed, and enlivened his columns with killings, law suits, murder trials and railroad accidents, and a thousand incidents of daily life in a humming, growing town—every last one of which he coined out of his own active brain.

Among the most exciting things with which he kept churning up his readers were a shooting scrape and divorce proceedings arising from a scandal in which the mayor's wife and a member of the city council figured. It dragged along through his columns for nearly six months. It was very interesting to read and implicitly believed—except by persons who knew that there was no mayor and no council at any time in the town where Jim's paper was published. He was called "Lying Jim" Townsend to the day of his death and could he have had his way it would have been graven on his tombstone.

The Comstock and environs surely had a rich mine of journalistic talent, and it experienced a newspaper boom which would have delighted the hearts of old James Gordon Bennett and Horace Greeley. Even to name the many other able writers who were there in early days, and in nearby Nevada towns, would be a task too long. Allen Kelly, John C. Lewis, J. F. Halloran, Donald Scrymgeour, Steve Gillis, H. Z. Osborn, C. A. V. Putnam, C. S. Preble, Allen Bragg, C. S. Young, T. E. Picotte, S. F. Sutherland, Will Austin, W. Frank Stewart, Andrew Maute, Andrew Cassamayou, R. R. and E. J. Parkinson, Robert Glen, D. R. Sessions, George Cassidy, W. W. Barnes, Ed Colnon—these are a few of the best-known ones, besides those already mentioned. Clement C. Rice, dubbed by Mark Twain "the Unreliable," Orlando E. Jones who, when a clown in a circus, was called Dan Conover, John K. Lovejoy, "the

old Piute," and W. F. Boardman, known as "Salty," the Pony
Express rider, were among those who added color to the profession.   Zoeth S. Eldredge, who developed into an historian
of note, was on the Comstock when I was there; and George
Wharton James, one of the most prolific of Western writers,
lived in eastern Nevada.   Timothy H. Rearden, jurist and classi-
cist, whose incisive criticism aided in shaping the style of
Bret Harte, resided on the Comstock; as did Charles Howard
Shinn, gifted writer, whose STORY OF THE MINE holds much
of lively interest about the old camp.[1]   Both were to me good
friends and true.

[1] Eliot Lord also wrote a splendid work on "Comstock Mines and Miners."

CHAPTER TWENTY-THREE

Typeslingers

Not the least of the factors enlivening Comstock journalism were the printers.

In the passing of the old-fashioned compositor the intellectual life of the craft—yea, of the country—suffered a distinct loss. The men who set type by hand were rather inclined to be "sporty" at times, but they were nevertheless a thoughtful, meditative class. Their dignity was something immense. They had a full appreciation of their own worth, and knew how to impress on others a realization of their importance.

We had some unique characters amongst the compositors in the old days.

Not, accurately speaking, a typical printer of the old school, Hazlitt the Pilgrim still had some traits in common with those charming disciples of the craft printorial who are held by typeslingers in affectionate remembrance. As strenuous as he, and almost as impetuous in maintaining their independence, like the Pilgrim they stood ever ready to quit work at the drop of a hat, and some of them would drop the hat themselves in the absence of any valid excuse for making a change. Yet the Pilgrim was not a typical journeyman typesetter, because he was much bigoted when it came to tramping.

He carried the roving habit to the extreme; he changed more often than the rest of the boys. Tom Watts, Charley Millard,

Dick Hicks, J. George Byron L. Rowe, Lying Jim Townsend, Eph Mangus, Frank Lee and several others of that clan ran the Pilgrim a good second, at times, but he was a more consistent performer—he was on the go all the time.

Few of the present generation of printers ever saw Hazlitt, and some of the youngsters never heard of him, yet in printing circles throughout the United States there was a time when not to know the Pilgrim was to argue yourself unknown. "I've just stepped up from Texas," he said in reply to the familiar greeting of the foreman of the Olympia, Washington, *Standard,* and there was no reason to doubt that he had actually trekked the entire distance. Many others of the craft duplicated this performance before the railroads made brakebeams a more speedy method of locomotion.

Every so often, the Pilgrim would show up on the Comstock. The last time I saw Hazlitt he was quitting, as usual. Our editor was an old-fashioned writer who insisted on spelling "honor," "labor" and words of that description with a "u". Hazlitt got a "take" of editorial and set it according to Webster, omitting the "u". When the proof came back the editor had marked in his favorite letter. Hazlitt refused to correct the galley. The foreman became sarcastic.

"Of course, the editor is an old fool, but we have to humour him, so just let him have his way."

"Not for me," said Hazlitt. "I'll not work in an office where they have such antique proofreading."

Slowly and with all the dignity of a Roman senator he rolled down his sleeves, drew on his coat, cashed his string for the half-day's work, and shook the office dust from his feet. He may be going yet. As he always carried his "International" card while on earth, why should any one doubt that in the realms beyond he goes heeled with the credentials of the "Interstellar Typographical Union", as he meanders through the coming eons?

A touch of class antipathy existed between speedsters and those not so rapid, and this was indicated in one of the Western offices along in the '70s when a "fast crab" and a "slow-coach" mixed it. When Henry Becker came to work one evening he found his frame decorated with a hammer which belonged in the pressroom, a vise used in bending rules in the "ad alley" and the office bellows, bearing the legend, "I am a blacksmith", these words being set in Becker's stick with no two types alike. The line was justified with a ten-penny nail, a small piece of broken bottle and a wooden plug at one side and the stump of a cigar at the other. This most elaborate joke was accompanied by the following inscription:

> "I am the slow, the beautiful slow,
> Setting less type than the rest, I know;
> Setting it dirtier, shoemaker style—
> But setting it steady and saving a pile."

When Henry Becker arrived everybody laughed, and he thought he detected the identity of his tormentor, so the next day he piled the collection of junk on the cases of a fellow-workman, with these lines:

> "I am the fast, undoubtedly fast,
> Setting more type tonight than last;
> Hogging, slogging, the type I sling—
> My name is McCutcheon, the Irish King."

Every printer on the Comstock remembered the day when the *Enterprise* was pied, which was in the midst of a squabble over personnel. The chase containing the type to print the inside form of the Comstock's premier newspaper (with columns of standing matter) was dropped—a dolorous accident, for which several later lost their jobs; they were lucky to escape Joe Goodman without loss of their lives. The *Enterprise* came out that day with its center spread an absolute blank. The Gold Hill *News* chortled editorially, recounting the story of an old inebriate who fell out of his tilted chair in a saloon, his hands to his brow, moaning in horror that he had gone blind— the *Enterprise* was a blank before his eyes!

Still, though rival editors snickered, a fellow-feeling was cherished among the compositors. All the printers on the Lode gathered in a "bee" to aid in distributing that infinitesimal pied type in the *Enterprise* office. And when, as I have recounted, in the conflagration of 1875 that office was destroyed, we set up and printed the *Enterprise* in the Gold Hill *News* plant. I recall that it was there I first met my closest friend among my fellow-craftsmen, Virgil Borst, now a veteran of half-a-century in active work. Dave Matthews, Charley Copp, Will U. Mackey, George W. Hoffman ("Toots"), Robert Glen, F. Slate, Al McCarthy (brother of Denis), Harry Fontecilla (he also was at Bodie when I was there), Daniel Connett, Peter Myers, Josiah C. Harlow, John Church—these were but a few of the printers I knew and worked with on the Comstock. The *Enterprise* alone had twenty compositors in its heydey.

Many of the workers on the editorial side in those early days were practical printers—Joe Goodman, Denis McCarthy, Steve Gillis, Mark Twain and Jim Townsend, among others.

Among the ablest and best-loved of the Comstock printers was Edward T. Plank, who was foreman on the old *Enterprise* when Mark Twain and Dan De Quille were reporters on that paper. He was recognized as a leader in his craft, and for three years served as President of the great International Typographical Union.

Plank was true blue. I saw him tested many times and he never flinched. He was chosen a member of the Nevada Legislature, and his motto was always: "Equal opportunities for all; special privileges for none." His bass-drum voice was not the only impressive quality of his speech, for his utterances were marked by good sense, moderation and a practical understanding of the affairs of life, viewed from the standpoint of the employer as well as from the standpoint of the employee.

The Washoe Typographical Union, of which Plank had been President, affiliated with the Mechanics' Union of Storey County, which was similar to a modern Labor Council, being composed of journeymen of all crafts. Plank at once became prominent in the larger organization, and one day headed a delegation named to call on Adolph Sutro for the purpose of asking him to raise the wages of carpenters. The Sutro Tunnel was undergoing extensive repairs and 300 carpenters were employed on the work.

The Storey County Mechanics' Union had more than 2,000 members and they did everything in an open-handed way. A large coach drawn by four dashing horses was secured for taking the committee to the town of Sutro in Lyon County, fifteen miles distant. Sutro met the committee and invited it into his office. Plank stated the fact that the men hankered for a dollar a day more than they were getting. He mentioned that it was hard work and that the request was really not unreasonable.

"You gentlemen seem to be from the Storey County Mechanics' Union, while these carpenters are working in Lyon County. Now if I should receive an application from the Lyon County Mechanics' Union it might be more appropriate," said Sutro in his pleasantest manner.

"We thought of that," said Plank politely, "and so we came

PART OF VIRGINIA CITY, NEVADA, 1877

WELLS DRURY IN VIRGINIA CITY, 1880

prepared. Allow me to introduce the President of the Lyon County Mechanics' Union." A gentleman stepped forward and shook hands with Sutro.

Adolph Sutro was a man of nerve as well as tact. There was a twinkle in his eye that showed his appreciation of the situation.

"May I ask when the Lyon County Mechanics' Union was organized?" he said calmly.

"Certainly, sir," said Plank, consulting his watch. "Its charter was granted an hour ago and before we left Dayton (five miles distant) the organization announced its affiliation with the Mechanics' Union of Storey County."

There was a quiet laugh all round and in two minutes more the whole business was settled, the carpenters got their extra dollar a day, the committeemen joined Sutro in a few bottles of champagne and drove home.

Plank explained to the Virginia City Union that it might have hurt wages on the Comstock if men had been allowed to work so near by at reduced rates.

In January, 1874, a 17-year-old boy (under the spell of reading ROUGHING IT) went to Virginia City, and his luck deserting him at faro, he went to work at his trade—printer—on the *Enterprise*. He was Fremont Older, long the dean of Western journalists.

Fremont Older in his delightful reminiscences tells amusing stories about Babbitt, a tramp printer who applied for work in the *Enterprise* office one day. He had "beaten" his way from New York, and was covered with grime, grease and coal-dust; but he was put to work. "We soon learned that he was more than an ordinary tramp printer," recounts Older. "I found his conversation most unusual. Apparently, he had read everything and knew everything. He spoke and wrote fluently both French and German. Whisky was responsible for his becoming a wanderer. His mad passion for drink had so undermined him physically that he staggered even when he was sober. He would start for the door and miss it by two or three feet. He had a wandering blind eye. It rolled about in his head as if it were entirely unrelated to the other eye. He was also very hard of hearing. Physically, he was most repellant, hollow chested, stoop-shouldered, with a high-pitched falsetto voice, but with a mind that attracted every one who met him. No one seemed able to resist him.

"A few days after Babbitt arrived in town he appeared at the office in new apparel from hat to shoes. He was perfectly dressed, but too drunk to work.

" 'How did you get the clothes?' I asked him.

" 'On credit at Roos Brothers.'

"Roos Brothers had a thriving clothing store at that time directly across from the *Enterprise* office.

" 'I told Mr. Roos my story in French," said Babbitt, 'and he was so moved by my plight that he trusted me.'

"Within a week he had borrowed money from nearly everyone in the office, including myself; had charge accounts in saloons, and had worked himself into the good graces of a German restaurant keeper by talking German to him, and representing himself as a secret agent of the German government. To the women of the underworld, who had fallen for him, he was the traveling correspondent of Frank Leslie's magazine, in town, incog., to write and illustrate a series of articles for that publication."

This gay Lothario, after the splurge of a farewell banquet, finally departed for Winnemucca, tentatively to wed a school-ma'am there whom he had ardently and victoriously courted by correspondence, and to whom he had sent his portrait—

or rather, the photograph of a handsome faro dealer instead.

Not one of the old boys would object if I told some of the convivial customs of those jovial days. Not they. Stout-hearted, clear-minded, they took their groceries and their grog with unvarying poise.

They were not altogether flawless, those grand old masters of the stick and rule. I remember that one who fell somewhat short in those conventions esteemed by the ancient and honorable order of Good Templars started home after a night's work carrying a roll of carpet which he had bought at auction the previous afternoon. When he had toiled almost to the top of the Divide, after a painful and meandering struggle, he was hailed by a constable and compelled to take the carpet back down to the police station, which was within a block of the office where he had been working. The head pressman was sent for and identified the printer as a law-abiding though somewhat self-indulgent citizen, whereupon the police sergeant told him he was free to go, and advised him to take the carpet away with him. "Not much," he replied, "I'd be sure to meet some other fool John Law who would make me bring it back again."

When I was foreman of the Gold Hill *News* it became my unpleasant duty to fire incompetents now and then. One was a lush who exceeded even the bounds tolerated in that liberal community. Gold Hill is built in a canyon, and in the old days houses covered both sides—so that virtually the entire populace looked down upon Main Street, and heard all that passed thereon, as from a gallery at a play. What was my astonishment to learn that the wife of this discharged printer (she loved "a drop o' the craytur" herself) walked all day ceaselessly up and down that street with her apron over her head wailing, "Wells Drury has ruined our little home! Wells

Drury has ruined our little home!" I was suspected of home-wrecking proclivities alien to my character.

Another typo who had an overweening fondness for prime Kentucky Bourbon, was himself a native of the Bluegrass State. One day he arrived the worse for his frailty, and was casting about in his mind for some excuse for not working. As he passed the editorial sanctum, he heard the editor, Alf Doten, a staunch New Englander, say to his assistant, "Get up a rock-ribbed leader on Forefathers' Day." That holiday, while dear to the heart of the Yankee, is unknown in the South. But from the chance remark of the editor our hero took his cue. He went solemnly up to the foreman, and wagged his finger at him: "I'd have you know, sir, I wouldn't work for any man—hic—on Forefathers' Day."

"Go on," responded the irate foreman, "get out—you won't work for me on any day." But next week he was back at the cases again. Then, as always, work was the curse of the drinking man.

They were devotees of the drama, the old-time printers, and critics of no mean ability. In fact, many of them took editorial positions, and more of them would have done so had it not been for the fact that they could make more money and be more independent over the spacebox.

One night a trio of these rare spirits forsook their cases for the glare of the footlights. They had begun early in the afternoon and were well in tune before the curtain went up. Tom evidently had intended to go home for supper, because he had with him a lot of fat pork chops. These he carried in his outside coat pocket as he made the rounds of the thirst emporiums with Dick and Harry, who had persuaded him to join them in their night's entertainment. With constant handling and jostling against the throng the original paper was worn off the greasy chops, and Tom supplemented the covering with a section of newspaper. This did no service except to discolor the white of the fat when the ink on the paper began to "run." Our three friends had inside seats for the five-act play at old Piper's Opera House that night, and as it was a point of honor in those days to go out for a clove between acts they encountered some difficulty in making their way among the crowded seats. Those pork chops appeared to grow in size and juicy substance, and in order to more conveniently carry them Tom divided the load, putting one-half in each of his outside pockets. He resembled a scythe-bearing chariot, terrible to see. Out and in, time and again, the devoted trio struggled over the rows of impeding legs and feet, gaining the aisle that led them to the buffet and hurrying back to recover their places before the raising of the curtain. At each move the pork chops stuck out more ominously, threatening the clothing of those all around. A mild-mannered citizen made a half-hearted attempt at remonstrance, but was frozen into silence by Tom's withering looks, and meekly waved his hand in mute apology for having the presumption to criticise his superiors. At length the performance ended, and at 3 o'clock in the morning those pork chops were still journeying about—Tom, Dick and Harry eloquently discussing the merits of the play.

CHAPTER TWENTY-FOUR

Dan De Quille

Of all the men I knew on the Comstock I consider William Wright—*Dan De Quille*—the most thoroughly characteristic of the camp and its inhabitants. As in the case of Mark Twain, the early occupation of Dan De Quille in the West was mining, and it was while so engaged at Meadow Lake, California, that he sent accounts of mining developments in outside camps as voluntary contributions to the Virginia City *Enterprise,* thus first attracting the favorable attention of the proprietors, Goodman and McCarthy, and so he was invited to join the staff. The similar experience of Mark Twain sometime later, when he left his quartz ledge at Aurora, Nevada, to begin his successful career, joined two of the most original writers that have ever been members of the same newspaper staff in this Western country. Mark came down to take Dan's place on the *Enterprise* while he made a trip to "the States", and when Dan returned they both worked on the staff of the flourishing journal. "We wrote at the same table and frequently helped each other with suggestions," said Dan. "Never was there an angry word between us in all the time we worked together."

In the long years of his reportorial work Dan De Quille never shed his character as a miner. A miner he started out, and a miner he remained—in spirit, if not in deed. Whatever other changes were made in the staff of the paper, Dan remained, through good years and through bad years, through bonanza and through borrasca, and his conscience never swerved from the firm conviction that the true calling of a first-class newspaper is to publish items concerning prospects, locations, mines and mills, shafts, tunnels, drifts, ore developments, stopes, assays and bullion outputs.

All other matters to him appeared inconsequential and of no material interest. If there was a murder, a sensational society episode or a political contest, any of them were welcome to space after his mining notes were provided for. If they interfered with what he considered the vital mining news of the day they had to be condensed or left over till some more convenient season. Dan was right, judging from his standpoint. He was a miner in a mining country, writing for miners, who had a livelier interest in the latest mineral developments of the Julia, the Lady Bryan, the Ophir or the Belcher, than in learning the result of a Presidential election.

Dan's hope was undying. He never lost faith in the Comstock, and he was one of the first outsiders to solve the existence of the huge "plum" of the Big Bonanza in the Con. Virginia and California mines. One day he startled John Mackay and Jim Fair by pointing out the exact position of the ore-body that their diamond drills had uncovered to them, but which had not then been revealed to the public gaze. Dan had worked out the problem from his knowledge of ore developments on both sides of that wonderful deposit.

It must not be thought, however, that Dan could write nothing but mining items. He had a fund of quaint humor, and when his attention was not distracted by quartz or placers, produced some of the most readable sketches written in the West.

Journalism in Nevada, as you will know by now, was uneven—that is, sometimes there were big stories of killings, with the succeeding inquests and trials, and then there might be a lull which to a reporter who was not resourceful would be fatal. Here was where Dan could shine. His invention was inexhaustible. Out of the merest trifles he produced columns of solid type. From filmy threads of unreality he evolved postulates and spun theories that startled scientists and set the Barnums of the country by the ears.

Who of the old-timers will forget his pseudo-erudite account of "The Traveling Stones of Pahranagat Valley"? With feigned scientific minuteness he showed how these traveling stones were by some mysterious power drawn together and then scattered wide apart, only to be returned in moving, quivering masses to what appeared to be the magnetic center of the valley. Upon these pretended observations he predicated a new doctrine concerning electrical propulsion and repulsion.

"These curious pebbles," he averred, "appear to be formed of loadstone or magnetic iron ore. A single stone removed to a distance of a yard, upon being released at once started off with wonderful and somewhat comical celerity to rejoin its fellows."

Dan called this kind of a production a "quaint", and when this "quaint" reached Germany it caused a furore among a select set of men who were dabbling in the study of electro-magnetic currents. Their secretary wrote to Dan demanding further details. In vain he disclaimed the verity of his skit. His denial was treated as an unprofessional attempt to keep his brother scientists in ignorance of the truth concerning natural laws, the effects of which they were convinced had been first observed and recorded by "Herr Dan De Quille, the eminent physicist of Virginiastadt, Nevada."

The greatest circus-man of America sent an offer of "ten

grand" if Dan could make these magnetized stones perform under a canvas tent in the way described in his article.

Dan De Quille had a definite scientific bent, not only in geology and mineralogy, but also in meteorology and astronomy, though the camp was wont to laugh at his weather-wise prognostications, and some humorists once rigged up a telescope with cobwebs so that his startled gaze seemed to view an explosion of the moon.

An engineering journal took up and endorsed as entirely feasible Dan's proposition to have the next thing to perpetual motion in pumping machinery by causing a windmill to hoist loose sand during the hours when the wind blew, in addition to the usual load of water, and to arrange for having this sand operate turbine wheels and thus keep on pumping after the wind had died away. Dan's description of such an apparatus, which he said was invented by Colonel James W. E. Townsend of Mono Lake—"Lying Jim"—was so convincing that an engineer in Boston actually figured out the exact horsepower to be produced by the machinery in question.

Another clever "quaint" of Dan's was the account of the man who invented a helmet to wear when crossing the hot valleys of Nevada. It was fitted up with an ammonia tank inside and the evaporation of the ammonia furnished the cold air to neutralize the effects of the heat. The man started out, and, not being heard of for several days, a relief expedition was sent after him. They found him sitting on a boulder in the desert all covered with icicles and frozen stiff in July. Dan explained that he had loaded up the apparatus with too much ammonia, with the most unhappy results. The London *Times* took note of that "solar armor" story.

When the newspapers of the Coast took Dan to task for his trifling, Dan only laughed and resolved never to do it again, but the next time that items were scarce he was tempted and fell from grace.

These diversions, of course, were only occasional and desultory. In his regular work Dan was a model of method and accuracy. This made his hoaxes all the more dangerous.

The exciting times on the Comstock and its season of riotous prosperity are described by Dan De Quille in his book THE BIG BONANZA. The manuscript for this volume was produced while Dan was on a visit to Mark Twain in his Eastern home, with his friend's active encouragement and perhaps even collaboration in some of the high spots. It ranks with ROUGHING IT as an animated picture of the life in early Virginia City, though characteristically Dan shied from making himself the central figure of the narrative, but instead established himself as an incomparable chronicler of affairs grave and gay which marked the annals of the Comstock.

THE BIG BONANZA, profusely illustrated, was published concurrently in San Francisco and in Mark Twain's home town of Hartford, Connecticut, in 1876, and Mark indited the introduction:

"One easily gets a surface-knowledge of any remote country, through the writings of travellers. The inner life of such a country is not very often presented to the reader. The outside of a strange house is interesting, but the people, the life, and the furniture inside, are far more so. Nevada is peculiarly a surface-known country, for no one has written of that land who had lived long there and made himself competent to furnish an inside view to the public. I think the present volume supplies this defect in an eminently satisfactory way. The writer of it has spent sixteen years in the heart of the silver-mining region, as one of the editors of the principal daily newspaper of Nevada; he is thoroughly acquainted with his subject, and wields a practised pen. He is a gentleman of character and reliability. Certain of us who have known him personally during half a generation are well able to testify in this regard."

At the last moment, Dan De Quille was called on by the publishers for a preface. He complied:

"PREFACE

"I have put all I had to say into the body of this book; but, being informed that a preface is a necessary evil, I have written this one.   THE AUTHOR."

Dan was royally entertained by his friend, at whose well-won affluence he marveled, but without trace of envy, for while he realized that he had allowed Mark to outstrip him, he always rejoiced in the other's good fortune. Still, it was in wistful mood that he commented, "A picture of the little dugout cabin in which Mark and Bob Howland lived in Aurora, Nevada, in 1862, would form a striking contrast to Mark's present fine residence in Hartford. The Hartford dwelling is a structure of many gables and angles, and at the rear or east end projects a veranda, intended to represent the hurricane deck of a Mississippi steamboat. In summer, with the shade of the surrounding chestnut trees cooling the air, this open deck is a pleasant lounging-place. Seated in it, dressed in white linen, Mark imagines himself on board one of the floating palaces of the Father of Waters, while his thoughts often revert to the still earlier days of reportorial work in the mining regions of the wild Washoe."

Dan expressed to me the warmest gratitude to Mark for his kindness and generosity during the time of tribulation, which every author will recognize as the period when he was in the hands of the publishers and proofreaders. This ought to settle for all time the cruel whispers that there was estrangement between these old companions. As a matter of fact, the strongest attachment existed between them, and this was undisturbed to the day of Dan's death. At least that is what Dan often told me, and one of his last letters, written not more than a month before his passing, had a friendly reference to Mark's sense of humor. It told of a day in Hartford when Joaquin Miller was with them, and how together they managed to bring the poet of the Sierras from the summits of his mountains to the consideration of everyday affairs.

Joaquin Miller, in his Western miner's garb, had been a literary sensation in London, and when Mark Twain was there he had introduced the humorist in the circles in which he moved. The two became warm friends. Joaquin told me that it was while he was out walking in New York City some years later that he was accosted by Mark and invited to spend the week-end at his Connecticut home. The poet smiled reflectively in the recountal when he intimated that Mark Twain was under the domination of his wife in more than a literary way. A walk after dinner was suggested and the party arose, but "Mrs. Mark" interposed an objection. Her insistence was so emphatic, with all its politeness of manner, that Mark like a corrected boy resumed his seat, and did not go out. It was a gentle tyranny.

Joseph T. Goodman, for whom both Mark and Dan worked, said to me: "Isn't it so singular that Mark Twain should live and Dan De Quille fade out? If anyone had asked me in 1863 which was to be an immortal name, I should unhesitatingly have said Dan De Quille. They had about equal talent and sense of humor, but the difference was the way in which they used their gifts. One shrank from the world;

the other braved it, and it recognized his audacity. To show how shrinking old Dan was, when I first brought him out of the brush in 1861—as I brought Mark Twain just a year afterward—he couldn't write in our one-room, helter-skelter press, composition and editorial quarters, so I had to hire a cabin for him just back of the office, which he had all to himself, and he did his work there for some months. But he got bravely over that, and in the end could write undisturbed in any confusion."

Though Dan never reaped the full fruit of hopes which he secretly cherished, he was not embittered. Few knew the nobleness of soul, the absolute intrepidity, and the generous nature that dwelt under the modest demeanor that was so natural to Dan De Quille. He was born a Quaker (his immigrant ancestor, Anthony Wright, came over with William Penn), and not even the rude experiences of frontier life could completely change the subdued and quiet manners which he inherited with his father's faith, and the dignity which belongs to the character of a gentleman.

As another wrote of Charles Lamb, so say I of Dan De Quille:

> "Free from self-seeking, envy, low design,
> "I have not found a whiter soul than thine."

Although he was a voluminous contributor to some of the leading magazines of America and England, and was the author of the classic book on the Comstock, yet it is as a newspaper writer that I like best to consider him, for to journalism he devoted his life.

For nearly forty years Dan held his situation on the *Enterprise* at a salary of $60 a week. Finally, when the camp went down and the old paper followed suit, Dan was left without a place, sick and worn out. He wrote to me that he had hoped to end his days on the old Comstock Lode, but that the pains of rheumatism might compel him to bid farewell to those cherished scenes he loved. He did not whimper, but began a series of syndicate letters by which he eked out enough to live on. He sent me a sheaf of his humorous sketches, which were placed with a San Francisco newspaper and the money was forwarded to him, thus affording him temporary relief; but he was no longer physically able to produce enough of these to support him. He hesitated to confess his poverty to anyone on whom he had a natural claim.

If there was any man on the Comstock Lode that De Quille most admired, it was John Mackay, and to "The Boss of the Comstock" he had dedicated his book, THE BIG BONANZA. One day when Dan's sad plight was mentioned to Colonel Billy Wood, who was Mackay's lawyer, he suggested that I send Dan's letter to Mackay, with a note explaining the needs of his old friend, who though bowed with affliction and age, was too proud to apply to him for assistance. In less than a week Dick Dey, friend and onetime confidential secretary of the millionaire, hunted me up and asked me to interpret a telegram which he had received from Mackay in regard to my letter. It told Dey to find Dan De Quille, pay all his debts on the Comstock if he had any such incumbrances, buy him two suits of the best clothing the town afforded and employ a companion to go with him back to the home of his folks amidst the pleasant fields of an Iowa valley. But that wasn't all. It directed that Dan should have a weekly allowance, equal to his former salary on the paper, during the remainder of his life. A year later Dan wrote to me:

"I am living like a fighting-cock, and don't do a thing but swing in a hammock under a shade-tree, surrounded by my children and grandchildren. My hardest work is to nurse my rheumatism while I drink milk punch (which the doctor kindly prescribes) and listen to the singing of the birds. It's all mighty smooth and nice, but I often yearn to be back in old Storey County, where there is some snap and vigor in the air, even in summer. Next winter I'm going to visit the plantation of a Kentucky friend who has promised me a banquet of baked 'possum and sweet potatoes."

But Dan didn't live to enjoy that promised meal. The gentle cornfield breezes, so different from the fierce Washoe zephyrs with which he had been familiar, had lulled him to sleep.

The last time I saw John Mackay in his office in the Nevada Block, San Francisco, he said:

"Yes, Dan is gone. He was a good man and a good friend. I am sorry to lose him."

As he said these words of affection there were tears in the eyes of plain John Mackay, the millionaire.

CHAPTER TWENTY-FIVE

Mark Twain, While "Roughing It"

*M*ark Twain—humorist, philosopher, prophet, sage, genuinely human in every fibre—was a keen observer and faithful chronicler of much that was picturesque in our Western life, that else had gone unrecorded. If ever a writer lived who truthfully can be said to have added to the gaiety of nations, Mark Twain is the man.

It is scarcely necessary to refer to the monumental hoax which first brought him to the attention of an astounded and exasperated public, a ghastly yarn—the story of the faked-up massacre in the giant forest surrounding Dutch Nick's, on the Carson River. All have been assured time and again that as a matter of fact no forest existed within miles of the place, the barren landscape having scarcely enough scrubby sagebrush to serve as a refuge for a jackrabbit.

There's no need here to insert a note that Mark's real name was Samuel Langhorne Clemens. Nobody cares for that, any more than they do for the gratuitous information that Dan De Quille's name actually was William Wright. What difference does it make what they were christened? Mark Twain and Dan De Quille they were called when among the people they loved, and so they will remain.

It was my pleasure to meet Mark Twain, but not in Nevada. He was there a few years before my time.

Mark Twain's life on the Comstock is recounted in his auto-biographical narrative, ROUGHING IT—his second book; INNO-CENTS ABROAD having been the first. As has been recounted, he and Dan De Quille were the reportorial staff of the *Enterprise,* under Joe Goodman. Being sent to Carson City to report the doings of the Legislature, he sent back his correspondence signed "Mark Twain," and that was his first public use of that famous pen-name. Later, when he had gone to San Francisco, he served as correspondent for the *Enterprise* and so hot were his personalities that he embroiled the newspaper in a series of libel suits, but Joe Goodman only smiled and shrugged, "If Sam can stand it, we can."

Already passing reference has been made to Mark Twain's aversion to practical jokes—partly due, no doubt, to the fact that no less a personage than himself was made a mark, the victim of a series of heartless jests in which he was the central figure. Steve Gillis was the perpetrator of several of these diversions.

It is an oft-repeated tale, how Steve and his cronies bought an imitation meerschaum pipe and had it presented to Mark with great ceremony in a gathering at the beer-hall in the opera house. Mark was primed with a response, and he gave his thanks for this token of esteem in words of fervent friendship, rudely disturbed a few days later when he discovered that the pipe was of papier-mâché, its mountings of base metal.

Never did he quite forgive his friends for that cruel thrust, and I think that the holdup on the Divide, with an account of which he concludes ROUGHING IT, somewhat soured him on the old camp and his onetime companions. After his sojourn in San Francisco and the Hawaiian Islands, he returned to the Comstock to lecture. His first talk was at Virginia, his second at Gold Hill. Following this latter, Mark was held up by robbers on the Divide and deprived of receipts from his lecture and of his highly-prized gold watch. In Virginia City, his old acquaintances commiserated with him, and drank deep with him at the bar. Finally someone contrived to get him back his watch, and Mark knew there must be some connivance between the robbers and his erstwhile friends. When he learned that the drinks which he and the crowd had imbibed were paid for from his own lecture-receipts, Mark's chagrin can be imagined. He had somewhat of a reputation on the Comstock of being a solitary drinker, which, if it were so, was a grievous fault, in that open-handed community.

Despite all this, Mark Twain always kept a warm spot in his heart for little Steve Gillis of the *Enterprise*. No wonder. Everybody loved Steve. The light of his countenance was like sunshine. He was happy, witty and companionable. He could laugh at the jokes of others as well as at his own. He was as full of cheerful fun and jollity as a schoolboy home for vacation. In his more serious moods he could play poker all night, always strictly observing the rules and ethics of the game, and, win or lose, pouring out a constant flood of banter, talking like a streak all the time, without repeating or getting tiresome. No matter how crowded a poker game happened to be, if Steve wanted a hand, there was always room for him. What more could be said? Steve was slow to take offense, but if he was angered he was fearless. He never looked for trouble, but he never dodged it. He had the instincts and breeding of a gentleman. He was an adept with the pistol and the foils, but was not averse to the use of his fists when necessity called. He hated a hoodlum as a cavalry mule hates an Apache, and resented the bumptious insolence of the young roughnecks who, with their slanted stiff-brimmed hats, in the '60s and the early '70s, infested the byways of San Francisco, insulting the unprotected and terrorizing non-combatants. This sense of chivalry on Steve's part, unusual as it was admirable, was the cause of most of his encounters. It was his ill luck to be over-matched in a majority of cases, but when he thought he was in the right he didn't stop to consider consequences.

You couldn't help admiring Steve's loyalty. It was of the old-fashioned Western variety, and few examples are to be found in these later days. If Steve was your friend you couldn't lose him. You always knew where to find him. If he gave you his word, you didn't have to page him the next morning, or the next week, or the next year. He was always there. You could stake your life on his fidelity, no matter what the hazard. Right or wrong he would stand by a friend to the last, and the greater the odds the better he'd fight. A diamond in the rough, some might assay him, yet nobody doubted that he was a man clear through; a trifle impetuous, possibly, but Steve's generous and forgiving nature was attested by the fact that he never held a grudge against a man after licking him. If he had faults, let others record them; his friends never noticed them, or at least never mentioned them in his presence. Even admitting that he was not entirely free from flaws, the world would be better off if we had more men like Steve Gillis—printer, editor, fighter. He has gone to his reward, and this modest chaplet is laid on his grave by one who loved him.

The cement of genuine friendship held Mark Twain and Steve Gillis. They were closer than brothers. They bunked together in the mines, sharing with each other all that they possessed in good times and hard times—in bonanza and borrasca. They worked side by side on the *Territorial Enterprise.*

They had been chums on the Comstock Lode, and *that* is a tie which cannot be broken.

They were chums in San Francisco, when the two had left the Comstock for a time. But notwithstanding all this Damon-and-Pythias stuff, Mark, being only human, finally grew weary of having to appear at police headquarters at all times of the day or night to go bail for Steve. It was enough to test the patience of a man even less irascible than Mark. One redeeming feature was that Steve was always turned loose without trial and his bondsman exonerated, because no hoodlum ever appeared to press the prosecution.

One night in San Francisco, as Steve was sauntering along the Embarcadero enjoying the reflection of the moonlight on the waters of the bay, and not thinking of adventure, he caught sight of a hulk of a fellow kicking a crippled tamale peddler from a saloon, and like an enraged panther Steve sprang to the defense of the weakling. The 200-pounder thrust out a huge paw, and clutching Steve by the collar lifted him and shook him till his heels rattled together like castanets. It was like a mastiff shaking a terrier. But Steve slipped out of his coat sleeves as if they had been greased, and putting a lot of dynamite behind his 140 pounds, with a few savage punches knocked the fellow insensible. As he closed his eyes a look of painful surprise overcame the pallor of the giant's face that a moment before was livid with rage. But, at that, it was a merciful blow that put him out. He never knew what hit him.

Steve was arrested on the spot.

Mark was summoned and went his bail in the usual mechanical way. It was becoming a habit.

"This business may get to be serious if we don't look out," complained Mark as he rescued Steve from the police station.

"We'll cross that bridge of sorrow when we come to it," was Steve's light-hearted response.

An hour later a hasty bulletin was sent from the emergency hospital. The man was thought to be dying from the effects of a blow, and his assailant must be re-arrested and held for manslaughter—possibly murder. It was a false alarm, but it threw a terrible scare into the boys, just the same.

Mark was the first to get wind of the ominous turn of affairs. He hunted up Steve who, with a cluster of cronies, was celebrating his victory in a bowling alley.

"Steve, you'd better vamoose," cried Mark, breaking into the merry party.

At daylight Steve lit out for Virginia City, his old stamping-ground. As he was starting he called back:

"Sam, if they try to stir up trouble for you, don't wait; but make tracks for the cabin of my brother, Jim Gillis, at Jackass Hill, up in Tuolumne County. He'll treat you white."

Mark was soon warned that the police, whom, by the way, he had attacked in his article, were looking for him. They wished to interview him about that bail bond. Besides, there was a dark hint that Mark would be accused of having taken part in the fight.

That instant Mark heeded Steve's admonition and began his flight to Jackass Hill. By anxious stages, walking at night and lying low in the daytime, he finally completed the journey. Jim Gillis was a prosperous "pocket-miner" on the Mother Lode, a region which still yields, to the industrious and the knowing, "pockets" of placer gold. Jim was a gentleman of the old school, a prince of good fellows, charming in personality and manner, and known as the boss story-teller in all the region of the Southern Mines. He received Mark with open arms and made him welcome to the best in the land.

If ever hospitality dwelt in the hearts of men it was and is manifested most generously among the mountaineer miners of California and Nevada.

Jim not only entertained Mark for several months, but told him all his best stories. He took Mark to Angels Camp and on his native heath had Ross Coon, one of the characters of the camp, give him the story of the JUMPING FROG OF CALAVERAS, besides myriads of other yarns, which later proved rich material for Mark's writings. You may read of that sojourn on the Mother Lode in ROUGHING IT.

Mark got permission to publish the Jumping Frog story as his own in consideration of the fact that his feelings were badly hurt by an occurrence in the Gillis mansion, and the tale of the saltatory amphibian was accepted as settlement in full for the shock sustained by his sensitive nature.

Gillis had been a lucky pocket-miner for years, and as his cabin was always stocked with plenty to eat, it was a popular place, its fame extending for miles around. Much of Gillis' success as a pocket-miner was due to the assistance rendered him by a pet hog named John Henry that had grown up with him from earliest pighood.

Some readers nowadays are not likely to know how pocket-mining is carried on, and for that reason perhaps may not be able to understand how Jim's pig could help him.

Pocket-mining is, in fact, just what the name implies—looking for pockets containing gold. These pockets are crevices in the rock, sometimes small and sometimes large, and it is the business of the pocket-miner to find them. To do this he adopts a plan at once simple and effective. It is known as the fanning process.

With his poll-pick, his gold-pan, his water can and his hornspoon, the latter being the most important, the miner begins work on the side of a hill which he thinks gives promise of gold deposits, and horns out the gravel here and there, changing his position from time to time until he finds what he considers a good "prospect"—a mere "color" not being sufficient for more extended operations.

The prospect being verified by repeated hornings, then begins the making of the fan. Here is a rude diagram which will explain the process:

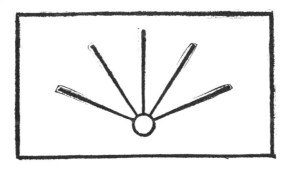

Starting from the initial point, where he struck the prospect, the miner diverges up hill, taking samples and making spoonings of the gravel in his progress. His theory is that the gold found at the spot where he started had been washed down from some place above, and that if he can only find that particular place he will be rewarded by a handful of gold. The fact that this theory proves true in so many cases shows why pocket-mining is so fascinating, and why when a man once gets into it he seldom cares to quit the excitement of such a life for any of the humdrum occupations of ordinary humanity.

The miner who obtains a good prospect and then carefully and conscientiously works out his "fan", seldom fails to get some kind of a prize. Sometimes it is large, but the thoroughbred pocket-miner never complains if it is small. He takes it thankfully as a gift from the gods, and hopes for more propitious fortune next time.

If while making the fan another prospect is struck, the place is marked, and after the original fan is worked out the place marked is made the point of divergence for renewed operations. In this manner the pocket-miner keeps his ground constantly under his eye, and any day can go out with his horn, knowing almost to a certainty that he will be able to make expenses, if not a little more. Many good gold ledges have been found in this way.

This mining lore I got from Steve Gillis. Steve and I tried it together on the northeastern slope of old Mount Davidson, near Cedar Ravine, which marks the north end of the Comstock Lode. We fanned a prospect right up to the dooryard of Dave Rowe, a miner who lived on the upper croppings of the Ophir, and then we abandoned it. Rowe afterward struck the gold by accident in his back yard, and soon cut into as pretty a ledge of gold rock as one would wish to see. He was getting rich fast and would have been all right if he had known enough to keep his good fortune to himself, but he began to put on style and make dark hints about having something better than John Mackay or Monte Cristo. This made the Ophir managers curious, and they soon pounced upon his sugarplum and gobbled it completely. Not only that, but they brought suit against Rowe for the several thousand dollars he had already taken out. They got judgment, but he defeated the execution. He had spent the money.

All this is a digression. The way in which Jim Gillis' pet hog, John Henry, helped him in his business was by rooting up the ground on the hillsides, thus giving the rain a chance to wash out the gold and carry it to the crevices.

Jim spent a month training his pig. The way he got the

pig interested in pocket-mining was decidedly clever. He took a lot of his big home-made biscuits, of which John Henry, Mark Twain and all the other visitors to the cabin were extremely fond, and buried them in the side of a hill. Then with his poll-pick he began to scratch up the gravel and toled the pig up to the biscuits one after another. After that whenever John Henry saw Jim start out with his pick he thought he was sure of a biscuit feast, and with squeals of pleasurable anticipation he would make for the hillside, where he would tear up the ground like a Panama Canal dredger.

John Henry had a companion, a bull-dog named Towser, that grew up with him. Towser was more ornamental than useful, but this did not lower him in John Henry's esteem.

The only time they disagreed was at night, and then they quarreled about the possession of the empty bunk which was located directly under Jim Gillis' bed. They had been "raised pets" and always slept in the house. You see, Jim's house had bunks in it, one above another, like almost all early California cabins. Jim's two partners, Tom Kelty and Sam Dinsmore, occupied bunks on the other side of the cabin.

Jim would wait until bedtime before he let the hog and dog in, and would enjoy the circus of watching them by the light from the big fireplace as they would struggle for possession of the bunk. The contest would usually end by both getting tired out, and finally they would settle down and sleep fondly locked in each other's embrace.

Jim said that lots of times it made the tears come to his eyes to watch how tenderly they regarded each other after the scrimmage for priority of right was over.

After starving around the San Francisco newspaper offices for a long time, when Mark Twain paid a visit to Jim's country home he knew he would be welcome, for his fund of anecdotes always assured him a reception wherever he went.

Along in the evening Mark began to think about his lodgings, and seeing that three of the four bunks were filled with the bedding of Jim and his partners he drawled out:

"Where are you a-goin' to stow me away tonight? You don't seem to have any extra beds."

Jim winked at his companions and said:

"I guess we'll make some kind of a shakedown for you in the bottom bunk under my bed, and tomorrow I'll go over to town and get a mattress for you."

That suited Mark well enough, and it was soon arranged that way. The supper of beans, bacon, flapjacks and molasses was soon over, and after the usual games of seven-up all went to bed.

Mark's couch was the hardest of all, but he was soon asleep. The others were awake, waiting to see something happen. The night was cold; the wind whistled shrilly along the foothills, coming from the snow-line above. John Henry and Towser were outside clamoring for admission. They felt that the winter of their discontent had arrived and they had been forgotten.

Jim could reach the latch-string from where he lay. Putting out his hand he pulled it and the door flew open.

Towser and John Henry rushed for the bunk. They did not sense that it was already occupied. On top of the sleeping Mark they clambered, the dog first and the hog close following. Then began such a battle royal as was never before seen in the Gillis cabin.

First it was John Henry on top and then it was Towser.

Mark was entangled among the bed-clothing and could not get up. He could only yell and swear. He was thoroughly terrorized by the suddenness of the onslaught, coming as it did to startle him from his peaceful dreams of piloting on the Mississippi.

The men in the other bunks roared with laughter and held their sides to keep them from splitting.

"Go it, Towser!"

"Give it to 'im, John Henry!"

"Hold 'em level, Mark!" they roared.

Jim in his eagerness to see what was going on under him narrowly escaped falling down into the struggling mass of hog, dog and Twain.

When the topmost contestants were exhausted Mark managed to escape. He was not much hurt, but was pretty well scared and unutterably disgusted. He swore vengeance on Towser, John Henry, Jim Gillis, and everybody else he could think of. He damned the golden earth by sections and quarter-sections, up-hill and down-hill, crosswise and lengthwise, but the more he sputtered and swore the more the others laughed.

At last Jim took compassion on Mark and took him in the upper bunk. It was a little narrow, but it was a great deal better than running the risk of another visit from the pets.

Next morning Mark packed up his collar-box and was about to leave, but Jim persuaded him to stay, and by giving him a clear title to the story of "The Jumping Frog of Calaveras," assuaged his anger. That tale was the beginning of Mark's fortune. John Henry did the business.

They all agreed not to say a word about the matter, and it was years later that Steve Gillis told me the story.

CHAPTER TWENTY-SIX

Downgrade

*B*ut to come back to the Comstock—
which Mark Twain never did, after
that hold-up on the Divide.

Despite fire, stock panic and bank crash of '75, the Comstock came back. In that year the bullion produced on the Lode amounted to almost $26,000,000; next year it rose to $32,000,000, and in 1877 it was more than $36,000,000—the maximum production. In that year the sales upon the stock exchange of San Francisco, virtually all Comstock securities, totaled about $120,000,000.

The disastrous conflagration of 1875, which wiped out $12,-000,000 in property, including most of the hoisting-works at the mines, had resulted in a severe stock depression; but the big break in the mining-stock market came in January, 1877, when the Con. Virginia passed its regular monthly dividend. The market crash was a terrific disaster for the West. The Comstock itself and San Francisco were hardest hit, thousands being beggared almost over night. The bitterness of the losers rankles after half a century.

It was later in 1877, after the Con. Virginia had resumed dividends, that the Sutro Tunnel, to which reference has been made, entered the Comstock mineral belt. This four-mile tunnel, or adit, to carry ore and drain water from the mines and to improve their ventilation, was conceived by Adolph

Sutro, and by him carried through to completion in the face of bitter antagonism and many engineering difficulties. Sutro was a Jew from the Rhineland, and the story of his achievement is a record of persistence and tenacity seldom matched, even by that race.

At first the mine-owners gave him encouragement, but their aid was suddenly withdrawn, and he was obliged to gain financial support in Europe, as well as among the Comstock miners. He charged that the Bank of California, because it feared the creation of a formidable rival, opposed him and his work; but he carried his fight to Washington and won victory in Congress.

The last finite obstruction in the Sutro Tunnel was blasted away on July 8th, 1878—and Adolph Sutro was the first man to crawl through into the Savage mine! The contending parties finally compromised their differences, and the tunnel served to drain the mines, where unusually heavy flows of water had been struck, though it was not used as an easier exit for ore, as its originator had planned. Throughout the contest, Sutro never accepted defeat, and was undismayed by the opposition of the most powerful interests. He was hailed as "king of the indomitables."

About this time, high hopes were entertained for the Sierra Nevada mine, north of Virginia City. Johnnie Skae was President and "Joggles" Wright was Superintendent. He sank a 1200-foot incline, all in ore, and drove a short cross-cut in ore; and people were saying and some were believing that a bigger bonanza than the Con. Virginia-California treasure was to be revealed. Alas, it was only a narrow "pipe" of ore that had been followed downward, and the bubble burst. Thousands were made poor by that debacle at the end of 1878, which was attended by riotous scenes amongst stockholders in

Virginia City. The Sierra Nevada works were shut down a year or so afterward, and genial Johnnie Skae migrated to Utah.

In 1878 deep mining on the Comstock began in earnest, but in the next year the swift decline commenced. With terrific rapidity, the output fell off. The columns of assessments in the newspapers became longer and longer.

As the mines declined, there was more temptation for "salting" activities, though there had been all too many of these nefarious practices on the Comstock even in the boom days. The greatest excitement was caused by the salting of the Lady Bryan mine, down in Six-Mile Canyon, early in 1880. Scandal touched the Lady's reputation.

Captain John Kelly was superintendent of the Lady Bryan, and came in for fierce censure, although finally most people judged him to be without blame. Kelly was a fine-looking man, tall, stout, impressive in person and manner, and renowned as a practical joker.

The truth may have been that some of the miners held quantities of the Lady Bryan stock at low figures, and were playing for the rise. Anyway, somebody salted the drill-hole being sent ahead to prospect for an ore-body. When Captain Kelly learned of the apparent richness of the ore being tapped, he thought he had a bigger bonanza. The news leaked out, and in the flurry on the market, the scheming parties unloaded their stock at high prices. But when the drift was completed to the end of that drill-hole, no pay ore was found!

So crestfallen was Kelly that he felt it incumbent on himself to clear the atmosphere of accusation and insinuation. He called the miners together and had them questioned in a public hearing; but all denied complicity. Not content with this, Kelly had each one in turn advance to the table where a massive Douay Bible lay, place his hand upon the good book and solemnly swear that he had no part in the deal.

There is a story that when Captain John reached for the Bible to swear on his own behalf, the cover came off at his grasp, and it was seen that the pages of the Bible had been taken out and had been replaced with a bulky patent office report. Those who told this story agreed that if miners would salt the Holy Bible, they were capable of any degree of guilt in the salting line.

Kelly insisted that the culprit must be one of the six men who were working on the drill-hole, though which one of them it was he never ascertained. The Comstock journals, which were full of half-savage, half-humorous allusions to the swindle, shouted, "Let no guilty sixth man escape!"

Denis McCarthy, owner and editor of the *Chronicle*, was a chum of Kelly, and sympathized with him in his trouble. At that time I was the city editor of the *Chronicle* and wrote all the mining news of the paper.

While the talk of the salting was still raging, an advertisement reading something like this appeared under the heading "New Today":

SALT MINE FOR SALE

The undersigned offers for sale a fine salt mine. It yields rock salt, mining salt, smelling salts, and so on. Specially recommended for salting mines and mills. Situated in Six-Mile Canyon, the output can be shipped to mines and mills lower down the canyon at minimum expense. This is the best opportunity in Nevada to buy and own your own salt mine. For full particulars address,

CAPTAIN JOHN KELLY,
Superintendent, Lady Bryan Mine.

There was blood on the moon that evening as soon as the

Chronicle appeared on C street. With a growl like a grizzly bear, Kelly rushed to the *Chronicle* office, and Denis McCarthy, who was innocent of the transaction, was so surprised he couldn't even swear. The offending notice was "yanked" before the main edition was run off.

The copy had gone in through my department, and naturally I was suspected—but it was never proved.

Bold, bad Bodie attracted many adventurers from the languishing Comstock, in 1879 and 1880, and I went there myself for a brief spell, on the staff of the *Bodie Miner,* one of the four fiercely competing newspapers in the camp. This town in the barren mountains north of Mono Lake is in California, just a few miles from the Nevada line. Geographically, it pertains more to the Sagebrush State.

When I lived there, at the peak of the mining excitement, there were almost 20,000 people in the camp, which altogether produced more than $50,000,000 in gold. A hectic career that boom-town had, and I am here to state that the bad-men of Bodie were no mythical personages. John Hays Hammond recalls that six men were killed in shooting-scrapes the week he arrived in Bodie in 1879.

"I was in Bodie," spoken in a reminiscent tone, was a bond of fellowship amongst men of the West who had sojourned in that restless camp, perhaps the wildest of all.

Though Bodie was then booming, other camps in the mountains round-about were on the skids. When I visited it, Aurora (which lies about ten miles down-canyon from Bodie) was a big town with whole rows of deserted brick houses. The Aurora mines were not yielding any bullion, though great things were promised for some new locations, whose wealth did not pan out. Best-known of the Aurora mines was the Real del Monte, and the Cortez, Coffee Mill, Antelope and a few others were worked tentatively. Of boom days in the Aurora region, read in Mark Twain's ROUGHING IT.

For a long time there had been uncertainty whether Aurora was in California or Nevada, which led to much friction, but in 1863 a survey showed it to be 4 miles east of the boundary.

A Comstock undertaker in 1880 was heard to complain of his hard luck. "The toughs hang around these diggings long enough to think that they are fighters," he moaned, "and the first break they make after leaving they get plugged, while Bodie undertakers get paid for planting them."

It was in that same year, when the Comstock camps were on the down grade, that two undertakers of Virginia City staged a street fight in a quarrel over the possession of a corpse, until bystanders interfered and separated the combatants. So had the mighty fallen!

This sense of departing glory was heightened by the gradual disappearance of select drinking-places, as the community declined.

Alf Doten was just placing the neck of the ginger-ale bottle across his thumb, as was his custom when called on to do his own pouring, when all at once his attention was attracted by a sign behind Charlie Price's bar. The sign read: "At Midnight All Drinks in this Saloon Reduced to Ten Cents."

It was a terrible blow to the pride of Gold Hill, for up to that time the camp was able to boast the possession of one two-bit saloon.

"Thus passeth the glory of the world," exclaimed Alf.

"It doesn't seem to me that I can endure this humiliation," the veteran editor said, addressing a faithful companion who was always willing to stand by in such trying times.

The clock showed the hour to be 11:55. In a few minutes

the brag of Gold Hill that it was able to support at least one first-class drinking place would be wiped out.

"I want to have the honor of buying the last two-bit drink in the old town," said Alf. He was asking a favor, but in this instance his companion was obdurate. "Let's shake dice to see who shall have the privilege," was the best he would grant.

So they rattled the bones and Alf won, but I never saw any winner more sorrowful.

The clock made that premonitory w-h-r-r-ing sound to indicate that the fateful hour was about to be struck.

"Here's to the departure of Gold Hill's glory and pride," was the toast they proposed, and they drank in silence.

"Not much use trying to run a nonpareil paper in a long-primer town any longer," said Doten. "I was willing to stick it out as long as there was a living chance, but now that there is nothing but ten-cent shebangs, the old *News* might as well suspend."

And it did.

CHAPTER TWENTY-SEVEN

Candelaria

*T*o the east of the Mono Lake district lies a rough, mountainous area then embraced within the Esmeralda country. Already I have mentioned that I resided in this scenic region for a few happy autumn months in 1880, when I went up to aid John Dormer on his enterprising sheet, the *True Fissure,* in the hopeful camp of Candelaria, while he went off prospecting. This part of the Esmeralda country was officially called the Columbus mining-district. Its principal camps were Candelaria,[1] Belleville and Columbus. It was organized by Mexicans in 1864, the preliminary meeting being held a hundred miles distant by men who recently had been in the district but who had vamoosed when the Indians went on the warpath. For that reason a special regulation was passed by the organizers of the district allowing the Recorder to live outside its boundaries until it was sufficiently populated to make it safe to remove there.

In the laws adopted by the miners it was decreed that the owners of claims should have the free use of all streams crossing their property, and also of all timber growing on their claims. These points go to show that the men who discovered these mines did not have much time to examine the country at their first visit, or else there has been a great change since that time. When I was there, the only timber to be seen was

---

[1] Candelaria is now in Mineral County, Nevada, not in Esmeralda County.

the dwarfed greasewood, which grows on ground that is too poor to sustain the more aristocratic sagebrush. As for water, there was none to be found in the district—except what was hauled there in barrels and tanks.

In Candelaria, the Mexicans at first held a virtual monopoly. By degrees, however, a few Americans, Slavonians and Germans managed to get their names on the notices of location, and the control of the district finally passed from the hands of the original claimants, together with the ownership of the property. The intrusive Anglo-Saxon even went so far as to rob the claims of their sonorous names, substituting his own ruder nomenclature. Such Nevada mine-names as Bully Boy, Big Bilk, Hoodoo, Accidental, Home Ticket, Buckeye and Bullwhacker scarcely compare favorably with the names of the Mexican claims around Candelaria—Guadalupe, Zaragosa, Sanco Pansa, Sacramento, Encarnacion, Refugio, San Lorenzo, Victoria, Pueblo, Sinaloa, Severiano, San Pedro, Juana Ordones, and the like. Bartosenagachi was a little harsher. The Esmeralda was one of the claims located; and the Candelaria mining-claim, from which the town no doubt received its name, was located on May 22nd, 1865, by S. Aruna, Jose Rodriguez, Antonio Rojer, Ventura Veltran and Francisco Pardo. It comprised 1200 feet with all the usual dips, spurs and angles, and in the original location is spelled *Candelarea*. It should be noted that this is the name of one of the holidays of the Catholic Church, which doubtless accounts for its having been applied.

Candelaria, the leading mining camp of the Esmeralda region during my generation, produced about $55,000,000 in bullion. The Northern Belle, the principal mine, had a better record than most mines in Nevada. To the end of 1880 it had paid 47 dividends and had never levied an assessment. Next in importance were the Mount Diablo mine, which however had not paid dividends; the Victor mine, long idle on account of litigation; the Mount Potosi, Enterprise and hundreds of other "locations."

A likely camp, Candelaria still had its drawbacks. Water was scarce, being then transported by wagon eight miles from Columbus and costing about five cents a gallon. Baths were a luxury not excessively indulged in, nor was water as a beverage popular. It is a libel, though, to say that a Candelaria barkeeper threw a chunk of glass into the tumbler in place of ice. Another malicious report was that conditions were so primitive that, the camp lacking a dentist, sufferers resorted to blasting for tooth-extraction. Rugged mountaineers they were, though, for with hardihood they fought off ants, horse-flies, rattlesnakes and tarantulas—"them hairy cusses," as the miners termed them.

Some of the canards anent Candelaria were spread by its rival and neighbor, Bodie—it was only eighty miles away by stage. Candelarians derisively referred to Bodie as Bad-Shot Gulch, and this slur on its marksmanship was resented by the wild-and-woolly camp of the Sierras. The number of shooting-affrays in Candelaria and its mill-towns of Belleville and Columbus was appalling.

One of the killings was the shooting of County Commissioner P. S. Traver by Mike Owens early in 1880. Owens was captured by Deputy Sheriff Alex McLean, but his friends interfered and took him away from McLean. He was recaptured, but was acquitted on the first ballot. Dobe Willoughby, implicated in the same slaying, was finally freed by the district attorney because of insufficient evidence after ten months in the Aurora jail.

Doc Callison killed Joe Turner in McKissick's Saloon, and

was acquitted, as so many were, on grounds of self-defence. Said he, " I could not have done otherwise." In many of the newspaper accounts of such frays you would read, "both citizens of prominence." Whisky was the cause of most of the fighting, but not when Bart Greeley mortally wounded Tom Logan in Candelaria in December, 1880. Tom was one of the most popular saloon-keepers in the place, but John Dormer wrote, "Neither man used liquor in any form. Logan was a quiet, peaceable gentleman, with a disposition as gentle as a woman's. Greeley was not given to quarreling." Still, they quarreled—as the aftermath of a card-game in which Greeley lost. Logan died saying he "blamed no one," and all flags were at half-mast.

"Dog-fights are very numerous for a town of this size," commented the editor of the *True Fissure* on a dull day, apparently with pride. John Condron's dog "Boss" ruled the canine desperadoes in Candelaria and Pickhandle Gulch, much as one Blue Dick swaggered amongst the *hombres*.

Pickhandle Gulch, otherwise known as Metallic City, was a mile distant from Candelaria, in the canyon between the Mount Diablo mine and the Metallic and Equator shafts. The gulch echoed with the sound of revelry by night—*all* night.

There were quite a number of other active settlements in that same general region of Nevada, and some of them have endured till this day.

Yerington was known in the '70s as Pizen Switch, until a Committee of Vengeance was organized by its citizenry to murder and scalp anyone who called it such. Stinking Wells was another station, on the Carson & Colorado narrow-gauge.

Hawthorne, overlooking Walker Lake, became the principal town of the Esmeralda region. It never had more than a few hundred people, but its ambitious projectors laid it out "on the plan of the city of Sacramento," and divided it into 90 blocks. Whisky Flat lies south of Hawthorne, and a road leads thence through Marietta, on Teel's Marsh, to Belleville.

This mill-town, which rejoiced in its reputation of "one of the best sporting camps in Nevada," was almost as tough a place as Candelaria, 7 miles above, and J. S. Longabaugh, courageous peace-officer, had his hands full. Feuds were responsible for many of the killings. Tom McLaughlin, an old Comstocker, was there shot from his horse, from ambush, in 1880. He had killed two men and wounded another in a street-duel in Marietta, and this revenge shooting was attributed to the aggrieved Brophy gang. As to McLaughlin, the public prints recorded that "he was pleasant and genial in disposition, and the very embodiment of a gentleman when not in liquor."

My gambler friend Ramon Montenegro had come over to Belleville from the Comstock as proprietor of "The Club House," where parties could at all hours "hold special or stated seances with the goddess of Fortune," as Ramon phrased it in his florid manner. Quite a leader in the community, he even had a couple of short-lived newspapers, one of them named the *Self-Cocker* and the other the *Tarantula,* he told me. But a long-standing feud with Judge A. G. Turner flared up. The two men met on the street and turned loose with their pistols, shooting as fast as they could. In the fusillade Ramon Montenegro was hit twice and fell. Turner was taken to Candelaria for trial, but no complaint was entered and he was released.

Over to the east of Candelaria is the Tonopah country, but it was not till the first year of the present century that Jim Butler's straying burros led to the Tonopah strike near the summit of the San Antonio Mountains. Two years later came the Goldfield discovery, to the south, and soon thereafter the Bullfrog and Manhattan developments—wonderful new treasure-finds that revived the excitement of the old days.

Just southeast of Candelaria on the other side of the ridge lies Columbus, which in the '80s besides a quartz mill had extensive borax works. It was there that Borax Smith (Frank M., of Oakland) got his real start, in association with his brother, B. G. Smith, who was a leading merchant of the district, with general stores in Candelaria and Marietta. The brothers Smith, whom I knew well, first worked the borax deposits of Columbus Marsh and Fish Lake valley, but later devoted their attention to Teel's Marsh and still later F. M. Smith gained fame with his 20-mule teams in Death Valley. Lucky Baldwin also was often in Candelaria, looking into mining-properties. About that time he bought Yank's place at Tallac, on Lake Tahoe.

Fish Lake, "a fashionable watering-place for the elite of Candelaria, Belleville and Columbus," as Judge Richard Becker waggishly described it, is only a little sheet of water, fed by warm springs. The Judge, deep in Indian folk-lore, told me a tale as to why the tribesmen shunned its shores.

The legends of the Indians preserve the fact that in ages past this lake was the favorite resort of their ancestors. When the first white settler visited the lake its margin was dotted here and there by the picturesque wickiups of the natives, and in the evening the water was almost alive with these dusky children of the valley, enjoying aquatic sports.

It is different now. The red man no longer frequents the neighborhood. The lake and all its surroundings have been turned over to the paleface without a protest. The *campoodie* has disappeared from its banks, and its waters are no more disturbed by aboriginal bathing parties. A great fear has fallen upon this people, because of an accident which brought grief to their hearts.

At the end of the hunting season in 1873, a brave named Nak-Tah-Kotch sought the lake to enjoy with his family the peaceful rest which all his tribe were accustomed to take at that time of the year. The sun was still about an hour high, so runs the story, when the little party arrived at the lake. Nak-Tah-Kotch's younger squaw released from her back the wicker basket in which all that long, hot day she had carried her papoose, and depositing it in a comfortable position against a sagebrush near the water's edge, busied herself in preparing for her lord his frugal meal of dried venison, pine nuts and *out-chu,* the latter article being a species of wild potato. While thus engaged she was startled by an infantile cry, and turning, saw her child in the water.

The little wicker-basket, moved by a passing breeze, had rolled down the bank into the lake. With a mother's instinct she sprang to the rescue, but in the frenzy of her maternal feeling became powerless, and sank almost instantly. Nak-Tah-Kotch plunged in to assist her, but with the desperation of a drowning person she clasped him around the neck, drawing him with her as she went down the third time. He was unable to release himself from her death-hold, and they both perished.

In the meantime, the basket, being of light materials and impervious to water, had floated to the middle of the lake with its human freight. The superstitious natives were all afraid to venture near the water, being convinced by the fearful catastrophe before them that the Great Spirit was angry with them for some sin that had been committed by them or their ancestors. It would have been sacrilege for them to have attempted to rescue the child.

Night came, and watches were set around the lake, all hoping to reclaim the little waif, but none daring to enter the water. Finally, the moon came up and the little wicker basket was discovered where it had drifted down among the tules which grew at the lower end of the lake. When reached, the babe was found to be asleep, blissfully ignorant of danger, while rocked by the gentle motion of the waves and soothed by their musical murmur as they broke among the sedges.

That child lived, a brown-cheeked maiden. Her name was Tah-Peta Yool-Kalla, which being interpreted means "Saved-by-the-Moon." Tah-Peta was greatly loved by the members of her tribe.

Each autumn Tah-Peta visited the lake and strewed wild-flowers and branches of the wild artemisia upon the pyramid of boulders reared by her tribe to mark the spot where her father and mother last imprinted their footsteps before plunging into the lake. Having performed this filial duty she went back to her people in the mountains.

After the day of that double tragedy no Indian so much as put his hand or foot into the waters of Fish Lake. As the bodies were never recovered, the Indians think they were conveyed to the nether world by some evil demon. They believe the saving of the infant was the result of a direct interposition of the Good Spirit, and would have made a goddess of the girl if she so desired. She, however, had no such wish, but was content with no greater fame than that she was the fairest daughter of her tribe.

Southeast of Fish Lake lie Red Mountain and Silver Peak, and Lida Valley is still farther south. The adobe town of

Silver Peak, where there was a big mill, was like a Mexican village.

Montezuma was a smelting camp of some importance. Other little places in the Esmeralda country, many of them abandoned now, were Dead Horse Well, Elbow, Gillis Mountain, Hog's Back, Military Station, Baldy, Blind Springs.

CHAPTER TWENTY-EIGHT

Blue Dick's Funeral

*O*ne of the fearless gun-fighters on the Comstock was Blue Dick—few knew him by any other name. Working as a miner, a premature blast had peppered his face with gunpowder, endowing him with a remarkable blue complexion. He had almost a piratical aspect, this formidable desperado, but he was "on the shoot" only when aroused.

When the rush began to the Esmeralda country, Blue Dick drifted over to Candelaria and soon became established as the premier bad-man of the camp—not the camp bully, for that title was reserved for a black-browed buccaneer known as Shagnasty Joe, hanger-on at the Northern Belle mine and the Roaring Gimlet saloon on Main Street. Joe was jealous of Blue Dick's eminence, and growled out disparagement covertly behind his hand, though never daring openly to challenge his over-lordship. Maybe Dick learned of these and other slurring remarks, but he seemed to take no notice.

Then, the camp was startled out of its boots one morning to hear that Blue Dick was dead—shot dead, of course, and by an unknown hand. Rumor said that he was down in McKissick's Saloon, on the south side of the Plaza, and the crowd hurried thither.

"Yes," said the barkeeper, brushing away a stray tear, "there he lies over there, and he'll never pull trigger again."

Over in the corner of the bar-room, Blue Dick reposed in state. Apparently he had "died with his boots on," for these sizeable brogans protruded from beneath the long, white sheet which covered his face. His broad-brimmed Stetson lay beside him on the green baize of the table.

"A good sort was Dick," mourned Grab Brown (G. R. A. Brown), one of the leading sportsmen of the place, "a sure-enough credit to the camp."

"He sure was," chorused the others, as they crowded up to the bar. "We ought to give him a right send-off—a reg'lar funeral."

"Jus' what I was a-sayin', boys," said the barkeeper, "and this house has put up a stake of $20 to start the collection to see Blue Dick's buried proper."

A murmur of approval went up.

"Step right this way, then, gents," said the barkeeper, "and throw your contributions into Dick's hat here on the table."

The boys crowded around, raining gold and silver (it was all hard money then in the West) into the sombrero. When a treasure hoard had been piled to mountain height, Grab Brown hesitatingly asked the proprietor if they might gaze once more upon the face of him who had been at once the pride and the fear of Candelaria.

Gently, the barkeeper drew back the sheet and they looked upon that sinister but yet handsome face. There were the blue marks along the forehead which had given the hero his name; there, the grim mouth, set in a half-smile; there, the steel-gray eyes that had been afraid of nothing in this world, gazing sightlessly now at the ceiling.

But suddenly Grab Brown gave a start. He fancied he had seen a quiver of the eyelid.

Sure enough—and the crowd drew back in amaze. The right eye of Blue Dick was seen solemnly to wink. A great shout went up as Dick rose to a sitting posture on the billiard table—a shout which developed to a cheer as he descended and swaggered over to the bar as alive and alert as ever was frontiersman—all whalebone and cat-gut, as the saying was.

The barkeeper toted the sombrero with its heavy treasure-trove, and heaved it onto the end of the bar. "What'll we do with all this bullion?" he ventured to ask.

"Set 'em up!" rose the universal chorus, and with the pious fund which they had so generously donated, the boys proceeded to drink to the health of the subject thought recently to have permanently lost his health.

As the celebration rose to a crescendo, suddenly the drink-dispenser raised his hand in warning and looked up at the big clock behind the bar. "Boys," said he, "the second shift is coming off the mines in Pickhandle Gulch. They'll be here at any moment now, and I suggest you all hush up until they arrive."

The room was stilled and the celebrants drifted into the far corners. Blue Dick, flushed, but with his azure scars blazing more vividly than ever, lay himself down on the billiard table and was sheeted over as before.

The miners from Pickhandle Gulch straggled in, and bellied up to the bar, as their wont was. As they "nominated their poison," the barkeeper mournfully repeated the news of the passing of Blue Dick.

"A friend of all of us, he was," said a shiftboss from the Mount Diablo mine, "a big force for law and order in this-here-now camp, and we ought to plant him handsome."

Whereupon a collection was started again, and the miners were ushered over to the billiard table to inspect the corpse. This time the exhibitor granted only a fleeting glance at the departed, and quickly replaced the sheet. It was lucky that he did so, for just then Shagnasty Joe swaggered into the joint. John Dormer and I, editors of the Candelaria *True Fissure,* drifted in right afterward—I trust *we* didn't swagger. We paused spellbound at the dramatic scene. Joe went to the bar, but finding no barkeep behind it, he pounded with his ham-hand for the quick service so renowned a bad-man had a right to demand. Turning, he saw the group milling around the billiard table, and Grab Brown spoke up. "Joe," he said with the air of a parson, "Blue Dick is no more."

"What?" said Joe with a scowl, "that ornery coyote! I never did like that blue-blazed varmint nohow, and it's lucky someone plugged him proper, or I might have had to do it myself for the good of the camp."

An angry murmur of dissent arose from Dick's friends, but Joe went on unabashed.

"Why, that lop-eared cayuse—he was a quitter anyway. Just look cross-eyed at him and he would hunt the tall timber. . . . What! *Wow!!*"

With pallid face and startled eyes Shagnasty Joe turned toward the swinging-doors, for he was always a superstitious man and he thought he saw a ghost. With a panther spring, Blue Dick had jumped from the table, covered from head to foot with the ghostly sheet, which he fought madly to throw off.

Just as Joe was bolting out of the doors, Blue Dick got disentangled and began firing at the rapidly retreating desperado. Joe headed for the lower road to Columbus with Dick after him, shooting and shouting like a demon possessed.

Fear lent wings to the bully's feet, and Dick had to give up the chase. He came back graciously to the bar to drink with the open-handed sports who had contributed so nobly to his funeral expenses.

"A fellow in these days has got to know his *friends,*" said he, placing his arms around the shoulders of his companions at the bar. "I'm glad to learn the high opinion all you gents hold of me, and it's just as well the camp is rid of that white-livered Shagnasty Joe. If it hadn't been that I got all tangled up in that shroud, I'd have plugged him proper, and Nevada would have been rid of the worst rogue unhanged."

MILTON ANTHONY SHARP, STAGE-ROBBER   W. C. JONES (ALIAS DOW) STAGE-ROBBER, KILLED
MIKE TOVEY, WELLS-FARGO MESSENGER   J. B. HUME, CHIEF DETECTIVE FOR WELLS-FARGO

STATE CAPITOL, CARSON CITY, NEVADA

© Behrman Collection

CHAPTER TWENTY-NINE

Milton Sharp, Bandit

*P*robably the most industrious highwayman in all of Nevada was Milton Anthony Sharp.

Sharp, in a modest way, did what he could to reduce the wealth of Wells, Fargo & Co. on the eastern slope of the Sierras about 1880. He robbed stages whenever he wanted to, and with great thoroughness, never making a mistake and never finding an empty treasure-box.

Gold bars from the Bodie mines were very numerous in those days, and nearly all of them were sold to the United States Mint at Carson City. Quite a lot of these yellow ingots failed to reach their destination, because Sharp stopped them on the way.

He was not averse to coin or greenbacks, either, but just took whatever came along. One haul of $13,000 in gold notes of Darius O. Mills' Sacramento bank didn't do him much good, however. He hid them under a pile of rocks and when he went to get them again they were gone. Wells-Fargo sued a rancher living near the place for the amount, saying they believed he had dug up Sharp's cache, and offered to prove that the rancher had lifted a big mortgage from his place soon after the robbery, and that $13,000 of the redemption money was in gold notes issued by Mills' Sacramento bank. The "home" jury gave a verdict for the rancher, however, and the matter was dropped.

Early in June, 1880, Sharp and a companion stopped the up-bound stage from Carson on a little grade near Dalzell's, eighteen miles south of Wellington's. Sharp stood all up in a row, with their backs to him and to the stage, just like a spelling-class at a country school—driver, messenger and all. Then he got up in the stage, where the treasure-box was chained on, so the driver couldn't throw it out if he wanted to, and broke the chain with a big stone. After getting the treasure in the box he had the passengers empty the contents of their pockets on the ground, their backs being toward him all the time. Then he made them take three steps to the front, and going along the line picked up such things as he thought would be of use to him, including the massive gold watch of Chamberlain, the driver.

"This stage-robbing is a very nice business when artistically conducted," commented one old-timer, recalling that exploit, "and I never knew anybody who could do it better than Milton Sharp, not even barring the much-advertised Black Bart."

"He was one of the politest gentlemen I ever met," admitted another victim. "There was nothing vulgar or coarse about him. Everything he did was done in a business-like way, and there was no unnecessary rudeness. He was particularly gallant to lady passengers and always acted like a high-toned gentleman. I have yet to hear the first person complain of the treatment received at his hands—further than that they did not like to lose their belongings."

The shotgun messengers were the only ones he seemed to have any grudge against, but he never killed any of them, which shows that he had a forgiving heart. The most he would do would be to take their cut-off shotguns and break them over the rocks. If he'd kept them all he'd have had enough to supply an ordinary militia company.

After the robbery near Dalzell's, police officers and shotgun messengers, detectives and Piutes were supposed to be on the track of the Dick Turpins, whose trail was reported to have been followed to Walker Lake, and half across the State of Nevada. The surprise of Chamberlain, the stage-driver, may be imagined when, six nights later, upon arriving at the same spot where he was stopped before, he was again ordered to "Halt!" by the same two road-agents. The passenger on the seat with Chamberlain was ordered to throw up his hands and keep them up, and the driver was requested in polite, but unmistakably firm terms, to throw off the express box, which was not chained down. Both of these demands were acceded to with great alacrity. This time the highwaymen did not trouble any of the passengers except the one on the driver's seat, and apologized to Chamberlain for taking his watch, stating that if they had had it with them they would have given it back with pleasure; and at any rate they promised to return it next time they met him. Also they stated their intention to return all the watches and jewelry taken from the passengers the week before, at the first convenient opportunity. As they secured $3,000 in coin from one package on the previous raid they felt very flush and correspondingly generous.

Several other daring holdups by the same pair disturbed the tranquillity of the countryside—mountainside, rather, for that country stands up on end. One of the robberies, in August, was at Big Bend, but the box only held $200.

On September 4th, the up-stage from Carson was halted by two bandits at the same spot where it had been stopped twice in June. James Cross of Candelaria and Colonel T. W. W.

Davies of Carson were outside with the driver, and as they threw up their hands Cross called to Sharp, who was one of the robbers, "There are no messengers on board." Guns were lowered then, and the eight passengers (one of them was my friend Harry Fontecilla of the Bodie *Free Press*) were ushered out and allowed to sit on the ground. They were not deprived of their valuables, though when the robbers opened the two boxes which they dragged from the boot they were much disappointed with the small haul.

The down-stage (going north) met the robbed stage near the bridge on the East Walker River. Two redoubtable shotgun messengers, Mike Tovey and Tom Woodruff, were aboard, along with the route agent, Billings. When they reached the point where the robbery had taken place, Tovey got down to examine the tracks and walking beside the stage he easily followed the footsteps of the robber pair. It was then about three o'clock in the morning, and bright moonlight. The robbers in the meantime had gone north toward Wellington's, and near Desert Creek stopped to throw up breastworks of stones.

Tovey, who had left his gun on the driver's seat, was slightly in the lead of the stage when the two men rose up from behind their stone barricade and fired. Their bullets missed him but one killed the near leader of the horses, the other entering the apron between Billings and the driver. Tovey ran back and Billings handed him down his gun, and then jumped down with Woodruff, the three getting behind the coach. The smaller of the robbers advanced, and as he came into the light Tovey fired, killing him instantly. The horses were plunging about so frantically that Billings, who was unarmed, went around on the other side to quiet them, and as he did so saw the larger highwayman—that was Sharp—

coming down that side. Woodruff saw him, too, and took aim and fired. At nearly the same time Tovey was bringing down his gun to fire and did fire it, but Sharp was a little too quick for him and shot him in the arm, knocking the gun out of his hands. Mike Tovey called to the other messenger, "Tom, I'm shot and bleeding to death. You'll have to look out for that fellow on the other side of the road." Woodruff fired several shots, and he and all the others were certain that the bandit was killed and had fallen just out of the range of vision in the darkness; but it proved otherwise. Sharp seemed to have a charmed life.

The small robber, lying in the road with the top of his head blown off, was a stranger to all who saw his body. He had on a little red-leather mask.

As Tovey [1] was bleeding profusely and his strength failing, Billings started with him for a nearby farmhouse on Desert Creek, while Woodruff went scouting out into the brush to try to find the other highwayman. The driver then took the harness from the dead horse, tied its mate behind the coach to lead, and hitched up the others into a four instead of a six-horse team. Just as he was about to climb up to his lofty seat, he was startled by a voice saying from the side of the road: "Now I'll trouble you for that box!"

The demand was complied with, for Sharp had the drop, and a disgusted driver urged his four horses on toward Wellington's. Sharp had reconnoitered, and when he had seen the party start for the farmhouse he had waited a few minutes and then had sallied forth boldly again from the brush and had

---

[1] Mike Tovey was killed in California during an attempted hold-up of the Ione-Jackson stage-coach, on which he was shotgun-messenger, June 15th, 1893. A tablet in his honor marks the spot.

completed the robbery. Who ever heard of better nerve than that?

J. B. Hume, detective in Wells-Fargo's service, who was a veritable sleuth-hound, was called by telegraph, and he concluded that the two men concerned in the stage-robbing were California road-agents who were old hands at it. When men rob a stage for the first time, he reasoned, they are generally so frightened over their adventure that they hasten to leave the scene of their crime as soon as possible. These men kept right up to their job and did it in a manner so thorough that there could be no doubt regarding their experience. Such gentry seldom employ an outside man for the reason that a third person must not only have an equal share of the spoils, but every extra man increases the possibility of detection, and the accessory might turn State's evidence in a pinch.

From what he learned from the body of the bandit who was slain (his name was Jones, under many an alias) Hume knew Sharp was the man wanted; and he went to San Francisco and waited for him, for he figured that after the big haul and the loss of his partner Sharp would head for his home base. Finally Hume spotted a valise at the Market street depot marked with Sharp's name. He shadowed this, and Sharp was apprehended at his lodgings on Minna street. Under direction of those noted police officers of San Francisco, Chief Crowley and Captain Lees, two detectives lay in wait for Sharp and when he came in for his valise he was overpowered. He was wearing a hunter's outfit and a slouch hat, and carrying a roll of blankets. In these were a sixshooter and a formidable bowie-knife, and on his person was a Colt sixshooter. He protested his innocence, even though he had almost $3,000 of the stolen money, and in the valise were found a gold watch taken from Charles Shaw, a commercial drummer, in a holdup in June, and a revolver taken from the stage on September 4th. The revolver was being sent C. O. D. to a man in Candelaria.

Sharp was brought back to the scene of his depredations and incarcerated in the Aurora jail. He was tried and found guilty on one of seven indictments brought against him by the Grand Jury; but he made his escape while awaiting sentence.

I'll never forget the November morning it was announced that Sharp had broken out of the Aurora jail. No such excitement had been seen in the camp. A number of bricks were removed from the wall of the jail, and tools found outside showed that he was "sprung" by friends.

Wells-Fargo offered a big reward for his recapture and the stages went out without carrying the usual treasure-boxes. The Sheriff, the Governor and the County Commissioners offered additional rewards. The country fairly swarmed with men hunting the outlaw. About five miles from town they found the "Oregon boot," the fifteen-pound steel shackle, which he had on when he escaped.

After that all trace of him was lost. It was in the dead of winter and intensely cold, but the ravines and sagebrush plains were scoured far and wide in vain for a sight of the daring stage-robber.

One night about a week after Sharp's escape a lot of us were in Dobe Willoughby's faro bank room back of McKissick's saloon in Candelaria, when we heard somebody throwing pebbles against the window-panes. It was the signal of distress from somebody, but no one seemed to know whom it was intended for. A man in the crowd said tensely: "Maybe that's Sharp giving notice that he needs help."

Everybody knew that Willoughby had been in the Aurora jail for a time while Sharp was there and they supposed the signal was meant for him. But he pretended not to hear it, and kept on dealing.

Deputy Sheriff Alex McLean heard of the suspicious circumstances of the pebble-signal on the window, and said he believed that Sharp had made it. He made no move to arrest him, however, and some of the boys joshed him for being afraid to tackle the lone highwayman. Those who laughed, however, did not show any particular desire to face the dark and the probability of half-a-dozen bullets to get the rewards which had been offered.

A miner finally came into Donahue's saloon, where a big crowd had gathered, and said there was a man back of Coalter's restaurant who stated he wanted to see an officer. McLean plucked up courage and went around to meet the mysterious visitor, who was crouching behind McKissick's saloon.

It was Milton Sharp. He gave himself up without resistance. He said that he had expected assistance from friends in Candelaria, but they had gone back on him, and it was useless to struggle against fate. He was hungry and freezing, and with no one to help him, escape was impossible. With one friend and money, he said, he could have gotten away, but having neither he had to weaken.

When searched, no arms were found on Sharp's person. This helps to explain his giving up so easily, for he was a man of undoubted nerve and if heeled he certainly would have made as good a fight as possible. It is a question if he could have been taken alive.

The first thing Sharp did after adjusting the handcuffs so that they wouldn't hurt his wrists was to ask for something to eat; and when he was taken to Billy Coalter's chop-stand he proceeded to stow away a mighty meal. After his supper he was taken to Wells, Fargo & Company's office in the Bank building for safe-keeping until arrangements could be made for his transportation to Aurora. I had a good chance to talk to this terror of seven counties that night, and I found him a mild-mannered, pleasant-spoken fellow, but with a flash now and then beneath the surface which showed him alert and keen as a steel trap. A Missourian, he had a handsome countenance, swarthy, with jet black hair, mustache and goatee. His features were sharp and his gaze was sharp. About thirty-five years of age, I should say.

This inglorious Milton was not inclined to be communicative at first, and when asked how he got the shackle off his leg he replied, "Well, I got it off, and I was glad of it." Afterwards, becoming more talkative, he admitted he was compelled to wear the iron for three days and that all the time he was surrounded by men who were armed with shotguns and hunting him. "It seemed to me," said he, "that I could not get out of their sight. The shackle hurt my ankle and made me very lame."

After getting rid of the shackle he was able to make better progress, but didn't know which way to go, as it seemed to him that the whole country was alive with men carrying shotguns. "I am not well acquainted with this part of the country," he told me, "and don't know exactly where I went in my travels. I had to change my course every few miles to avoid men who were tracking me. I only spoke to one man and that was at the little town about seven or eight miles from here—Columbus. After getting in this neighborhood I concluded to come here and try to find a friend that I thought would help me, but I didn't find him and I didn't like to ask for him." Sharp declined to give the name of the man whom he expected to see.

"If I had had any friends I would have been supplied with

money and with means to defend myself, and they would not have taken me so easily, for I would just about as soon die as to go to the State Prison." As Sharp uttered these words there was a glitter in his eyes that expressed intense earnestness.

"It was rumored that you had friends who helped you to escape from the Aurora jail," I said. "How did you get out?"

"I just dug out through the brick wall. Anybody can go through that jail. That is, if they are not locked up in the tanks—nobody can get out of the tanks. All the other prisoners, Mexicans mostly, were in there."

Candelaria was filled with a heterogeneous population at that time, and I remember there was much division of sentiment as to whether it was giving Sharp a fair chance to take advantage of his necessitous condition and lock him up like that. Some thought the least that ought to have been done for him was to furnish him arms and provisions, and then let the officers take him if they could. Out there they used to believe in a fair field and no favors, and might the best man win.

I remember that Tommy Watson was particularly indignant, and he questioned the legality of Sharp's arrest, because Deputy Sheriff McLean, who received his surrender, had that very day been found to be un-naturalized.

"I think it is an outrage," complained Watson, "that a free-born American citizen should be arrested by an un-naturalized Canadian Scotchman, and if there was a court of competent jurisdiction here, I would sue out a writ of *habeas corpus* and set Sharp free in less than an hour."

But they held Sharp, notwithstanding such-like objections. The very night of his capture he was taken to Aurora and locked up in one of the tanks which he pronounced so secure.

He was sentenced to the State Prison for twenty years under his conviction of robbing the Carson and Bodie stage on September 4th, and was at once escorted to the penitentiary under heavy guard, as befitted such an illustrious prisoner. The remaining six indictments against Sharpe were dismissed.[1]

His companion, identified as W. C. Jones, *alias* Keith, *alias* Dow, had already paid with his life for his transgressions.

Why didn't Sharp stop some of the stages after he got out of jail and thus relieve himself from his distress? Most of the stages stopped running two days after he got out, and anyway it was no use to halt them as there wouldn't have been even so much as a smooth quarter to be won.

Why didn't he take in some ranch or miner's cabin? Tommy Watson answered that question: "No, sir; not much. Not in a hundred years. Milton Sharp was a stage-robber; but, sir, he would never stoop to burglary."

[1] Milton Sharp escaped from the State Prison at Carson City on August 15th, 1889.

CHAPTER THIRTY

A Banshee of Esmeralda

*D*espite its name, the Esmeralda region has never produced any emeralds. A few diamonds have been picked up, though. With no desire to perpetuate a "Great Diamond Hoax," I think it all right to tell a story of one such find, as it was told me, though for its historic accuracy I cannot vouch.

Patrick Murphy lived in a canyon, which takes its name from him, near Whisky Flat. Murphy, who took pride in calling himself "plain Pat," was a fine old Irish gentleman, whose hospitality was bounded only by the size of his house. As he had a productive ranch and a thriving garden, his comfortable cabin was a favorite stopping-place for such travelers as chanced to pass his way. He was of a genial, companionable disposition, and the wayfarer, be he rich or poor, was always sure of a welcome. As much for company as for anything else, Murphy kept a hired man, and for years his old friend and mining partner, Jeremiah Degin, had been with him in that capacity.

One evening in the fall of '74 as Jerry and Pat were wending their way home after a day's work Pat suddenly stopped.

"Fwhat's that, Jerry?" he nervously asked, his voice falling to a husky whisper as he clutched his companion's arm, at the same time pointing up the canyon.

"Sure I don't know fwhat ye mane," answered Jerry with

composure. "I don't see nothin' to make a man shiver like that."

"There it is, Jerry! Jist beyant that clump o' sagebrush. It's a corpse-light, as sure as I'm a Christian!" And Pat's knees knocked together.

The evening was dark, and up the canyon about 300 yards above the cabin a clear light was seen blazing with an unearthly gleam.

"Howly mother o' Moses!" groaned Jerry, as badly frightened as Pat. " 'Tis a corpse-light. 'Tis a banshee," and he devoutly crossed himself. "Sure there's goin' to be a death in the Murphy family, and it's right sorry I'll be to lose ye, my dear owld frind; but if it's the will o' Hiven that ye must go, ye will have the restin' consolation of lavin' a good name behint ye, and takin' the blessins of thousands to Hiven wid ye!"

"How do ye know it's burnin' for me?" blurted out Pat. "It's maybe for one of the Degin family."

"I niver thought of that," shuddered Jerry.

The men retreated to the cabin and locked the door. After a cold supper they went to bed, vainly seeking in sleep relief from their fears. Next morning they were astir early. Nothing could be seen of the light.

That day they did not go to work, but busied themselves around the cabin, cleaning up things and making such preparations as would have been necessary if they had intended going on a journey. They shaved themselves and put on their best clothes. Jerry even went so far as to grease his cowhide boots. The desire to make a decent-looking corpse was evidently in the mind of each.

That evening Pat and Jerry watched the sun go down, and with bated breath waited the appearance of the corpse-light.

The night closed in rapidly, and there in the middle of the narrow canyon blazed the ethereal beacon. The men sat on the cabin steps watching it, talking of banshees, ghosts, goblins, and the like, until the moon came up, when suddenly the light disappeared like a snuffed-out candle. They were unable to understand the reason for this, but familiarity with the fancied danger had begun to wear away their fears, and they went to bed in a comparatively peaceful state of mind. On the following day Solomon Sloan, the Hebrew peddler who furnished the country thereabout with such articles as are generally carried by those of his class, drove up to the Murphy mansion with his little wagon and asked for accommodations for the night. He was made welcome, and Pat set out the best in the house, including the demijohn. After getting the latest gossip from Aurora, Sweetwater and other neighboring mining-camps, Pat told Solomon of the strange apparition of the canyon.

"Vas you effer gone up to see vat it vas?" asked Solomon in business-like way.

"Howly murther! No! I want nothin' to do wid a ghost, good or bad!" cried Pat, holding up his hands. Jerry shook his head and turned pale at the thought.

"Vell, I guess I gone take a look for it. Geef me a light and I mighty kewick find out vat kind of a ghost it vas."

The terrified companions endeavored to dissuade him from his resolve, but he persisted, and improvising a lantern from a broken bottle and a bit of candle, started on his direful mission. Pat and Jerry held their breaths as they watched him from the cabin door.

The corpse-light beamed as usual, and Solomon plodded sternly and slowly up the canyon towards it. His form was lost in the darkness, but his lantern glinted dimly as he clambered from boulder to boulder and struggled through the sagebrush. Finally he reached the spot and lowered his lantern.

The strange light disappeared.

A second later the lantern went out and Solomon was heard rushing down the canyon as if the devil and all his imps were after him. Jerry's hair stood on end.

Upon reaching the cabin the peddler was breathless and very excited, but tried to appear unconcerned. He said his hasty retreat was owing to his candle being extinguished.

"Fwhat made the corpse-light go out like that?" anxiously inquired Pat.

"Oh, it vas only a lot ov rotten vood, dot made a phosphorous, und ven I kick it ofer you couldn't see der light no more."

It required a set lecture on phosphorescent light to convince Pat and Jerry that Sloan's explanation was the true one. They were not altogether satisfied. Solomon made an early start the next morning, saying he thought he would go to Elbow Station.

The corpse-light was never seen again.

There was trouble in store for Patrick Murphy and Jerry Degin. Solomon Sloan had mysteriously disappeared, and foul play was suspected. The peddler was last seen alive driving toward Murphy's cabin. The two men were arrested and kept in jail for a time, but there was no evidence against them and they were finally discharged. They rested under suspicion, however, until three months later, when it was learned that Sloan sold his wagon and goods in Dayton and left for parts unknown. Two years passed, and the incident was almost forgotten, when one day the mail brought a copy of a New York newspaper to Patrick Murphy. A blue pencil mark was drawn around a paragraph which stated that one

Solomon Sloan, after negotiations long in progress, has consummated the sale of a very large diamond to a representative of the Russian government, to be taken to Russia to hold a place of honor in the imperial diadem. The existence of this stone was a great mystery, said the article, as it was a new light in the brilliant galaxy of precious gems. Sloan admitted that it was found in the United States, but would not divulge the exact locality, though it was known he had come from the Pacific Coast.

"That's the thing we mistook for the light ov a banshee," ejaculated Jerry as Pat finished reading.

"The same is me firm conviction," solemnly replied Patrick Murphy,

ELLA BISHOP (MRS. WELLS DRURY)

WELLS DRURY IN LATER YEARS

CHAPTER THIRTY-ONE

Campaigning

*A*fter my Candelaria excursion, I returned to the Comstock. For a time I was editor of the *Territorial Enterprise*. But Virginia City was in the grip of depression; and no wonder, for the total output of bullion from the Lode in 1881 was only about $1,000,000. It had been almost forty times that, a few years before.

So when my friend John Dormer, who had been elected Secretary of State, called on me to become his right bower in that office, I went down to Carson City, in 1882. With a heavy heart, I left the Comstock.

It was a political job, and I entered with zest into the campaigning that went with it. I had always been an ardent Republican, since my young days as an office-holder under Lincoln, and I had participated eagerly in the partisan politics on the Comstock Lode. During the next few years, however, this activity was intensified, particularly in preparation for the selection of a United States Senator from Nevada. So much significance was attached to the getting of this office that it may not be amiss to cast our eyes back over the years, to see how it went.

A Senatorial campaign was a superlative happiness for the people of the Sagebrush State, for every voter of that enterprising Commonwealth participated in the contest—and that was long before the popular election of United States Senators.

In some more conservative communities political activity is left to those self-sacrificing patriots who have volunteered to run the government for the pittance which is allowed by law for office-holders, and in order to reward their own forbearance they scoop in all that the public business will stand, but in Nevada of old everybody was a politician and an aspirant for public position. Some complaint was made on occasion that there were not offices enough to go round, but it was hoped that this difficulty might be obviated by amendment to the constitution.

References to the political days of yore by Nevadans are always tinged with regret that such good things may never be expected again.

When Nevada won Statehood, James W. Nye and William M. Stewart went to the United States Senate. They drew lots for the long and short term (four and two years), and Stewart won. Both were re-elected for the regular six-year term. To succeed Nye, the vigorous John P. Jones entered the field in 1872.

There were Senatorial campaigns before Jones came up out of Crown Point ravine to do battle with the veteran politicians who were disposed to laugh at his pretension. There had been spirited contests in the Legislature before that, but when he made his appearance on the stage of national politics the magnificence of his exploits so outshone the triumphs of his predecessors that they were instantly effaced and forgotten.

It was at the close of this struggle that Jones gave expression to his famous remark that "in a Nevada Senatorial campaign a million might be spent and no man corrupted," signifying— well, nobody ever knew exactly what he intended to say, but some of his friends interpreted the mystic words to mean that he had rewarded for their support only those who were already his friends, and that as they would have voted for him anyhow, therefore they were not swerved from their original intention, and if not swerved, then they were not corrupted.

Whatever may be the solution of the enigma, it is certain that no one in Nevada ever saw a livelier fight than Jones put up at that time, and it has since been the criterion by which other contests have been gauged. It was by no means a peaceful episode in the history of the State and to Jones may be credited the distinction of having a body-guard as formidable as any that could be at present recruited from Chicago. Big Jim Cartter figured as Jones' minister of war.

One may well wonder what would become of some modern-day fighters who venture into Nevada if they should chance to encounter antagonists like Cartter, or like Farmer Peel, Al Waterman, John Daly, George Birdsell, Jack Perry, "Irish Tom" Carberry or others of that kind. John P. Jones himself had plenty of color, as has been indicated. Elected to the United States Senate in 1873, he held that honor for five terms—thirty years. He was renowned for his masterly Silver speeches in the Senate. I was an adherent of his cause, and aided Senator Jones in gathering data on the silver question for the enlightenment of our national legislators. Our enthusiastic crowds were wont to give "three cheers for the dollar of our daddies, and Senator Jones, the daddy of our dollar!"

The Jones campaign, as the first notable affair of its kind in Nevada, obtained a prominence which none of its successors achieved. Whether there was more "influence" exerted then than during subsequent elections has sometimes been questioned, but at least the display was more spectacular and no approach to it was witnessed except when William Sharon shied his castor into the political ring and took the prize from all opponents by the overmastering weight of his "sack." In non-Senatorial years Nevada, like California, usually chose fair legislative material, and not infrequently a fair class of citizens was found to support millionaires reputed to have assisted in the development of the country.

This was the battle-cry when William Sharon was a candidate. He was spoken of as the savior of the Comstock for the reason that he had put his faith and money into the task of resuming deep mining after the old Lode had been drowned out by the influx of water on the lower levels, and when many believed that its mineral resources had been exhausted.

The disastrous fire in the Yellow Jacket mine at Gold Hill had brought bitterness in its train, and it caused an attack on William Sharon when he aspired to be United States Senator. The accusation was made that Sharon's henchmen had started the fire, in which about 40 miners' lives were lost, as part of a plot to depress stocks. When campaigning for votes, he was threatened with sudden death if he spoke at Gold Hill. He went there, boldly mounted the rostrum, and denounced his detractors. He was not molested.

John I. Ginn, who was editing Adolph Sutro's paper, the *Independent,* wrote an ironical "history" of the Comstock ledge, in which he pretended to show that Sharon was present at the creation of the earth and furnished the plans and specifications for the laying out of the Storey County mining district, and mapped the location lines of the Consolidated Virginia mine, together with all dips, spurs and angles. The jokers comprising what is commonly known as "The Third House," or lobby, tried hard enough to induce Sutro to enter the lists as a rival to Sharon, but Sutro, although cordially hating Sharon (who called him "that damned Assyrian") after investigation saw no chance to draw any strength from the opposition and declined the contest.

Colonel Billy Wood and Colonel Abe Edgerton were the prime managers of the campaign for Sharon, as "Red" Frank Wheeler and Louis Wardell had been for Jones in his first campaign. After Jones' first election he needed no managers in addition to his old friends, for the reason that he so won the applause of Nevadans by his advocacy of the cause of free silver that he had practically no opposition. It was when Jones won his first victory that Stewart applied to him the sobriquet of "the Metallic Accident," which stuck to him for many years, and might account for Jones' lukewarm feeling toward the venerable Senator when he was seeking re-election.

In the James G. Fair campaign of 1880, which preceded Stewart's last series, "Bear" John Kelly was the harbinger who announced the candidacy of Fair on the Democratic ticket, and W. E. F. Deal and Dick Dey were confidential managers.

Fair made his campaign on the "honest miner" basis. I was in Candelaria when he visited Esmeralda County. He drove in from Columbus on a buckboard one afternoon clad in regulation frontier garb—red flannel shirt, broad-brimmed hat, and trousers thrust into his traveling boots. The first thing he did was to ask for the nearest place in which he might wash the alkali dust from his throat, and all citizens who were in the neighborhood were invited to assist in the ceremony. Then Colonel Fair made the round of the mines in Pickhandle Gulch, in which he showed an intense interest, because he was first and last an enthusiastic miner, whose heart beat quickly at the sight of a choice ore-specimen. He also had a genuine sympathy with the miners, and won their admiration by his thorough appreciation of their work and their skill, for in old Nevada to be known as a first-class miner was honor and distinction enough for any man.

Fair's managers had a difficult task at the beginning of their undertaking for they found it necessary to straighten out personal misunderstandings between their candidate and some of the leading Democrats of the State. The most obdurate was Lou Drexler, himself a millionaire, but too "careful" to launch into a political career. The trouble was adjusted on the day of Fair's return from his tour of the land; the brassbanding and speechmaking and burning of bonfires persistently continued until election day, and of course a majority of the Legislature pledged to Fair received seats in the State Capitol.

Fair's sackbearers were in every precinct. In thinking back about that election, one recalls the historic remark in *A Texas Steer* concerning Senator Maverick Brander: "Wasn't he elected honest? Didn't every man *get* his five dollars?" But votes ran higher than that in the Fair campaign, and even the cemeteries were invaded for votes.

After the general election, Adolph Sutro let it be known that he would like to be United States Senator, though during the campaign his name had not been to the fore. He gave Fair some uneasy moments before the Legislative vote sent the Bonanza king to the Senate.

John Mackay could have been United States Senator at almost any time, and many politicians tried to lure him into candidacy, but the prospect did not appeal to him.

After an absence from Nevada of several years Stewart returned to that State and again announced his candidacy for a seat in the United States Senate. He had for his manager then, as later, C. C. Wallace—Black Wallace—assisted by Sam C. Wright of Carson. The Stewart campaign of 1886 was conducted on the approved lines of Nevada politics, with Steve Gage, who managed and won in Stewart's original political ventures, as consulting engineer.

"Give 'em plenty of brass bands and lots of hurrah speeches," was Gage's prescription, and it was carried out to the letter. Every brass band in the State was chartered to lead Stewart clubs for the parades and torchlight processions, and musicians were even imported from Truckee and Lake Tahoe for service in the campaign. When the polls were closed it was found that the windjammers, the bonfires and the spellbinders had done their work, so that the Stewart majority was overwhelming and no other citizen was able to dispute with him for the prize of the Senatorship before the Legislature, although Rollin Daggett had aspirations. Fair had withdrawn from the contest.

Stewart, who had served four terms in the Senate, though not consecutively, won his fifth and last victory in the complicated election of 1898. His enemies had predicted his downfall, saying that the old lion had lost his teeth and strength; that he was no longer the Bill Stewart of former days, when in the majesty of his powerful individuality he swayed men by his personal magnetism and compelled obedience where others were content to plead for favors. Stewart was supposed to be backed by the Southern Pacific, and Frank Newlands, his opponent, had behind him the millions of the Sharon estate (he was son-in-law to William Sharon), together with the influence of a majority of the mining corporations with headquarters in Virginia City and San Francisco. The fight was bitter, but Stewart won the Senatorship by one vote.[1] His campaign was handled in masterly manner by Black Wallace—so called from early days because of the sable hue of his hair, but the passing years had wrought such a change in that regard that by then he was entitled to apply to the Legislature for a change of name to "White" Wallace.

Among Nevada's most noted politicians and office-holders

---

[1] Francis G. Newlands was United States Senator from Nevada from 1903 to 1917.

of the '70s and '80s, besides those who have been mentioned, were Governor Broadhorns Bradley, Judge Charles N. Harris, Christopher Columbus Powning, Colonel W. W. Bishop, Governor Jewett W. Adams, George W. Baker, Hock Mason, W. Frank Stewart, Uncle George Tufly, Sam Davis, Dr. S. L. Lee, Rollin M. Daggett, Harry Mighels, Matt Canavan, George Cassidy, A. C. Cleveland, Charles Stoddard, Adolph Shane, Tom Wren, C. C. Stevenson, J. F. Hallock, R. K. Colcord and Henry Cutting. All loved the political going.

In very early days, Henry Edgerton ran for United States Senator after being in the State three months and was nosed out by one vote by a man who had arrived on the Comstock Lode only six weeks before the election—showing that priority of residence was not the deciding factor in the contest.

Tom Fitch, "the silver-tongued," was owner and editor of several newspapers, but made a greater success as a speaker. With a pen in his hand he appeared to be uninspired, but on the hustings he had no equal. One of the famous duels of early Nevada was that one in which Tom Fitch met Joe Goodman about 10 miles from Virginia City, where they edited rival journals. Tom was wounded in the leg with a pistol-bullet, and he limped through half a century of his life; but explanations after the duel made him and Joe friends once more. Both had stood up like men, and they bore mutual respect.

A Republican warhorse, Tom Fitch was long an aspirant for a place in the United States Senate, but he did not have enough money. He invariably fell short of the necessary votes in the Legislature, so he never had the opportunity to make the Senate resound with his magniloquence, though he did serve with distinction as a Congressman.

It was my privilege to be a member of the Republican National Convention of 1884, at Chicago, as a representative of the State of Nevada. I adhered to the Blaine wing of the Republican party, of which all Pacific Coast men were enthusiastic supporters. Theodore Roosevelt was a delegate from New York, and as the seats were arranged alphabetically by States, we became acquainted, for his chair during the entire convention week was immediately in front of mine. Well I recall how the aggressive Roosevelt forcibly "sat down" a butcher in the New York delegation who was raising a dissenting voice against something "Teddy" favored. Practical politics dee-lighted him always, and he reveled in keeping that delegation in line.

When we got to Chicago we found that it was the field against the White-Plumed Knight. It was "anything to knife Blaine," among all the delegations which were not pledged to him. And the question of bolting was brought up then, as later. That was what gave George A. Knight of California the opportunity to make the greatest speech of his life. He directed his taunts against George William Curtis, then editor of *Harper's Weekly*. He said that there were whisperings of perfidy in the air, and demanded to know whether men who were sitting in the convention intended to abide by the decision of the majority, or whether they would violate the well-understood gentleman's agreement. Would they bolt or would they like honorable men stand by the ticket?

Curtis rose to reply, and in his dignity declined to stand on a chair, as Knight and the other speakers had done. But the delegates wouldn't listen, and at last he was compelled to submit. Then climbing a chair he said: "A free man I came into this convention; a free man I shall go out of this convention."

There were cries of "Bolter!" and "Treachery!" and Eli Denison of Oakland marched around the horseshoe aisle of the Exposition building, bearing aloft the famous California eagle, while the 30,000 people yelled themselves hoarse in cheering for Blaine.

Amid the confusion Curtis finished his speech. It was the last rally of the opposition. As one of the Blaine campaign posters displayed in the hall said:

> "Woe to the rider and woe to the steed,
> That falls in the path of their wild stampede!"

The Blaine men took heart, and by reason of the personal popularity of their candidate snatched victory from defeat. The forces of the man from Maine simply ran all over the rest of the field of candidates.

The extra-mural activities of the delegates to the convention furnished even more excitement than those within the auditorium. My comrade on the grand tour of Chicago was Dr. Simeon Lemuel Lee of Carson, a stalwart of Republicanism in Nevada for half a century. The evening after Blaine's nomination (we still had our Nevada badges on) we strolled into a glittering place of public refreshment. A slurring remark was made to which we took exception, and a fight was on. Our adversaries seemed fearless and willing, and were about to rush us when all of a sudden one yelled, "Look out for that man, he's from *Nevada!*" And all turned and fled out of the swinging doors. They had seen the Nevada badge on Lee's broad chest, and perchance had misinterpreted a movement to his hip-pocket. Chicago has the reputation for gun-fighters now. Nevada had it then.

That year I stumped Nevada for Blaine, and I covered a wide swath of country to get at the sparse electorate.

CHAPTER THIRTY-TWO

Some Wild Nevada Camps

*W*hen a tenderfoot asked an old-
timer in Gold Hill the bound-
aries of the Comstock Lode, he drawled, "Stranger, the foot-
wall is the diorite of Mount Davidson and the hanging-wall
is Salt Lake City. All quartz within them boundaries is the
Comstock Lode." For speculative purposes, that is the way
some of the treasure-hunters figured. The Comstockers, myself among the number, ranged pretty freely to the east and
west. I was particularly well acquainted with the camps
where I lived in southwestern Nevada—the Esmeralda country
—but became familiar with other sections of the State also, on
trips as a public official, on political stumping tours and on
newspaper "details." As not a few of the outlying communities are mentioned in these pages, it will be well to pay at
least some of them a visit, for better acquaintance.

Most remote of the southeastern camps was Pioche, which
in the early '70s was one of the livest towns in Nevada, with
about 10,000 hustling inhabitants. Not only were some of
these a trial and tribulation to the rest, but the community
was scourged too by fire and flood. In one of the fires, an
explosion of blasting powder killed or maimed more than
fifty bystanders. That was on September 15th, 1871, the anniversary of Mexican Independence and the conflagration,

which virtually wiped out the town, came at the time of a glorious fiesta of the miners from south of the Rio Grande.

Despite other fires, the town grew up as big and bad as before. Shooting affrays were frequent. In the young grave-yard were the graves of 80 men who had met violent death. Most exciting of the conflicts was a pitched battle on February 22nd, 1871, for the Washington & Creole mine, owned by Raymond & Ely but jumped by another company, who were taking out ore under protection of a fort they had built, defended by heavily armed men. Raymond & Ely gunmen charged the entrenchments and drove off the defenders, killing one and wounding many.

The great Raymond & Ely mine at Pioche was very rich, producing possibly $20,000,000. Ore was milled at Bullion-ville, a dozen miles to the southeast; and Panaca was just beyond. The Meadow Valley mine was another big producer near Pioche.

Las Vegas, far to the south in the narrow funnel-heel of Nevada, was an insignificant village, site of an early Mormon settlement, though the lush meadows to which it owes its name attracted pioneer wayfarers along the old Spanish Trail, with their livestock. The project to dam the Colorado River at Boulder Dam was in the unvisioned future.

In the White Pine district, high on a peak well-called Treasure Hill a find of silver ores was made in 1868, and Treasure City there, often above the clouds, soon had 6000 people. During the hectic rush, more than 10,000 were credited to Hamilton, on the northern slope of Treasure Hill, but a fire of incendiary origin wiped out much of the town, whose decline was hastened by the swift exhaustion of the mines, which proved rich only near the surface. In the Eberhardt mine, though, in this region, a mass of silver ore was found which was one of the richest of such deposits ever uncovered.

After a strike was made in 1872 at Cherry Creek, about sixty miles northeast, that soon became the leading camp in the district. As with its namesake in Denver, one can usually say, "No cherry, no creek!" Both streams have a satanic habit of coming to life, though, in a tearing rage.

Ely was then a minor gold-producing region. The vast development of copper there came long afterward.

Placer gold was discovered in 1867 in the Tuscarora district, on the headwaters of the Owyhee River, north of Carlin; and soon afterwards rich silver veins were found. Among the pioneers in the Iron Mountain region near Tuscarora was Emanuel Penrod—"Manny"—who had been one of the original owners of the Ophir mine on the Comstock, but his ledge here proved no bonanza.

The most noted camps of eastern Nevada are Eureka and Austin, about seventy miles apart on the historic stage route leading from Virginia City toward "the States," and each roughly a hundred miles (both were rough towns) south of the transcontinental railroad, with which they were linked first by stage and later by rail. Although mines were developed on Bullion Hill in 1864, it was not till Eureka was founded about five years later that the region amounted to much. High rose the hopes for "another Comstock," and a district which could produce $60,000,000 in bullion in about a dozen years, as that did, was not poverty-stricken. The lead production of Eureka also was immense. Like so many of the camps, Eureka was wellnigh destroyed by fire several times. The worst blaze, in 1878, cost a million—not a cool million. A cloudburst a few years before took terrific toll.

In their heydey, picturesque Eureka and its suburb of Ruby

Hill lived the carefree life of the frontier. They had a goodly but ungodly quota of gunmen—gun-fighters, they were termed then. One of the most picturesque events, in which the entire community participated, was the gorgeous funeral of Gus Botto, leading gambler of the place, slain in 1878 by Jesse Bigelow, the *casus belli* being tickets for the opera house.[1] Eureka harbored hard *hombres,* and the refining influence of womankind was not always manifest. Not a social event, but one which drew excited attention in 1876 from all classes was the fatal stabbing of Bulldog Kate (Kate Miller) by Hog-eyed Mary (Mary Irwin), denizen of Eureka's underworld, incited by a grudge of long standing. Stage-holdups, street-duels, nightriding activities by the Vigilantes known as "601," anti-Chinese riots in which several Celestials were slain—these disturbed the even tenor of Eureka's way.

I recall the intense excitement which swept Nevada in 1879 at the time of the Fish Creek War, resulting from a dispute between mine managers and the charcoal burners who from the nut-pine trees made the charcoal used in the smelters. The armed *carbonari,* mostly Italians, virtually took possession of Eureka, under desperate leaders who threatened their enemies with destruction. Militiamen were called out, and on August 18th a deputy sheriff and a posse of nine ran into a gang of more than a hundred at the charcoal burners' camp at Fish Creek, thirty miles from Eureka. In attempting to make arrests, the posse killed five of the coal gang, and badly wounded six. "Justifiable homicide" was the verdict of the coroner's jury.

The "Reese River rush" preceded the Eureka stampede by some years, for it was as early as 1862 that Bill Talcott, a

---

[1] In 1874 Gus Botto had shot and killed Brannan, who had threatened to kill him on sight.

pony express rider, discovered silver there. Some English interests early worked a group of claims called the King Alfred mines, and other fine properties were developed. Probably $50,000,000 in silver was taken from this district, of which Austin became at once the center, with stage-lines radiating to camps roundabout.

Around Battle Mountain, north of Austin on the main railroad, were clustered several mining camps which produced their millions in bullion. That region owed its name to early conflicts with the Indians.

The most refreshing sight which greeted overland emigrants of the pioneer days was the vast natural greensward at Truckee Meadows, near the eastern base of the Sierras. On the highland river which comes tumbling down from Tahoe, and which bears the name of "Captain" Truckee, one of Fremont's faithful Indian Scouts, a little community sprang up about 1859. Called for a time Lake's Crossing, with the advent of the Central Pacific Railroad in 1868 it became a real town and was named Reno, in honor of General Jesse Lee Reno, who had been killed at the battle of South Mountain in 1862.

In the *Territorial Enterprise* of Virginia City, September 2nd, 1868, appeared an article captioned, "First Birth in Reno." This vital historic event was thus chronicled: "Under the proper head, in another column, will be found recorded the birth of a daughter—a nine-pounder. The happy father, J. A. Carnahan, was formerly a citizen of this place, but concluded to change his residence, and having established himself at Reno, set to work like a good citizen to do what he could toward the improvement and advancement of the town. Charley Crocker having offered a prize of 50 acres of land for the first child born in the town, Carnahan went in to win and he has won. His nine-pound daughter is the first child born in the place and takes the real estate. We understand that several others were expecting to carry off the prize, and that there are some long faces in the town, but all appears to have been on the square."

The Charley Crocker mentioned was one of the Big Four of the Central Pacific. Reno, of course, was not a mining-town, though it became the point of departure for the Comstock. It was seized with wild excitement every so often, as news of "strikes" started rushes of prospectors to new mineral fields. One of these began in 1876 when "Doc" Bishop picked up a specimen of ore from a table in a house where he was visiting a patient near Pyramid Lake. The ore appeared much like Comstock ore, but though a mushroom mining-camp sprang up, it did not prosper and was soon deserted.

About eleven miles south of Reno on the way to Carson and the Comstock are Steamboat Springs, which so often figure in speculations of geologists as to the origin of the great Lode. Sulphur has been mined there; and to my loss I once owned a quicksilver claim in the vicinity. Old Washoe City and Ophir City were farther south, quite flourishing places for a few years. Franktown, on Washoe Lake not far from Bowers Mansion, was named for an early settler, Francois Poirier. The crude nomenclature of those times was represented by the appellations of Lousetown, south of the Truckee; Dogtown, a very early camp of miners; and forlorn Ragtown, on the Carson River, so called because of the ragged huts of the Indians. Dayton, the camp of the mule-skinners on that river south of the Comstock, was early known as Chinatown. Silver City is four miles northwest of Dayton, on the way to Gold Hill. Empire was a sawmill town east of Carson City.

Lest this geographical lore prove wearisome, let me desist

with the remark that there are more than two hundred min-ing-districts in Nevada, and each has had from one to a score of camps, many of them not even remembered. But enough has been said to give assurance that not all the gold and silver, nor all the fun, were on the Comstock.

CHAPTER THIRTY-THREE

Political and Personal

*L*ife in the little capital, Carson City, was charming. Already I have given some of my early impressions of the community. In the '70s and '80s the city had a population of about 5000.

The V. & T.—Virginia and Truckee Railroad—linked Reno and the Comstock by way of Carson City, and the Carson & Colorado line extended southeast to the Esmeralda region and beyond. From Carson radiated stage routes in all directions. Some already have been mentioned. One of these climbed up to Glenbrook on Lake Tahoe, where Yerington and Bliss had big lumber mills.

While I resided in Carson, during the summer I was often up at Glenbrook and at neighboring resorts around Lake Tahoe, in which I loved to swim. The Comstockers, no less than the Californians, delighted to sojourn beside the beautiful Lake of the Sky.

Another stage line ran south from Carson City to Genoa, overlooking Carson Valley. This old town, where Mark Twain dwelt for a time, was early a trading-post called Mormon Station. In its insecure position against the steep hills it was ever threatened with destruction by avalanche. Now it has almost vanished.

A road scaled the Sierra to the hermit county of Alpine, in

California. The main stage route continued south to the mining-towns of Aurora and Bodie, in the vicinity of Mono Lake, and to the lower Esmeralda region—notably Candelaria.

With all these radiating routes, Carson was "The Hub," as Comstockers facetiously conceded. Her people were hospitable and generous; her men noble and brave; her office-seekers the most persistent in Nevada; and her schoolmarms charming to the fullest extent of female attractiveness. All Carsonites who did not drink belonged to the Blue Ribbon Order, and those who did imbibe took only the best.

Carson was proud of her Capitol, of her Mint, of her Roundhouse, and of her State Prison. She plumed herself on her level streets and her shade-trees. In the matter of climate, her arrogance was simply unbearable to a Comstocker, whose habitat was described in the Carson newspapers as "an inhospitable mountainside."

Nearly every Carsonite you met was a candidate for office. Those who had not announced themselves were in the hands of their friends.

After holding several political offices myself, I was elected to the State Assembly from Ormsby County, and presided as Speaker *pro tem*. My main interest was in legislation aiding the development of irrigation in Nevada. With pleasure I recall, too, that I advocated a measure for woman suffrage.

Among my friends in the Assembly was George L. Albright, father of Horace Marden Albright, who has served with distinction as Superintendent of National Parks. Law-makers of that session included George Alt, Clemence Lemery, John F. Egan, C. M. Fassett (who years later became mayor of Spokane) and many other friends of mine.

The Legislature met early in 1887, and one of its first acts was to elect William M. Stewart to the high post of United

States Senator. I placed him in nomination in the Assembly, and he won by overwhelming vote over George Cassidy.

For many years the recognized political boss in the Silver State, as has been indicated, was Black Wallace, a genius at combination and a man known for his fidelity to his word. Becoming the legislative agent for the Southern Pacific Railroad, he managed the political affairs of that great corporation in Nevada, and for a time had absolute control. Since these are true confessions, I may set down the recollection of a pleasant conversation I had with Black Wallace when I was a member of the Nevada Legislature. He suggested affably, "Wells, why don't you run for Governor? We would support you. And we wouldn't insist that you make a pledge of any kind. All we ask is that you *be friendly.*" As gracefully as I could, I declined the gambit.

One of my closest friends in official circles was Dr. Simeon Bishop, to whom I have referred with affection in earlier pages. Often I was a guest at his home at Reno, on the spacious grounds of the new Nevada State Insane Asylum, of which he was Superintendent. He had a large family, as handsome as they were talented. Most of all, I was glad to see the eldest daughter—Miss Elvira Lorraine Bishop. Ella struck me as the finest girl I ever met.

When I went up from Carson on a visit, my brothers of the press inserted in their sheets this personal item: "Wells Drury was in Reno today, but was confined to the Asylum."

After our engagement, during which I was on an Eastern trip and she was in San Francisco, Ella and I were married, May 23rd, 1888. We left at once for our honeymoon beside the Golden Gate. I had definitely withdrawn from political life in Nevada, and in my new happiness was glad of the opportunity which presented itself, to enter the field of journalism again, in California.

CHAPTER THIRTY-FOUR

Borrasca

*7*he opposite of *Bonanza*, in the mining vocabulary inherited from the Mexicans, is *Borrasca*—the nadir of ill-fortune. The Comstock was destined to know all too well the meaning of the term.

In 1882 the bullion produced on the old Lode amounted to little more than $1,700,000; and it was then that a great flood of hot water was struck in the Exchequer, flooding many of the other mines.

Still, production continued, and deep mining was developed. In 1884 the Mexican-Ophir winze attained a depth of 3300 feet, the deepest of all the workings on the Comstock. In December of that year a diamond-drill tapped water in the bottom of the winze and the mine was flooded. There came some resumption of activity from time to time, and in 1888 the bullion produced on the Comstock had climbed back to $7,600,000—the largest annual output since the days of the Big Bonanza. This came from working the low-grade ores above the Sutro Tunnel level. Then the output fell off again.

The flagging fortunes of the Comstock mines had a disastrous effect on San Francisco throughout these years, as it had even in the late '70s, and that was one reason for the influence of Dennis Kearney, the Wat Tyler of the sand-lots.

The city by the Golden Gate owed much of its affluence,

though, to the bullion from the Comstock Lode. Lordly palaces on Nob Hill were built by the mining millionaires; the Palace and Fairmont hotels, and many banks and great office-buildings downtown were created by the wealth from that famous ledge in Nevada. For years, the Comstock kept the big San Francisco Stock Exchange boiling.

It is well to recall, too, that the Comstock put the Postal telegraph lines across the continent and cables under the oceans. And early in its history it gave Uncle Sam his piles of gold to buy ammunition and hardtack when the ark of the Nation was buffeted by the war-billows of the greatest rebellion ever known.

The gallantries of some of the Comstock millionaires and their scions have furnished the sensational court cases of San Francisco for three generations—but this is not a scandalous chronicle, and the recountal of suchlike mischief-making is to to be sought elsewhere.

James G. Fair's later years, we recall, were clouded by the family troubles which turned his thoughts upon business as an occupation for his mind. He had undertaken one voyage on the sea of politics and desired no more. To him the conduct of public affairs was not satisfying. He was an adherent of the doctrine that the citizen best fulfills his duty to the commonwealth who indulges a spirit of enterprise with a common-sense view to emolument.

After the decline of the Comstock, John Mackay spent most of his time in New York and on the continent of Europe. James C. Flood directed the activities of the Nevada Bank in San Francisco, though he was much abroad, too.

Their European associations involved Flood and Mackay in a deal to corner the world wheat market, through the Nevada Bank, at a time when war threatened between France and Ger-

many, in 1887, when Boulanger was "the man on horseback."
Only one on the inside could tell the real story of that deal in
wheat—it was worthy of the attention of my friend Frank
Norris. The facts have never been fully revealed, but it is
known that with the fall of Boulanger and the crash of the
market, Flood and Mackay lost millions of dollars on the speculation. James Fair, their old partner, came to the rescue of
the Nevada Bank, of which he became President. Flood died
in Europe the next year. Mackay was the last of the Bonanza
Four to pass away, living until 1902.

To complete the necrology: William S. O'Brien had died
in 1878; James G. Fair, in 1894. William Sharon died in 1885.
John P. Jones, for 30 years in the United States Senate, engaged
in the Panamint mining activities above Death Valley. While
these did not develop as expected, he prospered in real estate.
Aside from his eminence as a mining man and a statesman,
Senator Jones was a city builder, laying out Santa Monica, California, in 1875, on the old San Vicente Rancho. He died in
1912.

Adolph Sutro, who had come to America as a humble immigrant, became a multi-millionaire, honored as mayor by the
city which he made his home—San Francisco.

While the old Comstock Lode suffered *borrasca,* it is heartening to record that most of the magnates who derived their
wealth so largely from its development continued to prosper
through the years.

CHAPTER THIRTY-FIVE

So Passes the Glory

*A*fter the decline of the Big Bonanza on the Comstock, the diminished output of base ore at Eureka, the temporary eclipse of the White Pine region and the slump in the price of silver (that was before the discoveries at Goldfield, Tonopah and Manhattan) there was a general dispersal of the chosen spirits who had enlivened the camps and diggings of Nevada. Some of the old boys died there, but a majority of those brilliant fellows sought new fields to conquer, scattering in all directions. Butte, Montana; Leadville, Colorado; Tombstone, Arizona; Bodie, California—these mining-camps were on the rise at the time the Nevada camps were on the steep skids, and each welcomed a quota from the Comstock. San Francisco, always colorful, received its returning horde with open arms. It is of record that wherever the Comstockers went, they generally made good. A man who got his early lessons of life in the maelstrom of a Nevada camp and was able to keep his head above the tide, was equipped to succeed almost anywhere.

Virginia City now lies stricken and old—yet not dead. The mountainside which shook and echoed once with the stamps of a score of mills is silent. Some mines are worked sporadically, but without much profit. A few of the old-timers linger on, and C Street seeks pathetically to keep up the show, despite the grim staring ruins of the old brick Wells-Fargo Building [1] and

[1] The old Wells-Fargo Building was condemned, and is now demolished.

a host of other fallen-down structures. The churches stand staunch and unshaken.

Above, on the slopes of Mount Davidson, are rows of ramshackle wooden buildings—some of them four stories high at the back—leaning against each other in dissolute insecurity. A Washoe zephyr might huff and puff—and blow those tenements down like the houses of cards Ramon Montenegro used to build in the old Delta Saloon for the delectation of Needles, Sleepy and the other hangers-on.

Most of the houses which once clung to the slopes were torn down long ago, often board by board, and used as firewood.

Gold Hill has well-nigh vanished into the thin air of the sierra. Only six families dwell in "Slippery Gulch," where once thousands of miners milled around in the streets on Saturday nights. American Flat is almost deserted, Silver City is little more than a memory. Over to the north, about a score of miles away, is Reno—not much more than a hamlet when the Comstock was in its glory; now a populous, flourishing city.

Yet—who of the old-timers will call Virginia City a "ghost camp"? Here is a ghost hard to lay. Here burns an immortal flame, not to be quenched by all the water in the mines; a spirit which refuses to be buried even in the deepest workings in the heart of Mount Davidson.[1]

Not silver but gold may rejuvenate the old camp. The world's new demand for the yellow metal might bring life to Virginia City, even to Gold Hill. Whisperings of revival in the old mines come; mayhap these rumors are to attain reality.

The old-timers, be it known, never surrendered. With pathetic insistence they claimed always that the camp would come back; that the spot which had produced almost a billion

---

[1] In 1936 the Comstock Lode has enjoyed a revival. Production of the mines has averaged 1100 tons of ore daily, and a dozen mills have been in operation.

in bullion could not have been robbed of all is riches by mere groping processes. Untold treasure still reposes, they declare, within the warm heart of the mountain.

My old friend and true, Gilbert McMillan Ross, metallurgist and wizard of Comstock mining lore, points out that barely one-fifth of the Comstock Lode above the 1600-foot level has even been prospected—below that level, not one-tenth. Millions of tons of good ore may yet be worked from the croppings of the Lode, he and others believe. With modern methods and science, the Comstock once again may be restored as a great producer of the noble metals.

Such, at least, is the belief and fervent hope of most of the old-timers. I have not the slightest doubt, myself, that the metal will prove to be there, if only the new generation of miners has the nerve to look for it and the skill to find it.

Many of the grizzled veterans would like to go crowding back again to the greatest mining camp of them all. Others shake their heads, mindful of Joe Goodman's sad reflection:

> "I would not wish to see it now,
>   I choose to know it as I then did,
> With glorious light upon its brow
>   And all its features bright and splendid;
> Nor would I like that it should see
>   Me, gray and stooped, a mark for pity
> And learn that time had dealt with me
>   As hard as with Virginia City."

But not alone for the glint of the precious metals would the returning ones foregather, but to breathe once more the strange aromatic fragrance of the *artemisia*—for there is a subtle *Lure of the Sagebrush,* as Sam Davis wrote:

"Have you ever scented the sagebrush
  That mantles Nevada's plain?
If not, you have lived but half your life
  And that half lived in vain.

"You may loiter awhile in other lands,
  When something seems to call
And the lure of the sagebrush brings you back
  To hold you within its thrall."

FROM A COMSTOCK EDITOR'S SCRAP-BOOK

Here follow a few miscellaneous items, principally from Comstock newspapers, typical of the clippings in the collections of the author of this narrative. Many of the stories were written by him as part of the day's work. Throwing sidelights on various aspects of life in Virginia City and Gold Hill during the Big Bonanza era, they serve to illuminate passages in the text of this book.

(*In Gold Hill News, 22 August, 1876*)

TURBULENT

THE CITIZENS OF THE COMSTOCK MAKE A NIGHT OF IT.

Whisky, Fists and Pistols—Rows, Ructions and a General Howl—A Few of the Principal Disturbances.

Virginia and Gold Hill went on a jamboree last night. If a member of the International Peace Society had been on the Comstock last night he would have died of a broken heart. Donnybrook paled before the reign of riot that prevailed. Fists were shot from the shoulder with utter recklessness, and pistols came from hip-pockets with a frequency that causes one to marvel that the Coroner has not a pile of cadavers to sit upon to-day.

Just about dark a man named Christy and a friend engaged in a wrestle in the saloon at No. 62 South C street. John Clark thought the affair was serious and interposed. Then the war began. Pistols were drawn and it looked for a few moments as if a first-class fight was upon the cards. Chief of Police Lackey dashed into the crowd and arrested the three men.

A lively row occurred at the same saloon about 7 o'clock. Charles

Ryno and special officer Merrow became involved in a dispute which waxed warmer and warmer. Finally Ryno jerked out his pistol and thrust it into Merrow's face. Then Merrow pulled his gun and was going to bore a hole in the body of his antagonist, when special officer Bartlett rushed in with his revolver and threatened instant death to both if either dared to fire. This settled the matter and there were no arrests made.

Another disgraceful affair took place in the Delta Saloon about 3 o'clock this morning. About twenty men, some of them county officers, were engaged at the hour named in drinking whisky and talking politics. The disputants merged from politics into personalities. Bad names were bandied and over a dozen revolvers were drawn and held aloft. Officer Curby ran in and attempted to quell the disturbance and arrest the leaders. He was threatened with death and shouldered out of the saloon. Chief among those concerned in this outrage was an official whose duty it is to prosecute those who offend against the laws of the State. It is probable that officer Curby will to-day cause the arrest of the principal offenders.

At the St. Louis Brewery, on South C street, there was a lively little mill about 9 o'clock. One Billers, keeper of the Black Hills Saloon, went into the Brewery (which is not a brewery, but a beer saloon), and began abusing the proprietor because of certain business matters. St. Louis thereupon gave it to the Black Hills between the eyes, and the B. H. lay down and was carried home.

During the evening Assessor Gracey had an unpleasant set-to with a political opponent. About midnight a man in a saloon on North C street announced himself as the Secretary of the Crescents, and the "boys" got hold of him and painted his face black. Some of his friends objected, and a fight ensued. Black eyes and hot stomachs prevail on the Comstock to-day.

In Gold Hill things got along a little smoother, although there were several little personal collisions and considerable quarreling. The most prominent disturber of the peace was an officer chosen by the citizens to preserve the peace, especially on such occasions. He behaved in a very disgraceful, reprehensible manner. We do not care to show him up just now, as he did that himself pretty well last evening, but may refer to the matter again.

A LIVELY CORNER

(*In Gold Hill News, 24 March, 1877*)

The central point of Virginia is at the intersection of C and Union streets. That is where C street is divided, the International Hotel being No. 1 North C street, and the Sawdust Corner saloon being No. 1 South C street. All the other streets running north and south are divided and numbered in the same way. This is only an initial or starting point, but is probably the liveliest locality on the Comstock. First, on the northwest corner, towering above the surrounding buildings, is the International Hotel, five stories high. The upper portion is being fitted up as a first-class boarding and lodging establishment, while the ground floor is devoted to saloons and eating-houses. On the northeast corner stands the Fredrick House, an extensive arrangement with hundreds of furnished rooms to let. In the basement is the Alhambra Theater. The southwest corner is occupied by the Sawdust Corner saloon, with the Delta close at hand. Both these places are old time landmarks. The Fredericksburg and Milwaukie saloons monopolize the southeast corner. These are the two most famous beer houses on the Comstock. Rooms over these saloons are being fitted up, and within the next few weeks the royal beast will make his lair within those precincts. The main traffic of Virginia centers at this crossing, and it will probably remain as it has long been—the leading place of interest of the Mount Davidson village.

AMUSEMENTS

(*In Gold Hill News, 7 December, 1876*)

The Comstock is an improving place to live on. Both Gold Hill and Virginia are well supplied with schools, and there is no lack of churches. We have more saloons to the population than any place in the country. Every Sunday when there is a show in town we have a matinee and an evening performance. On the Sabbath, also, we are entertained with a horse-race or a fight between a bulldog and a wildcat. Every month or so the prize-fighters favor us with a mill, which we all go to see and then indict the fighters, as a sort of concession to the puritanical element. It is merely a form, however, as we generally take care that our favorite bruisers have bail, and it would be hard to find a jury of generous Comstockers who would convict them. Every Saturday night small boys parade up and down the principal street of Virginia, carrying transparencies which inform our sport-loving people where cock-fighting may be enjoyed. Faro, keno, chuck-a-luck and roulette may be found in every second saloon, and a special policeman, wearing his star, frequently conducts the game. Taking everything into consideration, there are few pleasanter places to live than on the Comstock. Our favorite recreations are all so delightfully open and above board, too. In the effete Eastern States a man would be sent to jail for doing those things which serve to daily and nightly amuse the Nevada gentleman. Thus it is seen how the mind broadens in its views as it travels West.

CAPTAIN JACK—THE POET SCOUT

(In San Francisco Alta California)

VIRGINIA CITY, June 29, 1877—At Buffalo Bill's benefit to-night, "The Red Right Hand; or, The First Scalp for Custer" was given. In the last act Captain Jack Crawford came on the stage, mounted in the character of Yellow Hand. At his entrance he and Buffalo Bill, also mounted, began firing at close range. Suddenly Captain Jack fell from his horse. He recovered himself, and was engaging in a hand-to-hand conflict, when blood was noticed streaming down his tights. Miss Graville, who was seated in the stage box, fainted. The curtain was suddenly lowered. It was ascertained that Captain Jack, in drawing his revolver, accidentally shot himself in the groin, the wad inflicting a painful wound, which bled freely. After being taken to his room he was found to be out of danger, though suffering considerably.

(*The New York* Herald, *in printing this dispatch, added: "Captain Jack, instead of being scalped, as in the above-mentioned drama, heroically killed and scalped a tall Cheyenne warrior at the Silver Buttes."*)

WILDCAT FIGHT

(*In Gold Hill News, 5 November, 1878*)

There was a fight advertised to come off at the Alhambra Theater Sunday afternoon between an Eastern fighting bulldog named Turk and a 42-pound wildcat, a vicious brute, for $100 a side—that is, the cat and dog to fight for their lives and men bet $100 a side on the result. The fight was to be followed by a grand olio on the stage. It was an immense bill, and it drew.

In due time the cat was introduced upon the stage and was immediately followed by Turk; but at the first kiss of the dog, the cat took to the audience, and the olio instead of being performed by the troupe, was done by the spectators, to tooth and toenail accompaniment. The first bound of the cat took it upon the piano of the orchestra. The pawer of ivory left the swelling strain unfinished and turned a back handspring. The next leap of the "varmint" was at the contrabass, and both player and instrument went down instanter with broken heads. The cat lingered lovingly a moment among the strings as if to test their quality, and then sprang out among the audience.

Then began an olio in dead earnest, but not the one advertised, although the fight was over. It consisted of grand and lofty tumbling, leapfrog, and such-like feats of dexterity, all having a single object—to amuse the audience by a glimpse of sunlight out-of-doors and under the free light of heaven once more. Time: shortest on record—1:59. Everything went off well, especially the audience. The cat was found a few moments later looking out of one of the boxes and waiting for an encore.

NEEDLES, THE TRAGEDIAN

(*In Gold Hill News, 24 March, 1879*)

Everybody hereabout knows "Needles," or has heard or read of him, and none but will feel sad to read the following accurate sketch of him as given by the Truckee *Republican* of the 22nd instant:

"Needles, better known as the Sagebrush Tragedian, has been registered at most of the saloons on Front Street. He is a genius on a small scale; he is also a 'lusher' on a large scale. When sober he is an actor of considerable merit, but, unfortunately he does not remain in that condition more than a few days consecutively. Hence his engagements are short and his drunks long. He spends most of his time in traveling from place to place. A saloon is his favorite haunt. He entertains the multitude by declamations, recitations and character sketches, humorous and grave. At one time his auditors will be convulsed with laughter; at another they will be moved to tears by his really wonderful elocution. It is all the same to Needles, and ends by his getting gloriously drunk. Nature made him a genius; his social disposition made him a tippler. Vice has triumphed, and the once gifted man is now a human wreck."

Needles called at the *News* office this afternoon, and levied an assessment of 50 cents. His nose was skinned, his face black with smoke and dirt, and his entire wardrobe in a most deplorable condition. As the tragedian's name does not appear among the arrivals, it is fair to presume that the great man hoofed it over the grade, or that he made his way hither by means of the friendly but dangerous brake-bar.

(An advertisement in the Carson Appeal, 29 May, 1875. Abridged.)

QUEEN'S ELEGANT MORAL CIRCUS

Montgomery Queen's Caravan, Circus and Menagerie—Brilliant ovation, grand centralization of genius, concentration of merit, monopoly of equestrian stars, avalanche of attractions, great double circus troupe—under one mammoth pavilion.

THE BEST SHOW ON EARTH

The royal family of arenic monarchs—Vast assemblage of undisputed artists. The world-wide riding celebrities Mr. Jas. Robinson and Mr. Chas. W. Fish—each fresh from his European and American triumphs—Contesting Champions: Mr. Chas. W. Fish, who has been riding in Europe for the past two years, comes to America to dispute with Mr. Jas. Robinson, the great bareback champion of worldwide celebrity. Mr. Fish has traveled 8000 consecutive miles with his horses to meet Mr. Robinson. Mr. Fish is the only equestrian who has ever dared to accept Mr. Robinson's challenge to ride for $10,000. . . . Mr. Fish, the unparalleled principal backward back and forward feet to feet somersaults and trick rider, having been recently declared champion rider of England, Prussia, Austria and Russia, returns to America to contest his superiority in the New World.

Miss Molly Brown, the pre-eminent princess of arenic celebrities, the only recognized female somersault rider on the face of the globe! The largest and strongest troupe of finished, high-toned and high-salaried Artists!

HUNTING A MURDERER

(In Gold Hill News, 26 January, 1877)

Quite a number of men are out hunting for Graham, the murderer of Elholm, in Six-mile Canyon. This zeal to catch a criminal is inspired by the reward promised for his capture. The county offers $300, and $200 will be given from the estate of the deceased.

A CHEERFUL MORNING

(*In Gold Hill News, 26 January, 1877*)

One morning not very long ago a *News* reporter was in the District Court-room when a man was sentenced to be hanged for murder. When that business was over another man was arraigned for murder, and another for an attempt at the same crime. As the reporter stepped to the door to ask the Sheriff where and how another man was to be executed, the official interrupted him by saying there was a first-class item down in Six-mile Canyon—another man had been killed there that morning. Western life may be marked by a little roughness, but there is something invigorating about it, after all. It's impossible for one to suffer from *ennui* when the pistol is perpetually popping.

(NOTE: This *News* reporter was Wells Drury.)

FRISBIE'S BAR—CARSON

(*In Carson Appeal, 21 July, 1875*)

Lyman Frisbie has just received an invoice of the best potables that ever were concocted for the stimulation and preservation of the human economy. The whisky is of the most humanizing and exalting character; the brandy is of the choicest flavor and most amiable propensities; the gin possesses those truly alternative principles which gin of the correct kind of motives is known to contain; the rum is of the quality which none but the most reckless of families are willing to be without; and as to the wines and ales,

A SALOON SHOOTING

(In Gold Hill News, 2 January, 1877)

This morning about half-past 5 o'clock a dreadful tragedy occurred at the Delta Saloon, C street, Virginia. One man met his death and another received a mortal wound. The men who suffered were Thomas Hughes and Richard Paddock. Hughes lies dead at the morgue and before this meets the eye of the reader Paddock will, in all probability, have ceased to live. The shooting which caused the death of Hughes and the mortal wounding of Paddock is not easily explained. Diligent inquiry on the part of the *News'* reporter develops the following facts: At the time above stated some Cornishmen were singing a drinking song in the Delta. A young man present objected to the sentiment expressed in the song, which seemed to be lacking in admiration of the Irish. This gave rise to words. All were drunk and a lively row was soon in progress. Officer McDonald hearing the noise ran in, as his duty demanded. The first man he met in the saloon happened to be Tom Hughes. The policeman commanded him to surrender. Hughes refused and Paddock, who was sitting behind the bar, ran out to quell the disturbance. Hughes was unruly and flourished his pistol in a threatening way and declared with the usual profanity that no policeman on the force could take him to jail. The officer was determined and shaking off the half tipsy peace-makers who crowded round him made at his man.

Hughes raised the revolver, and as a policeman came toward him brought the weapon down upon his head, making a long, ugly gash. It is supposed by the excited persons present at the time that the pistol, coming in contact with the officer's skull, went off and the ball crashed through the left temple of Paddock. Be that as it may, the man fell to the floor and a deadly fight began between Hughes and McDonald over the insensible body. Both men had cocked revolvers in their hands and were determined to hold their ground. Seven shots were fired and when the din ceased Hughes was lying beside Paddock with three shots in his body. One grazed

the right wrist and went in above the collar bone. Two others left
a couple of dark, red spots over the heart. Paddock, still alive, was
carried to the keno room and laid upon the table, while surgical
aid was sent for.

Hughes was dead, and was allowed to lie where he fell, for a
time. Both men were in the prime of life, neither being more than
forty years of age, and each had a wife and children. The wife of
Paddock, clutching a child by the hand, made her way through the
rough crowd which had collected, and the scene of grief which
followed in the gambling-room was too terrible to be described.

After the shooting, officer McDonald was arrested by Captain
Byrne and taken to the city jail. The ugly scalp wound inflicted by
Hughes' pistol had partly deprived him of consciousness.

The cause of the row is not hard to get at. A few nights ago a
man named Alex. Nixon, a prize-fighter, kicked up a rumpus in
the cock-pit owned and conducted by Hughes and Paddock. In
the struggle Nixon bit the finger of an officer severely, kicked
another in the chin and blacked the eye of a third. When the case
came into Court it was treated lightly and the police felt that they
could expect no adequate protection from the law. The officers
generally expressed the determination to defend themselves thereafter against ruffians in the most effective way possible. McDonald
happened to be the first whose courage was put to the test and he
did not hesitate to meet desperate men with desperate measures.

Hughes four years ago was elected Constable of the First Precinct
in Virginia, and filled the office worthily for two years. He was a
strong-headed, courageous fellow, without a particle of fear, and
died as all who knew him predicted he would. Paddock figured
in many shooting scrapes during the wild, early days on the Comstock, and was known as a man who would rather look down the
barrel of a gun than waste wind. He seems to have got his mortal
wound in going to the defense of a friend and partner. Neither of
the men were bad. They were merely specimens of the rough and
tumble men produced by frontier life. But for recent events which
have forced the police to become walking arsenals, neither of these
hard-fisted fellows would be dead. Both had worked for years
here and in California.

During the melee special officer Bartlett got a stray shot in the leg, and "Old Dave," the porter of the saloon, grieves over a clean cut in his breeches. Coroner Hodges will hold an inquest, which will, no doubt, develop all the particulars of the tragical affair.

A SHERIFF'S CIRCULAR—FOR RECAPTURE OF JAIL-BREAKERS

(In Gold Hill News, 9 December, 1879)

Following circulars have been sent all over the Coast:

Sheriff's Office,
Storey County, Nevada
Charles Williamson, Sheriff

The following described prisoners escaped from the Storey County Jail on the evening of Sunday, November 30, 1879:

"Red Mike"—Under indictment for murder. He is a native of Ireland; is about 5 feet 5½ inches high; about 35 years old; sandy, almost red hair and whiskers; red face; had short whiskers on chin; good, high, strong forehead; a restless blue eye—looks away as soon as you look at him; rather quick of speech; quite solid looking, without extra flesh, and wore, when he broke out of jail, a reddish or brown suit (overalls and shirt) of canvas. I will give $100 for him in any shape you may bring him. His real name is William or Billy Langan.

Mark Brown—Under indictment for horse-stealing. He is a young man about 23 or 24 years of age; decidedly good-looking, and of a rather cheerful disposition; quite social in his bearing; when he left, was smooth shaved; had on a colored calico shirt, light brown pants, shoes with buckles on them, long dark-colored overcoat; is about 5 feet 10 or 11 inches high; is a natural rider, and falls easily into the business of vaquero; dark brown hair and good features generally; quite stylish in make up, but easily comes down to the bearing of a vaquero and is liable at any time to be found with a "horse for sale"; if he don't happen to have one with him, he can always bring you one from his ranch; can't possibly resist the offer to buy a horse from him. Will pay the same reward for him as for Red Mike.

Lafferty, alias Rosenbaugh—About 5 feet 5 inches in height; rather pale; an inveterate opium smoker; rather good looking; about 25 years old; heavy eyebrows; smooth face; light moustache. Will pay ten dollars for him—he is not worth that.

Kline and Schofield went with them (these two and Rosenbaugh are in for housebreaking). Kline is a German, about 5 feet 5½ or 6 inches high; very heavy set; large head; has a defect in one eye. Schofield is a small man; rather dark complexioned; smooth face. We will pay the same reward for these last two as for Lafferty, but don't care much for them; they will naturally fall back into our hands—can't help it.

C. WILLIAMSON,
Sheriff of Storey County.

By M. J. McCutchan,
Deputy Sheriff.

---

*(In San Francisco Stock Report—quoted in Gold Hill News,
5 April, 1878)*

THAT JOURNALISTIC MILL

BY DANIEL O'CONNELL

They met upon the stony street,
Mount Davidson looked down
Upon those doughty champions,
And all the eager town,
With pale lips, clustered round them
In admiration still
Of bold McCarthy's martial front,
O'Brien's might and will.

Like lightning from a thunder cloud,
Like torrent from a hill,
Like crash of avalanche, they closed,
All panting for the mill.
O'Brien's peeper, blue before,
Is sombre now as night;
Another paste and still one more;
His bugle's now as big as four;
And drips and drips with awful gore,
The first fruits of the fight.

Hath seen a locomotive
Dash headlong down the line,
When careless switchman swung not
The red flag, danger's sign?
So rushed the bold McCarthy;
So sped his fearful fist;
O'Brien's down, his battered crown
The trodden dust has kissed.

Ho! maidens of Virginia!
Ho! grimy working men!
Lift up the battered leader;
The champion of the Pen
Has conquered; Washoe matrons
To your sons the story tell,
How McCarthy bold, in the days of old,
Gave the great O'Brien hell.

EDITORS AS FAIR GAME

(Ambrose Bierce, in his column, "Prattle," in The Argonaut, San Francisco, 3 August, 1878)

One day last week a journalist of this city was severely beaten for something—I do not know what—that had appeared in a newspaper with which he is connected. . . . Without reference to this particular case, I beg leave to state, in the character of an expert who has a practical experience with both methods of redress, that it is more agreeable to a journalist to be shot than beaten. . . . There is no recorded instance of punishment for shooting a newspaper man. The restrictions of the game law do not apply to this class of game. The newspaper man is a bird that is always in season; sportsmen and pot-hunter alike may with assured impunity crack his bones with a bullet, or fill his skin with buckshot, compiling his carcass in a bag and exposing it for sale. I am quite serious in the statement that nobody in the United States has ever been hanged for killing a journalist; public opinion will not permit it. . . . Although the American public will not deny itself the pleasing pageant of some blameless citizen accomplishing serpentine contortions under the editorial pen, neither will it inhibit the flight of the blithe bullet through the editorial body.

"THE SAZERAC LYING CLUB"

(In Gold Hill News, 15 March, 1878)

Fred Hart's New Book, "The Sazerac Lying Club," is a veritable record of the sayings and doings of that peculiarly Nevadan Club, and full of incidents and gorgeous lies to suit all tastes. It will be sold at a price involving a loss to the publishers on every copy. Following remarks from the introduction will give our readers some idea of the scope and aim of the work:

"Polite lying, as we all know, is a gentlemanly accomplishment, and is moreover—when successful—decidedly meritorious. It stimulates the mental faculties, varnishes unpleasant facts, promotes friendship and lubricates business. Besides, there is money in it, and that is sufficient to make it commendable, and surround it with a halo of respectability.

"Many prominent persons have gained colossal fortunes by lying. It is the lawyer's principal capital, the editor's chief support, the politician's trade, the diplomatist's trump card, and the monarch's mask. It is scattered in human nature like gold in quartz; in some instances as specks on the surface, and in others as great bonanzas, deep down in the recesses of the heart, and it is almost as universal as gold.

"The Sazerac Lying Club is distinctly devoted to moral lies. It does not treat of the lies of politicians, stock brokers, newspaper men, authors, and others who lie for money, and all such wickedness has been carefully excluded from its pages. Only those lies have been introduced which amuse, instruct and elevate, and lift the fancy from the cold region of facts to the high empyrean of wit and humor.

"It is a record of lies told in the Sazerac Lying Club, whose object, as its name implies, was lying.

"Every lie is true, and that is the strongest recommendation that can be offered."

A TRAMP PRINTER

(In Gold Hill News, 12 September, 1876)

Hazlitt, the "Pilgrim," is in town. The Pilgrim is known in every printing office in the United States and comes here from Washington Territory. It is his habit to work for a few days and then start off on his travels again. Tilden, reform and whisky occupy the Pilgrim's intellect at present.

BIG JACK DAVIS—BANDIT

(From Wells, Fargo & Co.'s Express—"Robbers' Record")

DAVIS, A. J.—alias "Big Jack Davis."
Robbed Overland Express train from San Francisco to Ogden, near Verdi, November 6th, 1870, in company with Squires, Cockrill, Chapman, Parsons, Jones and Gilchrist.

Prior to this train robbery, Davis, Squires, and Cockrill had robbed W. F. & Co.'s Express three times on stages between Reno and Virginia City, Nevada.

Received at Nevada State Prison, December 25, 1870. No. of commitment, ——. Crime, robbery. Term, 10 years.

Pardoned February 16, 1875.

Was killed September 3, 1877, by W. F. & Co.'s guards—Jimmy Brown and Eugene Blair—while attempting to rob the Express on stage between Eureka and Tybo, in company with Bob Hamilton, Bill Hamilton, and Thomas Lauria, accessory. Messenger Jimmy Brown was shot through the leg.

MILTON SHARP—BANDIT

(From Wells, Fargo & Co.'s Express—"Robbers' Record")

SHARP, M. A.

Nativity, Missouri; County, Esmeralda; Age, 39 years; Occupation, Laborer; Height, 5 feet 6 inches; Complexion, Dark; Color of eyes, Dark Brown; Color of hair, Dark Brown. Weight, 161 pounds, large Roman nose, scar over right eye, scar on back of head, scar across right forearm, scar on first finger of right hand, scar on back of neck, two scars on right knee-cap; does not smoke, chew, swear, nor gamble.

Robbed W. F. & Co.'s Express on stage from Forest Hill to Auburn, May 15, 1880, with W. C. Jones, alias Frank Dow.

Robbed W. F. & Co.'s Express on stage from Carson City to Bodie, June 8, 1880, with Jones, alias Dow.

Robbed W. F. & Co.'s Express on stage from Carson to Bodie, June 15, 1880, with Jones, alias Dow.

Robbed W. F. & Co.'s Express on stage from Auburn to Forest Hill, August 6, 1880, with Jones.

Robbed W. F. & Co.'s Express on stage from Carson City to Bodie, September 4, 1880, in company with Jones.

Robbed W. F. & Co.'s Express on stage from Bodie to Carson the morning of September 5th. At time of halting the stage Jones fired two shots, killing one of the stage horses. Mike Tovey, W. F. & Co.'s guard, then fired, killing Jones. Sharp then fired, seriously wounding Tovey in the right arm. Tovey being disabled, started for a neighboring farm-house to have his arm dressed, when Sharp returned to the stage, demanded the box from the driver, and robbed it of $700, while Jones was lying dead in the road, and the stage being detained by the dead horse still attached to the team.

On the 30th of October, 1880, was convicted of the robbery of the 4th of September.

Escaped from the Aurora jail, November 2, 1880.

Recaptured and returned to Aurora jail, November 8, 1880.

Received at Nevada State Prison, November 12, 1880. No. of commitment, 158. Crime, robbery; term, 20 years.

(EDITOR'S NOTE: *Milton A. Sharp escaped from the Nevada State Prison at Carson City on August 15, 1889.*)

OLD HANGTOWN

BY WELLS DRURY

The early approach to the Comstock mines from California led "over the hill" from Placerville. It was to this lively mining-town that some of the first ore from the Ophir diggings was taken for assay; and on the revelation of its richness "the Washoe rush" was on, many of the first treasure-seekers lighting out from the bars and ravines of Eldorado County, of which Placerville is the seat of justice. Some of the early justice was meted out in summary fashion, giving the camp in its pristine glory the name of Hangtown. On the original Hang Tree several miscreants were strung up in 1849; and there were other swift and sartain executions by Vigilantes to lend color to the name, which however was soon replaced by the present official appellation.

Across Johnson's Pass above Placerville was opened a highway into Nevada, soon developed into a route of primary importance.

Hank Monk and the other gallant stage-drivers rolled their coaches along this road. Great freight-wagons, heavily laden with supplies and machinery, toiled eastward over the route; cargoes of high-grade ore came westward, before the establishment of mills in Nevada. Hardy prospectors trudged across on foot, their blankets on their backs. During the brief life of the Pony Express, the riders spurred from Sacramento through Placerville to Carson City; and over this route in the depths of winter Fred Bishop and Snowshoe Thompson carried the mail. After the completion of the transcontinental railroad in 1869, Placerville was not linked so closely with the Comstock, but it always kept a warm spot in its heart for its Nevada neighbor beyond the range.

Although I have been often in Hangtown, I never knew it so well as when I visited the old camp on pilgrimage with John M. Studebaker on an April day in 1912, almost sixty years after he had laid there the foundation of his fortune. Studebaker, then the head of the great corporation at South Bend, Indiana, which bore his family name, went up from San Francisco with a handful of old Hang-towners—Stephen T. Gage, Daniel W. Earl, Alexander P. Murgotten, William Bell and Charles H. Townsend—and I was privileged to accompany them and hear their exchange of stories.

Nothing that happened less than fifty years ago was permitted as a topic of conversation, and they did not spare one another in recalling incidents grotesque or tragic, which punctuated the early history of the Golden State, and in which one or more of their number bore part.

They called one another by their first names—John, Steve, Dan, Aleck, Bill and Charley—with the easy familiarity of boys let loose from school. It was genuine, this comradeship, because the absolute equality of pioneer days and customs never can be obliterated.

The journey to Sacramento, by river steamer, enabled them to reminisce to the full. Billy Bell musingly remarked that the fare from San Francisco to Sacramento by steamer in the early '50s used to be an ounce of gold (worth about $16) except when there was opposition, and then it might go down to 25 cents—"two-bits."

Driving from Sacramento we passed Folsom and continued into the lower Sierra. The road from Folsom to Placerville passes through a country which so far as pertains to the forest was then as primitive in appearance as if fresh from the creative forces. The road-bed was hard and smooth, reminiscent of the era when Charley McClane was division superintendent of the Pioneer Stage Line, and such wizard drivers as Hank Monk, Curly Bill Garhart, Newt Spencer, Billy Hodges, Big Jake, Baldy Green and others of that class guided their teams of four or six wild broncos along these grades. The hand of man has made but little impression on the trees that line the highway. They are the same as when they sheltered Murietta and Vasquez and other bandits, lying in wait to rob plethoric miners bearing gold dust from the diggings, or to pillage a Wells-Fargo treasure-box. This road once teemed with thousands of emigrants. Eating-houses, stables for teamsters and stage-stations were numerous. In the drive through this mountainous region the fleet-footed jack-rabbit and the crested quail were frequently seen darting across the road. Noisy bluejays, and blackbirds with cardinal chevrons on their wings, and woodpeckers pecking on the old barn door, were in evidence.

When we arrived in Placerville, before Studebaker would sit down to the banquet in honor of his return he insisted on seeing some of the old places he knew. He saw not many. Hangtown was swept by fire while he was there in the early days; it was almost destroyed again many years after he left. But the old-timers who rode alongside of him pointed out the place where he went to work for Joe Hinds to make wheelbarrows for $10 apiece.

Everybody had a nickname in the halcyon days, and Studebaker's was "Wheelbarrow John," because of his fame in producing a miner's wheelbarrow after his own design, which proved superior to all others in that district. But by his own admission his first productions were crude affairs.

Studebaker retraced the steps which in days of yore led to the scene of his daily toil. He visited the old shop where with such rude implements as the place afforded he had worked at his trade. He shook hands with the bronzed and bearded men bending over the anvils and the benches, saying that he took delight in watching the work go on as it did under his personal guidance so many years ago and marveled that there was so little change. The same old wagons, it almost seemed, were standing in front to be mended, the same old tools, some of which possibly he had beaten into shape at this primitive forge, were in the racks above the battered old anvil.

"Boys, I never did better work in my life than I did in this shop," was his parting remark. A rusty hammer, which he recognized as one used by him for years, and which he had fashioned for a particular purpose out of a bar of steel, was handed to him, and he bore it away for a memento. Specimens of gold quartz and placer dust and nuggets were presented to Studebaker as souvenirs, but they were not as highly prized as was this ancient hammer.

Replying to a question he said: "So you would like to know what prompts me to make this trip to Old Hangtown, would you? Well, this may be the last time that I shall have a chance to see these old boys, and I just wanted to meet them around the table once more. Sentiment? Yes, it must be sentiment, or something of that kind, that makes me do this. You may call this sentiment a grateful remembrance of the place where I made my stake with which to begin business for myself. So I want to go back to the old stamping-ground for a day and a night, and indulge in a last look at the place where my early friendships were formed. I want to clasp hands with companions who knew me then, and who have been my friends through all these years. Our lives have led us far apart, but I have never forgotten them, and it is a pleasure to think that they have not forgotten me."

As our automobile drew up at the old Ohio House, Studebaker spied a familiar face at once in the crowd of grizzled men on the wooden porch. "Hello, Newt, you around here yet?" he called in salutation.

"Yes, I'm here yet," answered Newton Spencer in his Missouri drawl, "but they call me Jedge now, John Studebaker. Ye see, I'm the Justice of the Peace."

"Huh! what did you ever know about law when you and Hank Monk used to stop in the road and decide with your fists which of your stages was going to back up to let the other pass?" asked Studebaker in jocular tone.

All the pioneers in Studebaker's party had been members of the old Confidence Engine Company of Hangtown, and they all remembered when the Orleans Hotel was burned. McKean Buchanan was playing "Richelieu" that night, and he rushed from the stage with his cardinal's robes flowing in the wind and seizing the pump-bar of the old hand-engine helped the firemen to throw water on the blazing building.

The Lee & Marshall circus was the topic which brought up a vast number of recollections. Townsend recalled that several men who afterwards became prominent in public affairs made their first appearance with that prodigious aggregation of world-wonders.

The famous prizefighter, Yankee Sullivan, lived in Hangtown for a space. "Together with a lot of other Hangtown boys, I began to take boxing lessons from Yankee Sullivan at a dollar a lesson," said Studebaker, "and the first time I put on the gloves he told me to hit him right on the nose as hard as I could. I thought he meant it, so I let out my fist with all my strength. What happened was that my fist never touched his nose, but, Yankee Sullivan style, his fist touched mine, which made me turn a double somersault and see stars in the daytime. I never took another lesson. Sullivan was a tough, and when he got to San Francisco and was taken into custody he imagined the Vigilantes were going to string him up, and he cut the main artery in his arm and bled to death."

Murgotten was called on to tell about the preacher who took a notion to strike out for other diggings and made a raise in an ingenious manner. "Pass me a slug and I'll play you a trick the devil never will," said the minister accosting a group of gamblers. Without a moment's hesitation the gold was handed out and the recipient was about to retire, when he was halted. "Here, tell us about that trick which you say you will play us and the devil never will," insisted one of the contributors. "I'll leave you," was the retort, and the jest was so thoroughly appreciated that the get-away stake was doubled.

There was a lot of gossip about the "big fire" of July 6th, 1856, when Steve Gage saved a printing press by picking it up and carrying it out and throwing it into Hangtown Creek, from which resting place four men were required to rescue it. Studebaker added, "Yes, boys, I was here in the fire of 1856. You will remember that we had to abandon the old hand fire-engine in the street, and we took to the hillside, I running for dear life to reach our little shop with our home and all our belongings in the back end, above Stony Point. When I got there the fire was also there. I got hold of my old trunk, which contained all my wardrobe, trinkets, relics and some gold specimens. I started up the hill with my treasure, but had to abandon it on account of the great heat. After the fire the only things left were the gold specimens and the clothes on my back. But nobody seemed to be discouraged, and none were shedding tears. We were right cheerful with our campfires on the hillside, cooking our grub over the coals, and then taking our night's slumber in our blankets under a manzanita bush or a pine tree. A new town went up like magic."

"I remember seeing you, Steve, throwing the diamond hitch over a buckskin pack-mule," reminisced Townsend.

"That's no lie," said Gage, "and I can throw the diamond yet. I had as fine a train of pack-mules as ever crossed the grade. I bought those mules at Marysville for $5000 cash, in the winter of '59 and '60, when the Comstock Lode was drawing thousands of people that way. It was hard work but it paid. In 83 days I cleared $10,400 in twenty-dollar pieces, packing freight to Virginia City.

"The great Comstock Lode, uncovered in the summer of 1859, immediately attracted a throng from California. They wintered in Virginia City, and early in the season all the stores ran short of provisions, including whisky, so freight prices went ballooning. Packers got whatever they felt like charging for all the goods they could get over the snow-blocked trails. I frequently met Snowshoe Thompson, the famous mail-carrier, on the road between Hangtown and the Comstock."

The legend of how Strawberry Valley got its name came up for discussion as usual. Hank Monk always insisted that the name was derived from the keeper of a way station. "That son of a buzzard," drawled Hank, "used to steal the oats and barley from the horses of the teamsters, and put straw in place of the grain, so we all called him 'Straw' Berry, which stuck to the station; and that's how Strawberry Valley got its name."

"No such thing," Gage declared. "I was there long before Hank Monk, and saw the strawberries growing on the spot where the station was afterwards built. The house was right in the midst of the strawberry patch, and that was why it was called Strawberry Valley."

Like everybody in those days, these six pioneers worked placer claims. Studebaker said his first claim was 25 x 25 feet in size, and he did fairly well. He said that he still had in his possession $700 worth of the coarse gold taken by him out of the American River, near Hangtown.

Gage's claim was 16 x 16 feet in size, and proved profitable. "Not all my mining ventures were satisfactory," Gage admitted. "There were months when I didn't make expenses. The best I did was to take out $50 a day for six weeks. The local regulations made by the miners were the supreme law of the land, and from them there was no appeal. Apparently such a thing was never thought of by anybody. Tenure of claims depended on actual occupation and use. The specific rules differed in the different districts. If a miner left his claim for the time provided for in the rules of his district he lost all right and title to it. He could sell his right, but if a claim was left without any person in possession it could be taken up by the next man who in good faith went to work on it, as actual use of the land was absolutely necessary. It could not be held idle. But woe betide the man who tried to jump a claim legally held by another. Claim-jumpers were decidedly unpopular, and according to my impression they were few and far between. The best laws for gold mining in the world grew out of the miners' rules in California, just as the laws governing silver mining were developed from the regulations of the Nevada miners in regard to the working of the ledges in that State."

That was a great blowout, that banquet in the dining-room of the Ohio House in honor of "Wheelbarrow John" Studebaker. The "chuck list" included such items as Chili Gulch Rib-Warmer, Sluice-Box Tailings flavored with Chicken, Indian Diggins Spuds, Tertiary Moisture, Slab of Cow from the States, Bandana Fries with Bug-juice, Lady Canyon Chicken (Hangtown dressed), Shirt-Tail Bend Peas, Dead Man's Ravine Asparagus, Cemented Gravel *a la* Emigrant Jane, Assorted Nuggets, Amalgam Cheese, Riffle Crackers, Mahala's Delight *en tasse,* Hard Pan Smokes and Butcher Brown Fizz-Water—champagne, no less! for grizzled miners some of whom had not smacked their lips over fizz-water for half a century.

"It was nearly sixty years ago," Studebaker, in reminiscent mood, told the crowd, "that a healthy, robust lad of 19 years arrived here. He came of good old Pennsylvania stock, inheriting from his father and mother a sound body and a willingness to do his work—whatever it might be—to the best of his ability. He came with a determination to work out his own destiny. That youngster was myself.

"The first wagon I ever made was used in the company with which I came across the plains. I did the woodwork and my brother ironed it, and I gave it to the company for permission to accompany them to California. We were more than five months on the road, and landed in California right up here on this square in August, 1853, and I had but fifty cents in my pocket. Although that was my only earthly possession my spirit was not daunted, for we were all led to believe that all we had to do was to go out on the morrow and dig all the gold that the heart could desire. How many of us found out that this was not true!

"Of course a big crowd gathered around us, and while we were trying to get them to talk about the gold mines they insisted on asking questions about what had happened in the States since they had heard from their friends. While the hubbub was going on a man came up and asked if there was a wagonmaker in the crowd of new arrivals. They pointed me out and he asked: 'Are you a wagonmaker?'

" 'Yes sir,' I answered, as big as life, with my fifty-cent piece in my pocket. The man was Joe Hinds, whom all knew and respected. He offered me a job in his shop, but I replied that I came to California to mine for gold, and that I had never thought of taking any other kind of a job. Hinds turned on his heel and walked off—he was a man of few words.

"After he was gone a man whom I afterwards found out was Dr. Worthem, stepped up and very politely said: 'Will you let me give you a little advice, young man? I said yes, and he continued: 'Take that job and take it quick.'

"His manner impressed me. He said that there would be plenty of time to dig gold, which was not always a sure thing, and that the job just offered me was a mighty fine chance for a stranger. I thought it was a pretty good idea, and as there were four of us youngsters who had come together, and all of us were broke, I decided to go to work for the wagon-maker if he would take me. I followed Hinds to his shop. It was not above Stony Point, I remember, and was a log house, with the back wall made by digging into the hill. There were coffee-sack bunks in which we slept, and in the middle of the room was a sheet-iron stove on which the cooking was done.

"I explained that I had decided to see what he wanted me to do, and he said he wanted me to make wheelbarrows for the miners. He wanted twenty-five and would pay me $10 apiece. So I began the next morning. The tools were the worst you ever saw, and the only material was pitch-pine lumber. I got along very slow at first, and at noon found that I was hungry. So I went down to the square where there was a tent with a big sign, 'Philadelphia Hotel.' The rule then was to pay a dollar before you went in. But I had no dollar. And my three companions were in the same fix. In talking with Simons, the proprietor, I told him I was from South Bend, Indiana, and found that he was from a place nearby. He was Dutch, and I talked some of my Pennsylvania Dutch to him. Finally after I told him that I was working for Hinds he let us go in, and we ate enough for three days.

"Simons went over to find out from Hinds if we were lying, and he had plenty of time, we stayed so long at the table. The other boys were wild to get started at mining, so I took them over to Hinds and got him to trust them for pick and shovel and pan. Simons fixed up enough grub to last for two days, and the boys started out to try their luck. The miners had a habit of telling a tenderfoot to dig almost anywhere except in good places, just for a joke, and that was the way they treated my friends. It might have been funny for them, but it was hard on the boys.

"At the end of the second day I got one wheelbarrow done.

Hinds looked at it. 'What do you call that?' he asked, puffing his old pipe.

" 'I call it a wheelbarrow,' I answered.

" 'A hell of a wheelbarrow,' was his comment. And he was correct, for as a matter of fact the wheel was a little crooked. But I put up the best excuse I could.

" 'You asked me if I was a wagon-maker and I said I was. I didn't say that I was a wheelbarrow maker; but I think I can do better on the next one.' He smiled grimly and said 'Go ahead.' I got myself provided with better tools and turned out a fair product, making a wheelbarrow a day. My comrades worked in the mines for a whole month and I paid their expenses, but they didn't strike anything worth while. Then they left, and I never heard of them from that day to this.

"Just about then we all heard many conversations something like this: 'Joe, how long you been mining here?'

" 'Six months.'

" 'How much have you got?'

" 'Not a d—— cent.'

"And so it went. Hundreds and thousands who tried the mines never made a success. But we who stuck to steady jobs at good wages and saved our money were sure of doing well. Joe Hinds and I worked many a night all night—he making new picks and I repairing stages that came in late and that had to get out at 6 o'clock in the morning. It was not always the fault of the mines, however, that the young fellows failed to make a stake, for they gambled away their gold dust like so many reckless sports that they were. On the way to California, I had an admonition from the lips of a gambler, who was accused of murder. A jury of twelve men was sworn in and after hearing the testimony the prisoner was found guilty and was hanged right there. With the rope 'round his neck he made a complete confession, saying that he committed the murder because the dead man made him believe that he had a large sum of money in his tent, but that all he found was half a dollar. The convicted murderer warned us all against gambling, "My dying advice to all you boys is to never play cards for money; never gamble or bet on the other man's game.'

"When the Adams Express Company failed I had $3000 in the bank—all the money I had in the world. Hinds, my partner, had $22,000 in the same bank. I remember that it was 2 o'clock in the afternoon that the bank was closed, and we all knew that if it didn't open the next morning the boys would come in and tear up everything, provided they thought there was any money in the place. That's where Hinds and his level head came in. He knew that the express people would try to get their money out that night, for the failure was caused by lack of money elsewhere, and not at Hangtown. The bank backed right up against Hangtown Creek, and without saying a word to anybody Hinds made up his plan. He hid in the brush back of the bank just across the creek, and watched.

"Sure enough, as he expected, he saw the express people creep out of the building at about 2 o'clock in the morning with the bags of gold. He trailed them and saw them put the money in old Joe Douglas' safe. The rest was easy for Hinds. He waked me up and told me what had been done, and said he was going to levy an attachment on the safe, and from what he saw he was confident there was enough to pay us both, so he asked me if I wanted to stand in on the attachment suit. Of course I did, and we got out the papers bright and early. You can depend on it we didn't waste any time. Douglas, the old sinner, denied that the money was in his safe, but the officer found it and served the attachment, and as there was no defense we got the coin in short order, every dollar of it, while hundreds of others, after long waiting, received only 15 to 30 per cent. Hinds threw that money into a wheelbarrow and trundled it through the streets of Hangtown.

"It was the money that I got out of that busted bank and the savings of five years that went into the business of Studebaker Brothers, and so far as I am concerned it all came from the start that I got in old Hangtown."

Steve Gage, whom I knew well in Comstock days, was an old-time settler in Placerville. He was elected to the California Legislature from that district in 1857, and served as City Marshal in '58 and '59, afterwards (as has been told) engaging in the freighting business between Placerville and Virginia City, and for years held a prominent part in the development of Nevada, before finally returning to California.

"Thousands upon thousands came here in search of gold," said Steve Gage at the memorable Studebaker dinner. "Their like was never seen before. Through the main thoroughfare of Placerville swept this vast concourse of people. Lured by gold they braved the dangers of the plains, the hardships of the frontier, the toil of the mines.

"The experience of those who crossed the plains has never been written and never will be. No person ever did or can describe those scenes. It was estimated in round numbers 100,000 crossed the Missouri River in 1852, and for the most of those Hangtown was the objective point, the only place they had heard of. 'To Old Hangtown or Bust,' was their slogan. How many fell by the way never will be known. Of those who got through about 15 per cent branched off and went to Oregon. The remainder came to California, and almost every one of them passed through old Hangtown.

"It was while at Hangtown that Professor W. Frank Stewart, noted mining expert and scientist, invented a new earthquake register or seismograph, but Mark Twain wrote up for the Virginia City *Enterprise* a fake account of its first trial, pretending that a mangy hog scratching his back against the clapboards of Professor Stewart's cabin threw that learned gentleman into a paroxysm of fear, and caused him to report the occurrence of a terrible earthquake which never happened. Mark meant it for a jest, but Stewart took it as a deadly insult, and challenged the joker to a duel, refusing to be placated with anything less than a retraction and an apology.

"Among the venerated names of old Hangtown stands that of Penn Johnson, that brilliant genius, who introduced to this community the ancient and honorable order known as *E Clampsus Vitus*. Only pioneers will understand this reference to the most elaborate and stupendous josh organization that ever was known on earth.

"When I received my invitation to be here, many reminiscences began to pass before my vision. I could see the old bull ring on the hill where the school house now stands. It was erected by Ben Nickerson. I remember the last exhibition—neither the bear nor bull would fight. The crowd got mad, tore down the pen, killed the bear and rolled it down the steep hill. The mob led the bull through the streets, beating him. As he passed my father's store on Main Street, the bull got tired of the fun and turned and kicked one of the tormentors in the forehead, laying him out. He was taken into our store and old Dr. Worthem brought him to.

"The few women that were here in the early '50s, my mother among them, had a mining claim near the mouth of Log Cabin Ravine. One day some Chinamen jumped the claim. The women called a miners' meeting and decided to eject Mr. Chinaman. They went over in a body, threw the Chinks and their tools out and told them to 'git,' and they 'got' while a number of white men stood by and enjoyed the sport."

After singing "Auld Lang Syne," the final hand-clasps were given and the company separated, many never to meet again. The return trip from Placerville was begun as the sun was sinking. The rhythmic throbbing of the automobiles fretted the echoes of the hills and canyons. At the foot of a sharp grade a heavy, slow-winged night-hawk swung athwart the gathering shadows. An owl spoke from the dismantled casement of a tumble-down stage station.

> "Above the pines the moon was slowly drifting,
>   The river sang below;
>   The dim Sierras, far beyond, uplifting
>   Their minarets of snow."

Placerville is the best place from which to begin a tour of the Mother Lode Country, as we in the Studebaker party proved. It is only a jaunt of a few miles northward to Coloma, where the gold-rush began, and thither we went, to view the spot on the South Fork of the American River where, on the morning of January 24th, 1848, James Marshall picked up the yellow flake of gold in the mill-race of Sutter's mill. This was the discovery that startled the world and lured countless thousands to the new El Dorado.

Above the village, and above Marshall's old cabin, rises the striking monument to the discoverer. As I stood there, I thought back to the time when I knew James Marshall, at the old What Cheer House, in San Francisco. He was a grizzled miner, somewhat embittered by the neglect of the people of the land which his "find" had made prosperous; but to me, then but a boy, he was friendly and kind. Like Comstock he had been a trapper; and like Studebaker he was also a wheelwright and blacksmith, and today you may see his old forge at Kelsey, east of Coloma.

It would be a delight to visit all the quaint mining-towns of the Mother Lode, but a description of that trip would fill a book; so Placerville, which had closest associations with the Comstock, may serve as the typical example.

But let me mention one more storied site, in conclusion. Just a few miles from Tuttletown, you may turn off the main road to Jackass Hill, where a reconstructed cabin stands—the home of the Gillis boys, where Mark Twain lived for several months as a prospector and "pocket-miner." Tuttletown, with its stone store—a veritable fortress of commerce in the wilderness—is hardly even a hamlet now, but it has haunting memories.

My friend Steve Gillis spent the evening of his life in this region with his brother Bill Gillis, and not long before his death in 1918, as American soldiers were departing for the struggle overseas, I received my last message from him, "I stick my head out of the coffin and yell, 'Hurrah for the boys!'"

All along the Mother Lode, here and elsewhere, you see prospectors even today panning for color on the river-flats and up the gulches. Not only the lure of gold is here. Light clouds hang in feathery whiteness above the snow-covered spurs of the Sierra Nevada that dominate the landscape. Meadow-larks springing from the manzanita along the roadway warble their welcome. The red madrones are ranged below the pines, and it is here—as my old crony, Joaquin Miller, would say—that the

> "Rabbits play, and the quail all day
> Pipe on the chaparral hill."

INDEX